Silent
Running

Other Books by James F. Calvert

Surface at the Pole
The Naval Profession
A Promise to Our Country

SILENT RUNNING

MY YEARS ON A WORLD WAR II ATTACK SUBMARINE

JAMES F. CALVERT
Vice Admiral, USN (Ret.)

FOREWORD BY
EDWARD L. BEACH
Capt., USN (Ret.)

John Wiley & Sons, Inc.
New York • Chichester • Brisbane • Toronto • Singapore

4 4 8 7 1 4 2

Library of Congress Cataloging-in-Publication Data:

Calvert, James F.
    Silent running : my years on a World War II attack submarine /
James F. Calvert : foreword by Edward L. Beach.
        p.   cm.
    Includes index.
    ISBN 0-471-12778-7 (cloth : alk. paper)
    1. Calvert, James F.   2. Jack (Submarine : SS-259)
3. Haddo (Submarine : SS-255)   4. World War, 1939–1945—Naval
operations—Submarine.   5. World War, 1939–1945—Naval operations,
American.   6. World War, 1939–1945—Personal narratives.   7. World
War, 1939–1945—Campaigns—Pacific Area.   8. Sailors—United States—
Biography.   9. United States, Navy—Biography.   I. Title.
D782.J33C35   1995
940.54′26—dc20   95-15447

Printed in the United States of America

10 9 8 7 6 5 4 3 2 1

To Peggy

Contents

List of Charts

Foreword

Edward L. Beach
Captain, USN (Ret.)

The scandalous misbehavior of U.S. submarine torpedoes—in fact of all the torpedoes provided for our armed forces during the first two years of the war—has been described by many others. The well-justified dismay over this poor performance has obscured a salient fact related to the use of these underwater missiles in submarines. Where destroyers were expected to shoot all their "fish" in a single "shotgun" salvo, ideally against a distant enemy battleline, submarines worked the other end of the spectrum. In submarine doctrine shooting a torpedo was like firing a rifle. We took big risks to aim them individually and carefully, and we fired them at close range.

Accurate aim was as important to torpedo performance as the proper working of its mechanisms—but no more. Poor aim could cause a miss, but so could a bad performance from our underwater missile. Both had to be simultaneously on the mark, or the fish, and all the effort, were wasted.

Aiming a torpedo involved a combination of two talents: accurate periscope observation, which was the skipper's responsibility, and meticulously accurate operation of the torpedo data computer, the TDC, the complicated instrument used to aim the torpedoes.

The early years of the war saw many failed torpedo shots, and a controversy erupted over what had caused them. The argument was finally sorted out late in 1943: the torpedoes had been carelessly designed and built, and insufficiently tested. We were aiming them well, but no amount of good aim could get a hit with a torpedo that did not run as touted.

Since there was a multiplicity of faults, it took until nearly the end of that year before our submarines could go to sea with confidence that all (or nearly all) of the congenital malfunctions of their torpedoes had been corrected. By the fall of 1943, nearly two years after the war had begun, our accurately aimed fish were beginning to do the job they should have been doing since the start of the war.

It was early in 1944 that I first began to hear about Jim Calvert. Because of the overweening importance of good aim, a real "TDC expert" was truly worth his weight in gold coin. Jim was obviously such a person. I first learned his name in connection with one of the more amazing submarine attacks in the reports we regularly read of the exploits of other subs: the USS *Jack*, in which he served as TDC operator, had fired long-range (about five thousand yards or more than two nautical miles) at a convoy of troop transports speeding away from it, and had sunk three of them. We submariners had been indoctrinated to believe that even four thousand yards was far too long a "torpedo run"—that we could not be sure of adequate sharpshooter accuracy at that great distance. Yet, because the *Jack* had been unable to get closer to the flying targets, here was someone who had hit a target at maximum range and thereby converted failure ("the targets got by") to success. Three of them did not "get by" the *Jack*.

As Calvert describes his experiences in the *Jack*, it becomes clear to all submariners acquainted with the wartime conditions of service that he must have been virtually one in a million. He was a TDC operator with that extraordinary ability, often bragged about but less frequently demonstrated, to make a TDC sing when it came to aiming the weapons. He describes how his skipper, a fairly senior officer renowned for his ability to make rapid and accurate observations with a periscope, following the submarine dictum that all on board should be able to perform all appropriate jobs, put him on the TDC "for exercise." Jim called his first hits luck, and maybe there was some of that in the beginning. Nevertheless he worked the problem with surpassing concentration, and was able to put his exercise fish under the target the very first time he took over the instrument. While only a junior officer on board, just out of submarine school, he wound up with the TDC job in combat; and the *Jack* quickly became one of the legendary torpedo shooters in our Pacific Submarine Force. His skipper shared in that accolade, but to us more junior persons, Jim Calvert was the bedrock of the *Jack's* outstanding success.

Here now we read Jim's version of how it happened, told mod-

KRUS, N P

4415

Thursday, July 6, 2017

32395004487142

estly, as it has to be. Nevertheless there is enough between the lines to make it clear that the author and his TDC had an affinity seldom seen. His awards for his wartime service reflect it, and his subsequent naval career has borne out the promise of those early years.

There was, indeed, much more to Jim Calvert's career than just the war years or his naval service afterward. Most of this is left undescribed or only hinted at, for this book is only about his service in World War II. For the record, however, the reader should know that he became one of the outstanding officers of our Navy, was Superintendent of our Naval Academy in Annapolis (in which post he was promoted to vice admiral), and had come within an ace of being picked to be the Chief of Naval Operations (the senior naval officer in service) when he decided to terminate his naval career and go into private business. In this, too, he did extraordinarily well, but it is not a part of his wartime story except insofar as his early performance presaged that of his later years. One has to remember that he was "Jim" at the time of which he writes. The Vice Admiral and corporate executive he grew into later.

Some of his escapades are told with the impact of a confession—to himself if to no one else. Jim had a propensity for daring and risk-taking, something that later observers, knowing him only as a sober-sided vice admiral, might be surprised to discover. Risk was, of course, inherent in submarine warfare. We all took risks, sometimes big ones, in the course of wartime duties, but there were other sorts of risks too.

It is with a certain relish, therefore, that one reads how Vice Admiral Jim Calvert, then a lowly lieutenant, within a week after the war's end and before the formal surrender on board the USS *Missouri*, with a few other submariners went beyond the boundaries established for our preliminary occupation zone in Yokosuka, rode a train to Tokyo, and took an unauthorized tour of Japan's surrendered capital. The young men received some curious looks from the city's bemused inhabitants, but they got away with it as far as the Japanese were concerned. On their return to Yokosuka that afternoon, however, they found themselves in deep trouble for their violation of strict emergency occupation rules. No one was in deeper than Jim himself, for—owing to rapid promotion during the war—he found himself named as the senior officer of the malefactors, technically in charge of them, and therefore himself personally responsible for the military crime they had all committed!

It was only the timely intervention by one of the submarine

force's foremost leaders, who was able to see the escapade as the innocent end-of-the-war euphoria that it was and happened fortunately to be on the spot, that saved the day. This gentleman, still revered by Jim, at the risk of his own career tore up and threw away the official reporting papers that would have put Jim in the dock before a general court-martial. Jim Calvert's naval career was saved, and an esteemed future superintendent of our Naval Academy was preserved for the guidance of a later generation of young officers. We may today be glad that someone took a more liberal view of the incident than the individual who had written the charge.

And now Jim Calvert is seeing his later years. He has had a rich and full life. He fought for his country in the greatest war man has ever waged, and he served it loyally through the fifty years of troubled peace that followed that Armageddon of our era. Through it all he remained faithful to the ideals with which he began his service. But now, as he relives some of those early days, he must wonder, as we all must, what has become of the exuberant youth he once was. In writing these reminiscences he cannot but be struck that those years, at the very beginning of his eventful life, were the ones when he was able to make his greatest contribution to everything he has since held dear.

Preface

This book is a record of the impressions and memories of my submarine experiences in World War II, covering nine war patrols made in the Pacific against the Japanese.

I have attempted to restrict myself to what I knew and experienced at that time and how I felt about it then. I have done my best to ignore those layers of knowledge, cynicism, and worldliness that have inevitably come in the decades that have passed since these experiences. This book is about a small-town Ohio boy who, knowing very little of the world, was caught up in a titanic struggle between two nations being fought halfway around the world with complex and dangerous weapons.

These are the memories of a young man who started out as the freshest and greenest of the officers in the USS *Jack*, one of the war's most successful submarines, and progressed upward to become the second-in-command of that ship by the end of the war. This book also deals with his experiences ashore in Australia between war patrols, a time that left an impression that lasted all his life.

To many readers, steeped in the cynical and deprecating way in which so many veterans of World War II have spoken of their officers and of the branch of the armed forces in which they served, my enthusiasm for the submarine service and my senior officers may seem naive or uninformed. I can only repeat that I am attempting to reflect honestly what I felt at the time.

I have included many conversations and pieces of dialogue. It should be clear to everyone that, after nearly fifty years, the exact words, except in one or two memorable cases, are no longer available to me. But in each case I have been careful to make the words reflect the gist of what was being said at the time.

James F. Calvert

St. Michaels, Maryland
May 1995

Acknowledgments

The writing of memoirs, of whatever time of one's life, is an act of considerable egotism, and without the encouragement of my stepson Kemp Battle, this book would never have been written. Kemp has written several books, knows the publishing business well, and had the persuasiveness to overcome my reluctance and inertia. He introduced me to a good literary agent and, in general, got me going. I am also indebted to Kemp's wife, Carolyn Slaughter, a well-known author, for many valuable suggestions and observations.

I have made no pretense to original research other than that pertaining directly to my submarine, the USS *Jack*, and this book is in no sense a history of American submarines in World War II. That task has been admirably accomplished by Clay Blair, Jr., in *Silent Victory*, to which I am indebted for some of my background material as well as for the confirmation of certain dates and statistics.

I want also to acknowledge my dependence on Rear Admiral Samuel Eliot Morison's fifteen-volume *History of the United States Naval Operations in World War II* for dates and a general perspective on the war in the Pacific, in which the *Jack* played only a very small part—but a highly important part to some of us.

Special gratitude is due to Captain Edward L. Beach, a veteran of World War II submarining and a distinguished author. Ned is a good friend and has proved it by writing the Foreword, but also by taking unusual care in going over the final manuscript and giving me some valuable corrections and suggestions.

I also want to thank Rear Admiral Chester W. Nimitz, Jr., for reading the manuscript, catching several errors of fact, and giving me some new and interesting material concerning the loss of the

Harder. Chester was a very experienced and successful submarine officer in World War II, both as a junior officer and as a commanding officer. He knows whereof he speaks.

In addition, I want to express my thanks to my *Jack* shipmate of World War II Terence J. McCabe for reading the manuscript, catching several errors of memory, and suggesting additional material. Terry's scrapbook also proved a valuable resource for photographs.

Very special thanks are due to Mr. William R. (Dick) McCants, the son of a Naval Academy classmate of mine, Thomas R. McCants. Captain McCants was a distinguished World War II submariner, and his son has done his memory proud with a fine book, *War Patrols of the USS Flasher.* Tom McCants participated in all six of the patrols made by the *Flasher,* the ship that topped the list of American submarines in terms of total tonnage sunk. Dick McCants did all of the patrol track charts for *Silent Running* and has given me other valuable assistance as well.

However vivid my memories of these war patrols, I would not have been able to set them forth with any real accuracy without access to the original patrol reports of the *Jack* and the *Haddo,* made available to me by the Naval History Department of Washington, D.C. Both the Historical Center and the Naval Institute Press were helpful in supplying photographs.

Thanks are also due to *Haddo* shipmate Jack Keller for the use of his diary of the trip to Tokyo. It was supplied to me by Al Viebranz, and it was very important to my telling of this tale—some of the details had fallen from memory after all the intervening years.

I want to express my gratitude to Rear Admiral Jim Finkelstein, the former Chief of Information of the Navy, for putting me in touch with several people who were helpful in the production of this book.

An agent is a critical member of any author's team of allies, and I would like to thank Alexander Hoyt of New York City for his advice and friendship and, not least important, for arranging the publication of this book by John Wiley & Sons, Inc., of New York.

At John Wiley I would like to express my appreciation to Senior Editor Hana Umlauf Lane for her understanding and patient help.

Considering all of the help I have received, it is particularly important that I make it clear that the responsibility for any remaining errors is entirely mine.

Finally, no one writes a book without disappearing into the warm embraces of a word processor for many long hours and days.

I want to state my appreciation to my wife, Peggy, for putting up with all of this. Her love, understanding, and patience knew no limits.

James F. Calvert

St. Michaels, Maryland
May 1995

Silent Running

1

Training for the
Big Show

The cold wind whistled by my ears, and I was grateful for the heavy Navy watch cap I had snuggled down over them. As we passed the New London lighthouse and left the Thames, I could feel the gentle rise and fall of the ship as it rode the seas stirred up by the brisk southwest wind. It was January of 1943. The wintry day was partly cloudy, and cold. When the sun came out, however briefly, it felt good. Occasionally the bow would catch a chop of water and send a quick dash of it up on the bridge. Somehow that felt good, too.

It was a clear day, and I could see the long, gray coast of Connecticut behind us as we left the Thames, and the more distant low profile of Long Island to the south. We were in Long Island Sound but headed for the deeper water of Block Island Sound.

I was on the bridge of a brand-new submarine just beginning its training to go into the Pacific to join the war against Japan. The sleek black bow of the ship stretched out ahead of me, and I watched it knife gracefully through the icy waters of the sound. More than three hundred feet long, it was the newest of the submarines being built in great haste at Groton's Electric Boat Company in 1942 to bolster the Navy's effort against the Japanese in the Pacific.

I was pretty new myself. I was the youngest and most junior officer on board—fresh out of the Naval Academy at Annapolis and the New London Submarine School. The other four officers were all men with significant experience in submarines and had served at least two years before that in surface ships. I was the baby of the wardroom in more ways than one.

Our skipper was Lieutenant Commander Tommy Dykers, Annapolis class of 1927 and a very experienced submarine commander. Lean, dark, and hawklike, he had a strong, clear voice that

1

was the very essence of command. His slightly aristocratic look belied the toughness underneath. A native of New Orleans, he still carried its characteristic drawl.

The next in command, our executive officer, was John Paul Roach, Annapolis class of 1932. His nickname was Beetle—because of his heavy eyebrows and his last name. About six feet tall, with jet black hair and an almost always cheerful face, he too was a veteran submariner but had not had command. He was a warm, friendly, and competent officer and was a big help to me as I tried to fit into the team. His Texas accent somehow seemed to fit his cheerful mien.

Our third officer was Miles Refo, Annapolis class of 1938. He was the son of a well-known naval officer. Miles had deep roots in Virginia and was, indeed, a direct descendant of Robert E. Lee. He was tall, slender, prematurely balding, and absolutely competent. He took a rather dim view of putting never-been-to-sea ensigns on submarines, but he tolerated me as a necessary evil of wartime.

It was a bitter cold day, and the bridge of our submarine gave no protection to its occupants. There was a metal shield forward that would stop some of the seas that frequently broke over it, but the bridge was essentially open air. It flooded completely when the submarine submerged. It was not a friendly or cozy place. For better or for worse, its watchstanders were out in the elements.

The three lookouts perched above and behind me on the periscope shears were bundled up to their noses in navy blue winter gear. Heavy face masks covered all but their eyes. The lookouts were, nevertheless, using their binoculars—not too important right then, but vitally necessary once we left the protection of Long Island and Block Island Sounds and ventured into the Atlantic, where German U-boats were known to be operating.

The *Jack*—for that was our submarine's name—had not yet been placed in commission in the Navy. Nearly, but not entirely, completed, she counted on these early sea trials to identify items still needing to be accomplished. We were on our way out for an early shakedown cruise on which we would also begin learning to dive our ship. Because I was too inexperienced to be the officer of the deck (OOD) by myself, our executive officer, Beetle Roach, was on watch with me. Since he was also the navigator, he frequently went below to the conning tower to use the charts. There is absolutely no way to keep charts safely on a submarine bridge. He had no choice except to leave me on the bridge alone.

We navigated carefully through the Race, the narrow straits that join Block Island Sound with Long Island Sound, a place known for swirling currents and treacherous whirlpools that can grab an unwary vessel and turn it around like a top. The beautiful stone Race lighthouse loomed large to our left, and heavy icicles festooned its walls. I looked down from the bridge at the angry, churning water and noticed that the spray being thrown up by the bow was beginning to freeze on the bridge structure. It was cold, all right.

In a submarine the helmsman is with his wheel down in the conning tower and can see nothing. All of his courses are ordered by the officer of the deck, and as we plowed through the Race, I warned the helmsman to be alert for currents and whirlpools.

I didn't mind being left alone on the bridge—I could pretend I was driving.

For our first dives, we chose a spot in Block Island Sound where we had about two hundred feet of water—deep enough to give us time to catch her if we had made a mistake in calculating our compensation, but shallow enough to catch her at a safe depth in case we were so far off that we went right to the bottom.

Compensation is the submariner's name for predicting just what weight will be needed to give the submarine neutral buoyancy when it is submerged and its main ballast tanks are flooded. The variable ballast tanks, both forward and aft, are carefully filled with seawater until the weights reach the calculated amount; after that they are not changed unless necessary. We had never been submerged before, so we had no way of knowing whether our estimates were actually correct.

We would soon find out.

We went at it in cautious steps. Since the officer of the deck was a key player on the diving team, we started out with our fourth officer, Claude Leyton Goodman, up there. Annapolis class of 1939, he was a thin, dark-complexioned Virginian who was not subject to excitement under any reasonable stress. He was a good submariner and an excellent choice to make these initial dives from the bridge. (He didn't like the name Claude so we all called him Leyton.)

For our first dive, we got everyone off the bridge safely, including Leyton, then shut the conning tower hatch. Next we sounded two raucous blasts on the diving alarm (OO-gah, OO-gah) while going ahead at about five knots on only one engine. Everyone in the control room watched the Christmas Tree—a panel about half the size of a card table top, filled with red and green indicator lights.

The engine shut down, its exhaust indicator light went green, the main induction light went green, and when Miles Refo (he was the chief engineer and the diving officer) saw that he had a green board, he ordered high-pressure air bled into the boat to test the seal. It held, as shown on the barometer at his station.

"Green board, pressure in the boat," he sang out to Dykers, who was in the conning tower where the attack periscope was located.

"Very well—take her to sixty-five feet," came the response from the skipper.

"Sixty-five feet, aye aye," from Miles. Submariners are meticulous about repeating orders back. There is too much at stake to risk a misunderstanding.

"Open all vents," ordered Miles. Normally this would have been done on the diving alarm to save time, but for this first dive we were taking it very slowly. Baby steps for baby feet.

"Open all vents, aye aye, sir," came the reply from the man on the hydraulic manifold that controlled most of the diving apparatus. The gleaming chrome-plated levers were thrown, and the roar of the main ballast tanks filling with seawater was all around us as the vent lights on the Christmas Tree went red. (The flooding ports on the bottom of the ballast tanks were always wide open. The sea was prevented from entering only by the pressure in the tanks—like an inverted glass held in water. When the vents were opened, the pressure was released and the sea came in.)

Down went the *Jack*, slowly but surely easing under the icy black waters of the sound. The bow and stern planesmen carefully controlled the angle of the submarine, keeping it modest, and she settled out near the ordered depth. Two huge, clocklike depth gauges sat squarely in front of each planesman, who also looked directly at bubble indicators showing the angle on the boat. An up angle would drive her up, a down angle the reverse.

Sixty-five feet is about periscope depth for a fleet submarine. Dykers took a look around while Miles made the necessary corrections to his compensation. Immediately apparent to me was the steadiness of the ship once we submerged. We had been rolling about noticeably on the surface due to the freshening wind, but once we reached even periscope depth, all motion was gone, and we were quiet and steady as a rock.

Miles continued to give the orders to flood in a little water here, pump out a little there, as he adjusted the variable tanks to give us neutral buoyancy.

"I've about got her now," called Miles to the skipper.

"Very well, prepare to surface, two engines."

The maneuvering room repeated back, "Two engines, aye aye, sir."

OO-gah, OO-gah, OO-gah went the raucous alarm. We blew the main ballast tanks and in a short time were on the surface with two engines running. We prepared to make the next dive a little faster, at about eight knots, which would take us down with more force.

This time we left Leyton on the bridge to sound the diving alarm himself from up there. No lookouts were on the bridge, so he scrambled below, shut the hatch, and hung on to the lanyard while the quartermaster cranked it shut tight. Green board, pressure in the boat, open the vents, periscope depth. All OK.

After two more dives, done with lookouts on the bridge, we were ready to open the vents on the alarm. This meant there was no room for error. Once those vents were open, the submarine was going down. And anything that was left open or failed to shut could cause disaster.

So on the next dive, we sounded the alarm with all three lookouts up and a quartermaster on the bridge with Leyton. The ballast tank vents were opened on the alarm, and the bow was under and sinking fast by the time the bridge was cleared. The lookouts came down pell-mell, followed by the OOD. Green board, pressure in the boat as we were going down, periscope depth. All OK.

We had by then made a complete dive as we would out in the Pacific—except that the time from sounding the alarm until we were completely submerged was seventy seconds. Dykers wanted it between thirty and thirty-five seconds. We thought what we had just done seemed fast, but we knew we had to cut our diving time in half. We had lots of work to do.

High-speed diving is attained partly by using special tanks that are blown as soon as the submarine is below the surface, but it is attained mainly by driving the boat down faster at a steep angle. It is the angle that bothers you at first. You are sure that the submarine is going out of control and will soon be hitting the bottom or going beyond its test depth.

Quick diving takes training and confidence. Our first dives were made using only the battle station lookouts, who were our best bow and stern planesmen. The lookouts came roaring down from the bridge, through the conning tower, then dropped into the control room and grabbed the bow and stern planes.

As we got into steep, fast diving, we used only the battle station planesmen, at first. On later days, we began to train all the rest of the lookouts as planesmen. There were some twenty of these because they had to be relieved about every half hour on patrol due to eye strain. (A lookout on patrol had to keep binoculars up to his eyes without rest.) We dove and dove and dove until all of the complicated steps began to be second nature to us all.

The first really steep angles we took caused everything loose in the boat to come clattering down in every compartment, scaring everyone. Pots and pans, spare parts, books, dishes, coffee cups— all crashed down in an unbelievable din. The combination of uncommonly steep angles and the noise of things falling all around you was terrifying. Frightened looks from crew members seemed to say, "Do these guys know what they're doing, or are they going to sink this thing permanently?"

Eventually, everything was properly stowed for steep angles. We began to realize, despite our feeling of being out of control, that Miles really would get us down safely and that we might survive to get out to the war zone after all.

Dykers hammered home to us again and again that the ability to spot enemy patrol planes and to submerge quickly—in thirty seconds or so—was our main means of survival in the war zone. We made this our goal and all were determined to reach it—we had a sincere desire to survive this war.

The next task was to train other diving officers besides Miles. Out in the Pacific, there would be no warning of the need to dive; there it was up to the OOD to come down, take the dive, and get the boat under safely. Leyton and I were the main objects of this training effort, and after a short time, the focus was all on me. How was this freshly graduated, never-been-to-sea greenhorn ever going to learn to be a trusted diving officer?

I did dive after dive until my legs and arms were weary from going up to the bridge, scampering down, glancing at the Christmas Tree, putting pressure in the boat, and coaching new bow and stern planesmen on how to reach the proper depth.

In due time I began to feel the necessary self-confidence, and, as is usually the case, when that happened others began to feel confidence in me.

I was beginning to be a submariner.

Well into our second week of training, we had a serious mishap. We were still shifting all of our teams around to be sure that everyone had equal time on the critical diving stations. Also, we were still attempting to make that thirty- to thirty-five-second mark. We weren't there yet, but we were closing in on it. Our dives routinely took around forty-five seconds, and we knew that only by getting a steeper angle could we reach our goal.

The mishap occurred while we were diving in Block Island Sound in about 150 feet of water. Another routine dive, I thought, as I worked on some papers in the wardroom. All of a sudden it was clear to me, even from a distance, that this was *not* routine. I heard shouts from the control room, then the diving officer called, "Blow all ballast!"

Shortly we were on the surface but wallowing in an unaccustomed matter. I went to the control room to hear Chief Earl Archer, the senior engineman and a very experienced submariner, saying in a quiet voice, "The main induction must be open—we had green water pouring into the engine rooms before we got the flappers shut." Archer simply never got excited, thus the quiet voice. But what he said was exciting enough. Everyone looked at the main induction light on the Christmas Tree. It was red, but the face of practically everyone in the control room was white. We all realized what a close call we had had.

The main induction valve, located under the after end of the bridge, is about three feet in diameter. It supplies most of the huge amount of air needed by the diesels to run. It was the failure to close (or keep closed) the main induction valve that had caused the *Squalus* to sink off the Isles of Shoals before World War II with a serious loss of life.* As a result of that accident, quick-acting backup flapper valves were installed in all fleet submarines to give the engine room crew a chance to prevent flooding if the main induction valve were left open.

Without these newly designed main induction flappers in our engine rooms, we would have flooded at least a large part of the *Jack*, and there would have been another rescue operation under way. The redesigned flappers took only the flip of a long handle to shut—but even then our men had seen a lot of green water come down before they were able to shut the flappers.

---

*The *Squalus* was later raised, rebuilt, renamed *Sailfish*, and did yeoman service against the Japanese in World War II.

What had happened? We had had a green board and pressure in the boat. How had the main induction valve opened? We would never know for certain, but the best reconstruction was as follows:

The only lever anywhere on the boat that controls the main induction is at the main hydraulic manifold, located under the Christmas Tree in the control room. This manifold, through hydraulic pressure, operates not only the main induction valve but also the main ballast tank vents and a number of other important pieces of machinery involved in the diving process. The man on the main hydraulic manifold, almost always a chief petty officer, has one of the most critical jobs on the dive.

In our everlasting drive to get under in less than thirty-five seconds, there was a lot of pressure on the main hydraulic manifold operator. He had to do everything both swiftly and correctly. That morning the chief on the manifold must have thought he was opening the vent of one of the auxiliary tanks meant to hurry the dive and, instead, grabbed the main induction handle and reopened that critical valve. The main induction handle is shaped entirely differently from any other hydraulic handle, and thus it is not easy to see how the mistake was made. Nevertheless, that is the only way the accident could have happened.

It took more than an hour to drain all the water out of the induction piping leading to the two engine rooms. (The piping is more than one hundred feet long and about two feet in diameter.) Lots of water. We all took a moment to thank the men who had redesigned those engine room closure valves. We also thought about those men of the *Squalus* who had given their lives in the accident that resulted in this design change for our fleet submarines. Without much question, they had saved all the men in the two *Jack* engine rooms, perhaps more.

When we were drained down and ready to go, Dykers put exactly the same team on the next dive and had them go through several quick dives until everyone's nerves were settled—kind of like getting back on the horse right after you've been thrown.

Believe me, we were all main induction conscious after that day. In hindsight, Dykers did the right thing by keeping that same chief petty officer on the hydraulic manifold. Many skippers would have bounced him out of submarines after that gaff—and the chief knew it. He knew what a break he had been given, and he developed into one of the *Jack*'s best chiefs and best hydraulic manifold operators.

Obviously, submarines are a complicated and dangerous business. How had I gotten myself into this nerve-racking game at the tender age of twenty-two? Well, to begin with, I had gone to the Naval Academy at Annapolis, Maryland.

I had been a premedical student at Oberlin College in Ohio for two years when it became apparent that there wasn't enough family money to send me to medical school. (This was before the days of student loans.)

I took the exams for the Academy, received a principal appointment, and in June of 1939, found myself on the way to Annapolis—farther away from home than I had ever been.

I really knew very little about the Naval Academy. I had read several old *Lucky Bags*, the Naval Academy yearbook, at the public library, but my firsthand knowledge was close to zero.

The letter I had received from the Academy explained that the class of 1943 (it was the summer of 1939) would be entering the Academy in small groups, about eight or nine a day, all through the summer. By the luck of the draw, I assume, I was to be in the very first group. I was also informed that I would have to find a room out in town while I was taking my physical exam. If I failed the physical, I would return home at my own expense.

Fortunately, I passed the physical and spent an exciting and rewarding period of my life at Annapolis. The attack on Pearl Harbor and America's entry into World War II occurred while I was there. The Academy's normal four-year program was shortened to three. Hence my class would graduate in 1942, a year earlier than planned.

As we prepared for graduation in June, the newspapers were full of stories about the war. I read them all with interest, but the articles that really caught my eye were those about the American submarines in the Pacific.

The Navy's carrier strikes in the Pacific seemed so massive and so much in the hands of the admirals that it was hard for me to get enthusiastic about them. What could a mere ensign do there? But submarines—that was a different story. Submariners were younger men, and they were right there in the front lines delivering telling blows.

One of the submarines that got lots of attention in the newspapers was the *Seawolf*. Her visit to the Naval Academy when she was on her shakedown cruise a year earlier was still fresh in my mind. I had even briefly met her fabled skipper, Frederick B. Warder. One of the chief petty officers on the *Seawolf* took an hour from his busy day to show me around the submarine. It was apparent from all he said that the men of the *Seawolf* were proud of their ship and proud of their skipper.

Little did I realize at the time what an important part Frederick Warder would later play in my life.

As I read the *Washington Post* articles about that same *Seawolf* and that same Frederick Warder out there in the Pacific putting Japanese ships on the bottom, I wanted to get out there and join them!

It was clear from talking with classmates who had visited the submarines at the Academy that the undersea boats are not everyone's cup of tea. Living spaces are cramped, and getting in to work on some of the machinery takes a contortionist who has absolutely no fear of being trapped in a tight space.

But these same visits convinced me that submarines were for me. I liked the confined, neat spaces and the cut of the jibs of the men on board. In addition, I was fascinated with the machinery—particularly that which aimed and fired torpedoes.

I was bursting to have a go at the submarine navy, but as is so often the case in life, there was a snake in this Garden of Eden. The Navy's rules required two years of sea duty in surface ships before one could even apply for Submarine School, the six-month entry gate to the undersea navy. In two and a half years, I thought, this war will be over and I'll have had no chance to see action in the Pacific in submarines.

There was, however, a faint ray of hope. I had a classmate, Howard Clark, whom I admired very much and who was just as anxious as I to go directly to submarines. Howard's father was a submarine officer.

One day, talking to Howard over the phone from his duty station in New London, Captain Clark said, "If you guys are so determined, why don't you go over to Washington and talk to Commander Suits, the detail officer. He's the one who can change the rule, and he's an old friend of mine."

The submarine detail officer is in charge of all personnel assignments, including those to Submarine School. We went over and talked as persuasively as we could but were turned down. Cold. No way. His closing words were very final: "Nobody wants an officer on a submarine who has never been to sea. What would they do with him? He would just be in the way."

We left Commander Suits's office resigned to the fact that, somehow, the Navy was going to have to fight the submarine war in the Pacific without us.

In March or April, I was assigned to the *Boise*, a fairly new cruiser operating in the Pacific. Actually, it was a good assignment—it just wasn't a submarine.

Then one day in late May, Howard received an urgent phone call from Commander Suits.

"If you and that classmate of yours, whose name I can't remember, can find twenty-three other guys in your class who want submarines and can pass the physical, you're all set. We're starting a three-month class in New London on July first."

Howard and I tirelessly tromped the corridors of Bancroft Hall, the Academy's huge dormitory, looking for volunteers and found, once again, that not all of our classmates were as desperate for the undersea navy as we were.

I had lived my entire time at the Academy with the same three roommates, and they were naturally where I started. However, Bill Chip had long since been signed up for the Marine Corps, and Max Harnish was waiting for Pensacola and flight training. We did, however, sign up my third roommate, Bill Bissell, and went on, somewhat encouraged, to other possible candidates. We found that many of them were happy with their surface ship assignments and had no desire to change. Others just plain did not like the idea of ships that were designed to sink.

We never did fill the entire quota of twenty-five. We got about half that number; the rest of the class came from officers in the fleet, some of whom had the required two years of sea duty and some of whom did not.

Submarine School was a great experience. I loved every day of it. Shortened as it was from its normal six-month length to three, it was pretty strenuous. But my fascination with submarines only increased as I learned more about them.

Even though every day, and indeed every hour, at the school was filled with work, I found time to marry my Naval Academy sweetheart, Nancy King, who was living in Annapolis. After a one-day leave for the wedding, which took place in Annapolis, we traveled that same afternoon to New London. There we found a tiny house that looked like something Hansel and Gretel might have lived in. It was small and modest, but it was also both home and heaven to us.

As my time at Submarine School drew to a close, the question of ship assignments became more and more a matter of concern. Choice of duty was given in order of class standing, and fortunately I stood high enough to get a good selection. While I was anxious to get out to the war, I was also anxious to get a new submarine and to be one of the commissioning crew . . . and I had a new bride at home.

The three top students in the class chose new-construction submarines being built at Electric Boat. We were assigned to the submarines in the order in which they were being built, which was alphabetical. Sam Logan, the number one man, went to the *Harder;* the number two man, Bill Willis, went to the *Hoe;* and I went to the *Jack.*

Thus were our fates decided . . . and little did we know what a profound effect these assignments would have on our lives in the years to come.

And so, that was how it was decided that I would report to the *Jack* while she was still on the building ways at Electric Boat. She had been launched in the fall of 1942, and we were soon out on the sound learning how to dive.

We also had to learn how to shoot torpedoes. During the building period, we had worked at Submarine School on the attack teacher— a sort of training device built to simulate, reasonably well, an actual torpedo approach on an enemy ship. Each new-construction submarine was given a generous allotment of time on the attack teacher.

We had developed the usual team for an attack party. Dykers was the approach officer, of course; Beetle Roach was assistant approach officer; Leyton Goodman was on the Torpedo Data Computer (TDC); and, as junior man, I had the plot, a sort of do-by-hand backup for the TDC. Miles Refo, of course, was down in the control room as the diving officer and was not part of the attack party.

All of us knew we had a real pro for a skipper. When he took that periscope, he knew exactly what he was doing—mainly, he was concerned with training the rest of us. Particularly the TDC operator. During the building period, while waiting our turn for the attack teacher, I had had the opportunity to observe several other submarine attack parties at work. It was soon apparent to me that we had the most polished man on the periscope but not the best attack party.

In the submarines of World War II, the TDC was a vital part of the torpedo-shooting team. It was an analog computer that displayed the target course, speed, bearing, and range on a continuously updated simulation behind a large, vertical piece of plate glass. Four knobs, or cranks, were located on the machine just under the simulated picture. The operator used three of them to set in the observed bearing, range, and target course, as seen by the captain. The fourth knob was used to set in the estimated speed of the target.

As the periscope observations continued and the range and bearing differentials (between what the TDC generated and what was observed) were noted, a skilled operator could soon deduce the correct target course and speed.

The TDC made significant use of the feature that enabled the "fish" (as we called a torpedo) to turn to a predetermined course after leaving the tube. This was accomplished by a spinning gyroscope inside the torpedo. The difference between the fish going straight ahead or turning to the new course ordered by the TDC was called the *gyro angle*.

Most important, the TDC was continually wiring the gyro angles necessary to hit the target down to the torpedo rooms, where synchromechanisms ensured that the torpedoes were always ready to shoot with the TDC's latest lead angles. The spindles that set the gyros inside the torpedoes were automatically withdrawn exactly at the moment of firing. It was an elegant system.

Although we had not been doing too well in the attack teacher, we were all sure that when we got out for our really serious training we would do better. Our target was a submarine rescue vessel, a sort of seagoing tug equipped to help a sunken submarine get its men to the surface. It wasn't a very glamorous target, but for our stage of training it was fine.

We went at the first few approaches with great confidence, yet we really didn't do any better than we had done on the attack teacher. We were missing the target speed too often, and our practice torpedoes (set to run under the target) were missing the mark. The target vessel could see the bubble track of a torpedo and thus could give us an estimate of how widely we had missed. A perfect shot was called a *middle of the target* (MOT), but we weren't getting any MOTs.

After a series of practice approaches out on the sound with more or less the same unhappy results, I could see that Dykers was becoming very unhappy with his attack party. One day, to my complete surprise, he said, "Jim, you take the TDC on this next run—Leyton, you move over to the plot." Goodman, understandably not pleased, moved over. The plot was traditionally the job for the most junior officer on board. I was surprised, all right, but also delighted. I realized this was my chance.

The TDC was mounted vertically in the after port corner of the conning tower, about three feet from the attack periscope. In truth, the TDC operator was the skipper's key partner in the attack party.

The next three runs went beautifully, with almost exact solutions each time. We had three MOTs. It was beginner's luck, but I was excited about it. The next day when battle stations sounded and the attack party assembled in the conning tower, Dykers said quietly, "Jim, you take the TDC again."

I never left the position after that day.

To give Leyton Goodman his due, he was three years senior to me, much more experienced in submarines, and had every reason to think he would be the TDC operator. To his credit he never mentioned the change and backed me up 100 percent in his job as the plotter.

To put all of this in perspective, I should tell you that the TDC was not taught at Submarine School when Leyton attended it. There had been no TDC in the old prewar submarine he had served in. Torpedoes had been aimed then with an awkward hand-held device, the Mark VIII Angle Solver, usually called a "banjo."

With the banjo it was necessary to preset the gyros and then wait for the target to come onto the right bearing for shooting. It was a cumbersome and slow way to shoot torpedoes. Comparing the banjo to the TDC was like comparing the Wright brothers' plane to a modern fighter.

In his businesslike and quiet acceptance of the new arrangement, Leyton proved to me, right then and there, that he was a true team player.

We were not the only submarine to make such a shift. Our division mate, the *Harder*, made a similar change, putting my Submarine School classmate Sam Logan in as TDC operator over a much more experienced submarine officer. Sam had stood number one not only in our Submarine School class (as mentioned before) but also in his class at Annapolis. He was tremendously capable and, I believe, became one of the great TDC operators of the war.

By then our attack party was developing beautifully. Dykers was ringing up one MOT after another. Most of the crew, understandably, did not understand all the details of torpedo fire control—but all wartime submarine crew members were *very* sensitive as to whether or not their skipper could shoot torpedoes. They knew full well that their lives would depend on it someday. Our crew was beginning to feel more and more confident about the captain of the *Jack*.

And so was I.

It was customary after each firing to surface immediately and to help the torpedo retriever, a medium-sized motorboat, locate the torpedo, which would come to the surface after its run was completed. Following one very nice approach and another MOT, we were starting up the engines, feeling pretty good about everything, when a chilling word came up from the forward engine room:

"We have a serious casualty on number two engine."

On attempting to start the engine, a cracking, crumbling noise had emanated from the forward gear casing. Inspection showed that the whole complicated train of gears in the forward end of the engine had been wrecked by a broken gear at the top of the complex arrangement. It had fallen down through the other gears with disastrous results.

The *Jack*'s engines had an interesting and somewhat distressing history. During the 1930s the Navy had asked a number of American diesel engine manufacturers to undertake a very important project. The result was one of the best instances of cooperation between the Navy and American industry up to that time.

When the Navy laid out its needs for a lighter-weight, more flexible diesel that could be tied to an electric generator for use both in charging batteries and driving a submarine, it became clear to a number of people in the Navy that such an engine-generator combination could be very useful on a railroad locomotive.

It was known that the railroads were anxious to find a lighter and more flexible locomotive to replace the heavy and expensive coal-burning steam locomotives of the day. The Navy representatives went to the railroads and had very little trouble in convincing them that these new engines could be the answer to their search. They were interested and let it be known to the companies working on the new Navy diesels.

Encouraged by the promise of such a large commercial market, as well as by the chance to supply these engines for the Navy, a number of American concerns undertook the project. The two winning builders were the General Motors Winton Division in Cleveland (GM) and the Fairbanks-Morse Company of Wisconsin (FM). Both of these engines, particularly the GM Winton, went immediately to use in the railroads, and a revolution in locomotives was under way.

The new fleet submarines used GM and FM engines that were essentially identical to those being used in the railroads. This extensive use in private industry contributed enormously to the final successful development and wonderful reliability of these engines.

For reasons that I will never understand, a group of men in the Navy's Bureau of Ships was deeply impressed with the engine built by the Hooven-Owens-Rentschler Company (HOR) of Hamilton, Ohio, based on a design licensed from the Maschinenfabrik-Augsburg-Nürnberg (MAN) organization of Germany. The initials of the American manufacturer and the German designer were combined to designate these engines as *HOR MAN*s. They were referred to, in polite company, as *HOR*s, with each letter pronounced separately. As the 1930s progressed and submariners had more experience (almost all of it bad) with these engines, they came up with some saltier names.

These HOR MAN engines were installed in eight of the twenty-six fleet submarines built in the mid- and late 1930s. No sooner were they put into service than they began to cause trouble. They were, to my knowledge, never used by the railroads.

To everyone's dismay, in the rush to build new submarines after Pearl Harbor, the Bureau of Ships decided to install these same HOR MAN engines in the first squadron of twelve submarines to be started at Electric Boat. Although we were at war with Germany, and in spite of the HOR's poor performance in the early American fleet submarines, the plans went forward.

Given these concerns, we were all very interested to learn that the MAN engines powering German U-boats were definitely not using the particular design found in the HOR MANs. For all these reasons, we worried about the HORs in the *Jack* from the day we reported on board.

With this ominous report from the engine room of the *Jack*, our worst fears about our German-designed engines were becoming a reality.

The HOR people and the Navy's Bureau of Ships had a remedy—they thought. Spring-cushioned gears would be placed in the train to provide some flexibility and, voilà, we would be back in commission. The change was to be made on all twelve of the submarines in Squadron Twelve—forty-eight engines. But first, the new, cushioned gears had to be fabricated and installed, and this would take time. All of the ships in the Squadron would be delayed at least two months in departing for the Pacific, and we were not pleased.

We tried to make good use of our time with daily visits to the attack teacher, but we were all distinctly unhappy. The war was going on without us while we wasted time sitting at the dock.

We received a happier piece of news during this waiting period— happier particularly for me. We were getting another officer before departure for the Pacific—Ensign William Chisholm Coleman III of the United States Naval Reserve. My days of being the youngest, most untrained officer on board were over. What was more, Dykers told me that Coleman would be taking over the commissary department and would also become the assistant communications officer. To say that this was good news would be a serious understatement. Commissary was dull, time consuming, and to my mind, unrewarding work. Also, as assistant communications officer, Coleman could take over the tedious tasks of making corrections to classified publications and of drawing and cataloging codes and ciphers—both long and tiresome chores.

The day Billy Coleman reported on board was a happy one for many reasons. Bright, cheerful, handsome Billy was easy to like. His blond hair, blue eyes, and ruddy complexion went along with a spirit that was hard to suppress. A graduate of the University of the South at Sewanee, Tennessee, he was a welcome contrast to the steady navy blue of Annapolis that otherwise dominated the wardroom. Billy never tired of singing the praises of Sewanee—after all, he had to defend himself against the heavy Annapolis majority.

Like Dykers, Roach, Refo, and Goodman, Billy hailed from the South (from Charleston, South Carolina), and our dinner conversations about the Civil War (established early in the *Jack* wardroom's history) took on even greater enthusiasm. In particular, we covered

Stonewall Jackson's campaigns in the Shenandoah Valley in minute detail. Front Royal and Port Republic became as familiar to me as Groton and New London. I valiantly tried to uphold the Northern point of view, but it was a losing battle with five against one.

Finally the day came when, with all engine modifications completed and all other preparations made, we were ready to leave for the Pacific. It was April of 1943, three months later than it should have been.

Nancy and I had lived in the dollhouse much longer than we had ever thought possible. But now our chance to be together was over, at least for a long time.

"When will you ever get back, Jim?" she asked. "Is there any chance you will be sent back for new construction?"

I laughed, "We've had more than our share of new construction, thanks to all the delays. Now it's our turn to do some work."

Still, it was hard, dreadfully hard. Plans had long been made for Nancy to live with her parents in Annapolis while I was away—we had no real idea how long that would be. We both knew it could be forever. We heard about submarines being lost in the Pacific every month or so. Some of the new widows were friends of Nancy's.

It was a tough good-bye, and we were both grateful that there were no children.

It was a fine spring morning when we backed away from the pier at Electric Boat and the good-luck waves of our families and the workmen standing there. They all knew, and we knew, it was up to us now.

I was still not qualified as an OOD, so I was with Beetle Roach on the bridge as we plowed through the waters east of Montauk Point and out into the Atlantic. Beetle went down to the conning tower to set our course for the Mona Passage, which lay more than a thousand miles away, between the Dominican Republic and Puerto Rico. We were on our way.

Then Beetle joined me again on the bridge, and we began to talk about the adventures ahead. No officer on board had made a war patrol, and only one or two of our seventy crewmen had any war experience.

We were beginning to talk about the training we still needed when Beetle said something very important: "Jim, the only safety we have is in being trained so well that we are better than anyone we meet. We have to work the living bejesus out of everyone on this boat so that when we do meet the Japanese, we'll be the best trained submarine they've ever had to handle. We have no other protection—if we don't work that hard, they'll kill us as sure as we're standing here."

I was so impressed with these words that when I got off watch, I wrote them down and kept them in my desk.

They were with me the rest of the war.

2

On to
Pearl Harbor

After a few days at sea on the way to the Caribbean, Dykers called me into his cabin and said, "Beetle tells me you're ready to be a top watch stander now. It's pretty quick, but this is wartime. I know we can count on you."

I went out of the skipper's room walking on air—and right into Beetle's room to thank him. He said, simply, "You're ready for it—go to it. You get the twelve to fours, Miles as senior watch officer gets the eight to twelves, and Goodman takes the four to eights."

I had expected to get the midwatches, the traditional lot of the junior top watch officer. It's the toughest watch. Not only is your sleep broken up every night in the middle, but the times you are off watch are not the best to get sleep. But I couldn't have cared less about the details—I was a top watch stander. The rest of it just didn't matter.

Not long before we left New London, we received another new member of our wardroom, though not in the usual way. Our senior chief electricians mate, John T. O'Brien, was promoted to Ensign USN under a program where particularly outstanding enlisted personnel were being promoted to officer status when their records, age, and potential warranted it. The custom was to transfer such new officers to a different ship so that they would not have to deal with shifting their relationship to a group of shipmates they had gotten to know well as fellow enlisted men.

None of us, however, wanted to see O'Brien leave the *Jack*. Everyone—crew included—felt that he could handle the transition. So after several long phone calls to Washington by Dykers and a formal written request, Jack O'Brien was assigned to our wardroom. We were glad to have him there, and he fit in from the beginning.

Obie, as we sometimes called him, naturally had a lot to learn about standing deck watches, and he was put on the eight to twelves with Miles Refo, the senior watch officer. So it was clear to me that I would be the only OOD standing watches alone. Billy Coleman was on with Leyton Goodman, and Obie was on with Miles.

My first watch alone was scheduled to be the twelve to four that afternoon. I was so excited about it that I forgot all about lunch. Going through the control room on the way to the bridge, Chief Hunt, our chief of the boat, smiled at me and said, "Way to go, Mr. Calvert."

The word gets around fast on a submarine.

It was a beautiful sunny day when I got to the bridge to relieve Miles and Obie. I got congratulations from both of them, but I had the feeling that Miles was wondering just what the hell was happening to the Navy when a green Ensign with no sea experience was becoming a top watch stander on a new fleet submarine. However, he said nothing about this. I think he was resigning himself to the changes the war was bringing.

We were reaching the northern part of the Caribbean. Yellow pieces of sargasso weed drifted by from time to time, making a striking contrast with the deep blue of the Gulf Stream. Flying fish were about, taking their long, skittering flights away from some predator I could not see. The air was warm and balmy, a blessed relief from the biting cold of Long Island Sound, where even April could be bitter. My three lookouts were wearing their blue denim shirts with the sleeves rolled up and the ever-present blue baseball caps pulled down over their foreheads for protection from the sun.

All seemed right with the world. I was on a submarine, headed for the Pacific war, and as a top watch stander. I had taken a small but not insignificant step toward success in what I had so long wanted to do.

After about five minutes of this pleasant reverie, the quartermaster of the watch came to the bridge with a chart on which he had marked the location of the known U-boats in our general area as given to us by the Navy antisubmarine command about noon that day. None were in our immediate vicinity, but three had been detected within a hundred miles, and undoubtedly others were out there, invisible and unknown.

A surfaced submarine, as the *Jack* had been while traveling, was a sitting duck for a submerged enemy submarine. The U-boat, with only his periscope showing, had the drop on any unsuspecting surfaced submarine. He would be tensed and ready beneath the surface, poised for the kill. The first sign of danger for the unaware surface traveler might well be the ear-splitting torpedo explosion that spelled his doom.

Eternal vigilance is indeed the price of survival for a submarine transiting the ocean's surface. We were following a zig plan to make us harder to hit, but we knew from experience that a zig plan can often be deduced and then penetrated by a skillful submarine skipper. The only real safety lay during the day in a supersharp lookout for periscopes, and at night in a steady watchfulness for lurking, surfaced U-boats, usually down-moon where they would be least likely to be seen.

We hammered this danger into our lookouts day and night. Each was responsible for a sector encompassing one-third of the sea around us. "Never take your binoculars down" was the lookout's watchword. To make this possible, lookouts were relieved every twenty minutes by another set of lookouts. As the officer of the deck, I was not expected to keep my binoculars up all the time since I had no relief coming for four hours. But, believe me, they were up there about 90 percent of the time.

Again and again during our training at New London, Dykers had told the officers of the deck, "If you see those torpedo wakes, turn toward them—comb the wakes. If you see a periscope in firing position but no wakes, turn directly away from the periscope. If you see a periscope not in firing position, dive and turn away as you submerge. Go to three hundred feet—he can't shoot you there."

So despite the blissful beauty of the day and my elation over being qualified as a top watch stander, the dark thread of danger ran through that watch, as it would through every watch for years to come. Submarines, submarines, submarines—whether German or Japanese—were never far from our minds.

As we approached the Mona Passage, about our third or fourth day out, the enemy threat became a reality. It was on my afternoon watch, on a bright, sunny, calm day, when the port lookout said:

"I can't be sure . . . but isn't that a submarine, Mr. Calvert?" He gave me the bearing; sure enough, way out on the distant horizon was a U-boat. It was painted either white or light gray, and its silhouette, well-known to me from study of the identification books, was undoubtedly that of a Type VII U-boat. Though he was six miles or more away, we were headed very much in his direction.

What to do? I called Dykers to the bridge and, after studying the U-boat for some time through binoculars, determined that the German was on a course similar to ours but diverging to the east. Dykers decided we would attempt to skirt around him to the west. There was no way we could approach him successfully submerged—he was going away from us at a speed higher than we could make if we dove.

Dykers gave the order for the new course and speeded up to hasten the process. About fifteen minutes into this effort, a loud and clear report came from the same lookout who had originally spotted the U-boat.

"I'm pretty sure he's diving!"

Both Dykers and I looked carefully; sure enough, the U-boat was gone. Now what to do was again the question, and I was glad I did not have to answer it. The German had undoubtedly seen us and could be—probably was—closing on our track right now. This was our first enemy contact, and I know Dykers wanted to pursue it aggressively. But how?

If we stayed on the surface, we could be a sitting duck. If we submerged, we had no way of getting closer to him. We did not have sonar that was even remotely capable of fighting a duel with another submarine. It would be like two blindfolded men fighting in a pitch black cellar, each armed with a baseball bat.

Dykers decided to dive. I remembered his instructions from our training days in New London: "If you see a periscope not in firing position, dive and turn away as you submerge."

We dove and turned away from our last bearing on the U-boat, then proceeded slowly to the west. Although there were some scares from the sonar men, who thought they heard screws but couldn't be sure, we had no more positive sign of our German friend. He was probably as wary of us as we were of him.

Well after dark we surfaced and got on our way again with a supercareful lookout, and following a cautious zig plan, we continued our transit to Panama.

During our long, calm, sunny days en route from New London to Panama, we had plenty of time to read. We would gather around in the wardroom, a space maybe twelve feet long and eight or nine feet wide, containing a table about twice the size of two large card tables. We spent a lot of time there doing our routine paperwork and reading. The same table served as our dining table for all meals and as the site of the evening bridge game. At mealtime it was covered with a soft pad and a white linen cloth. At all other times, our table wore a green baize cover well suited for paperwork, reading, or the bridge game. There were bookcases at both ends of the room and a strictly low-fidelity record player not far from the locker holding the sacred chronometer, so essential to the navigators.

From the time that we had been under construction at Electric Boat and housed in a temporary office up on the hill near the building ways, I noticed that Dykers and Roach spent a lot of time assembling, organizing, and reading our file of patrol reports. These were detailed, classified documents written by each submarine on the conclusion of its patrol. A copy was sent to each active submarine as well as to any under construction. Each patrol report was complete with endorsements (comments, sometimes acidly critical of the way the patrol had been conducted) from its chain of submarine command. Patrol reports ranged in length from thirty to sixty pages, very occasionally more. Dykers and Roach recommended that I read each one carefully, and believe me, I did.

We had a carefully framed, large National Geographic chart of the Western Pacific on the inner bulkhead, or wall, of the wardroom. The chart was very useful for orienting ourselves while studying the patrol reports.

The reports were not all literary masterpieces, but each one contained a detailed record of a submarine's experiences while on patrol, written personally by the skipper. This task was never delegated. Every torpedo or gun attack was thoroughly described, its results were analyzed, and enemy tactics were appraised. The reports also contained a rundown on any difficulties experienced with the submarine itself, which, in the early days of the war, were many.

When I reflected on the fact that I would soon be out there putting my life and the lives of my shipmates on the line in the same environment, I didn't need anyone to tell me that these reports were important. I read each one so many times that I almost memorized them—particularly those about patrols that Dykers marked as having been well conducted, in his opinion.

"Here's one from a boat that really gets in there and slugs. Look this one over carefully," Dykers said as he handed me a report received just the day before.

To my great interest and surprise, I saw that it was from the

Seawolf, my old friend from Naval Academy days. Having visited her at Annapolis and then read about her war exploits in the newspapers, I felt as though I was greeting an old friend. After reporting to the Pacific Fleet, the *Seawolf* had been assigned to the Asiatic Fleet in the Philippines and had become one of the first in action against the Japanese.

I read every word of the *Seawolf* patrol report over and over. In reading it I noted the professional way in which it was written and also the emphasis that her skipper, Commander Warder, placed on the performance of the TDC operator. It seemed that my feeling, developed during our training period, about the key role of this machine was not far off the mark.

Later all of us in the *Jack* were given even more reason to be interested in the patrols of the *Seawolf.* We were told that Frederick Warder, who had by then completed seven very successful patrols in the *Seawolf,* would soon be reporting for duty as our Division Commander, a position critical to prepatrol training at Pearl Harbor.

As nighttime arrives on a submarine at sea, the ritual of shifting to night lighting takes place. Of course, we were running darkened topside, leaving the bridge absolutely black. No smoking for the OOD or the lookouts. Fortunately, on a submarine you don't have to worry about a light showing from the interior.

Nevertheless, down below, anywhere that bridge personnel might go, the bright white lights that had blazed during the day were extinguished and red lights substituted. Because night vision was a precious commodity on a wartime submarine and red light impairs it less than white, the control room, the crew's mess, all of officer's country, and the torpedo rooms (where most of the lookouts slept) went to red light soon after sundown. Only the engineering spaces stayed white.

Once you got used to them, the red lights had a sort of comfortable, homey feel, and the shift helped to set the rhythm of long weeks at sea.

Eight hours after completing my first afternoon watch alone, I was wakened for my first midwatch (midnight to four). I had gotten caught in the after-dinner bridge game and had not turned in until about 10:30. I had just gotten into my deepest sleep and was sure someone was making a mistake. But when the temporarily off-watch lookout who had been sent to wake me thrust a pair of red glasses into my hands, I knew what was going on. Sleepily I put on the goggles, thrust on my shirt and pants, staggered into the deserted wardroom, and got a cup of bitter black coffee that had been sitting on the warmer for so long it was almost as thick as syrup. It tasted awful, but it had plenty of caffeine and soon did the job of jolting me awake.

I went to the conning tower, where the quartermaster showed me our position on the chart and gave me the latest reported U-boat positions—a matter of even more intense interest since our recent experience. He then handed me the small, green night order book in which Dykers had written the night's instructions for the OODs before turning in. I read it under the dim red light of the chart table.

The instructions were fairly routine: precautions about U-boats, a course change about two in the morning, and a warning that, since we were in range of the Panama-based aircraft looking for U-boats, we would probably need our recognition signals. We were to have the blinker gun ready on the bridge with the necessary signals for the time period.

Not long before our transit, our squadron mate, the *Harder*, had been mistakenly bombed by an American patrol plane while en route from New London to the Panama Canal. If this could happen to *Harder*, one of the best-trained submarines I knew, it could happen to anyone. To say we were on the qui vive because of the *Harder* incident would be putting it mildly.

Even after taking off my red glasses, the bridge was pitch dark. There was a thin moon and many stars, with little or no wind. Warm and pleasant. Miles and Obie were more than ready to be relieved. They repeated all the information in the night order book, as was the custom, and told me there was nothing in sight. Soon I was alone on the bridge with my three lookouts. Up went my binoculars for a careful look all around the horizon. We were near the shipping lanes running to the canal. Because of the U-boats, any shipping would be running totally dark and thus could pose a collision hazard to us. The battery charge had been completed, and we were sliding along in a smooth sea on three engines, making about fifteen knots. The sound of those HORs purring away back aft was reassuring, yet I could not help but wonder just how reliable they would prove to be. So much depended on them.

I gazed at the stars briefly, hoping to see a known constellation, then quickly dropped this effort, realizing that my only proper concerns were U-boats and the safety of the ship. It was now totally my responsibility. Seventy men and six other officers were counting on me to do what was needed should an emergency arise. All but the watch section were asleep. All the sleepers were counting on the ship's watch structure, and on me in particular, to keep them safe. I knew I was the least experienced of the watch standers, but if hard work and concentration could do it, I was going to give it my best. To be honest, I was scared; I didn't know what else to do except pray—and I did plenty of that.

The moon went down, and blackness wrapped around us like a soft, warm blanket. The stars seemed brighter than life and closer than I remembered ever seeing them. The phosphorescence of the tropical waters shone around our bow and in our long wake, stretching out astern. I reflected on the unusual darkness—was it so dark that a submerged U-boat couldn't see us through his periscope? I thought so but wasn't sure. If he were on the surface, charging batteries, would we see him before he saw us? I intended to make sure that we did.

Suddenly one of the lookouts said quietly, "I can hear a plane, but I can't see him."

I heard him too—but try as I might, I couldn't see anything in the direction of the sound.

Then, brighter than any of the stars, a light flashed near the horizon. It was sending code. I read *dot dash*, then *dash dot dot*—the letters *A* and *D*. It came again—*AD, AD*. As ordered, I had memorized the recognition signal challenge and the response. *AD* was the correct challenge, so I grabbed the blinker gun and sent the correct response—*dot dot dot*, followed by *dash dash dot*—*SG*. No answer.

I sent it again, twice—*SG, SG*. Still no answer. Had I gotten it wrong? Had the plane misread it? Was this going to be the *Harder* incident all over again?

Then from the plane: *dot dash dot* and again *dot dash dot*—*RR*, or *roger roger*, the welcome Navy response meaning "I have read and understood your response."

In what seemed like no time, the plane was overhead and waggling his wings in salute. He then disappeared to the east in his ceaseless search for U-boats.

Breathing a sigh of relief and trying to sound as matter-of-fact as possible, despite my hammering heart, I called the captain on the bridge phone.

"Exchanged recognition signals with what looked like a Navy patrol plane. He banked overhead and went off to the east."

"Very well, thank you," was the casual response. Clearly I had wakened Dykers from a sound sleep. I was pleased to think that he had been sleeping and not lying awake worrying about his new top watch stander.

As my heart left my throat and returned to somewhere near its normal position, I reflected on the events just passed. Wartime was wartime, but this seemed like a dangerous way to live. Those patrol planes were anxious, terribly anxious, for a U-boat kill. Who had looked up that signal on board the plane? What if he had been so busy flying the airplane that he had gotten it wrong? Suppose I had gotten it wrong?

I reflected again on the *Harder* incident. Were we going at this the right way? The only alternative was to dive on sighting *any* airplane. But that, especially at night when you would be late spotting him, could invite a fatal bombing. I decided there wasn't any better way and began to concentrate on matters more immediately at hand. Up went the binoculars as I began an even more intensive search for that U-boat so much on my mind.

"Permission to come up and relieve the lookout, sir," came from the conning tower hatch in the forward part of the bridge.

"Granted," I grunted, and up came the shadowy figure of the relief lookout. He passed me and climbed up the periscope shears to his station.

In a few minutes, two more relief lookouts came up, and the routine was completed. Down went the other men to the control room for a cigarette and a cup of coffee.

Routine, routine, routine. It may be dull to those who live on the land, but it is a blessing to those who live on ships—particularly warships. Routine means that things get done safely and with a minimum of confusion and effort. Things are done exactly the same way, on exactly the same schedule, time after time until they are done almost unconsciously. Temperature and voltage readings are taken, oil is applied, food is cooked, watches are relieved, positions recorded, logs written—all without any orders being given and with a minimum chance of something being forgotten or done wrong. This gives the officers and senior petty officers more time to think ahead about what might happen and how to deal with it if it does. Especially the officer of the deck.

Watches are always relieved fifteen minutes early. So at 3:45

promptly, Leyton Goodman and Billy Coleman appeared, sleepy but in reasonably good humor and ready to take the watch. I told them of the plane and the exchanged signals. Billy had already memorized the new response, which would go into effect at 4:00 A.M. exactly. I briefly wondered if the clocks on the patrol planes were as accurate as ours.

I went below, turned into my nice soft bunk, and was sound asleep in two minutes. Before I knew it, our senior steward, Domingo, was waking me and asking if I wanted any breakfast. I had had about three hours' sleep, but hunger called. I weaved into the wardroom and had Domingo's pancakes and bacon, made as only he could.

Domingo was our senior wardroom steward and a remarkable man. A native Filipino, he was a veteran of more than twenty years in submarines and a wonderful cook. He had retired after completing his twenty years and had found employment in Hollywood as houseboy to Hedy Lamarr, a famous and beautiful movie star of the time. After Pearl Harbor Domingo had volunteered to return to the Navy, provided he could serve on an active submarine going to fight Japan. The Navy had granted his request, and he joined the *Jack* during our building period.

Needless to say, all of this absolutely fascinated the other men, who never ceased asking Domingo about Hedy. Was she really as beautiful as she seemed in the movies? Had he ever seen her without makeup? Without clothes? Did she have boyfriends? And on and on.

But Domingo was perfectly loyal to Hedy. So far as I know, he never said a word about her except that she "was a very nice lady." He refused to answer any and all questions about his famous employer. I believe part of this was genuine loyalty and part a desire to go back to his old job when the war was over.

Although in a submarine officers normally eat from the general mess, stewards pick up the food back aft from the ship's galley and bring it forward to the wardroom, where it is served to the officers. I soon learned that having a steward who is liked by the ship's cooks can be important. There are good cuts of meat, and then there are other cuts. Domingo knew his business, and despite his refusal to come up with any information about Hedy, he was well liked by the cooks.

Landfalls are something very special to people who make long sea voyages and have at least some of the responsibility for the navigation. Actually, I had no such responsibility. But as one who had always been interested in navigation, I was watching it carefully.

Each morning, at that special time when the stars are still visible but the horizon is just becoming clear (maybe a half hour or forty-five minutes before sunrise), Beetle Roach and Olsen, the quartermaster, would be up on the "cigarette deck," as the after end of the bridge was called, getting as many stars as the weather would permit. Especially when I had the eight to twelves with Beetle, I had a front seat for the whole show.

Looking through the eyepiece and mirrors of the sextant, Beetle would bring the star down to the horizon, thus getting its exact altitude. When he had it just right, he would call out, *"Mark!"* and Olsen would write down the precise time to the second, using a watch he had just set by the chronometer kept in a special locker in the wardroom. Once every twenty-four hours, Olsen would come to the wardroom and, using a special radio for the purpose, get the time tick radioed to all ships in the Pacific. This time tick, together with the inherent accuracy of the chronometer, ensured that the time written down at the call *Mark!* was as accurate as possible. This was very important, since an error of only one second could cause an error of up to four miles, depending on the direction of the star concerned.

As I listened to these shows occurring on the cigarette deck, the names of the stars—Betelgeuse, Rigel, Arcturus, Aldebaran, Polaris, Vega—became as familiar to me as the names of baseball players or of the Civil War generals so endlessly discussed in our wardroom. Occasionally I reflected on the ancient Arab astronomers who had given these stars their names as they studied them in their long desert vigils. But that was long ago and far away. Now those stars were of vital importance to *us*, in 1943, as we prepared for our landfall.

Once in a while I would get to see the layout of the star lines on the large plotting chart that represented our part of the ocean. At times the lines would cross in a point as small as a BB. At other times they would enclose an area as large as a nickel. At still other times, with lots of clouds or in very rough weather, they would not cross well enough to mean anything. Accordingly, we might know our position within a mile, within five miles, or not at all.

By now it was late April and we were approaching Colón, on the Atlantic side of the Panama Canal. Naturally I was particularly interested in the navigator's work at this time. Since I had the midwatches, however, I had not gotten to see the morning and evening star shows. But I knew from listening to the wardroom conversations that clouds had interfered with stars and that we did not have a very good idea of our position.

The landfall would be the proof of the pudding. The entire string of morning and evening star fixes, checked with sun lines twice or more during the day—all would come to a head with the landfall. Did we really know where we were, or were we just kidding ourselves—adrift somewhere on the broad Caribbean? We would soon know.

Because all navigation lights in the Caribbean were extinguished to avoid giving help to the U-boats, Dykers and Roach wisely planned to make our landfall at Panama in daylight. Beetle said we should see the mountains of Panama sometime on the four to eight if all went well. When Leyton and Billy came up to relieve me, I said I would stay up awhile to help look for the landfall. I'm not sure they appreciated it, but at least they didn't kick me off the bridge.

About 6:30, Leyton said laconically, "I see the mountains."

He called the skipper on the bridge phone and reported the sighting. No big deal, I thought. But shortly Beetle came to the bridge, rather more excited. For the next half hour he and Olsen were busy using binoculars and charts to see if they could tell just *which* mountains we had spotted.

In another few minutes, we could see the very tops of the masts of a ship roughly dead ahead. Assuming he was heading for Colón, we were just about right—but maybe that was not where he was going. More than one ship has gotten into trouble following another, assuming that the lead ship knew where he was going.

One of the horror stories of Navy navigation concerns a squadron of destroyers that was following its flagship at high speed in a dense fog off the coast of California in the 1920s. Understandably, they thought the squadron commander in the flagship knew where he was going. Unfortunately, he did not. Seven of the destroyers went on the rocks, close to the shore. Their whistles and emergency signals warned the others away, but the seven ships and many lives were lost.

Happily, there was to be no horror story that day; soon the lighthouse marking the entrance to Colón Harbor came into sight. Beetle's navigation had been right on the button. We were all happy—but none as happy as Beetle and his quartermaster assistant. Before long we were tying up to the docks at the Submarine Base in Panama. Here Beetle had had his last active submarine duty, and it was also familiar territory to Miles Refo, Leyton Goodman, and Obie. Only Billy Coleman and I were wide-eyed newcomers.

We had a day or two at the base while some minor repairs were completed. During this time we had an experience ashore that left a deep impression on me. When in a new port away from home, the officers from small ships frequently go ashore in a group in the evening to "sort of see the town." This was old hat to the others but all new to me. Goodman and some of the others either had the duty or had work to do on board, so this sight-seeing group consisted of Dykers, Roach, Refo, and myself.

We ended up in a famous (or infamous) night spot, where you could have dinner, see a show of sorts, and have women of doubtful background come uninvited to your table to ask if you wouldn't buy them a drink. There was dancing, but what else they had in mind was not too hard to divine. Wisely, we all stayed seated firmly throughout the evening.

When the bill came, it was outrageous. Beetle said the place had raised its prices now that all the ships were coming through on their way to the Pacific, filled with officers and men that didn't know any better. We were all in uniform, and apparently the management had spotted us as easy marks, unfamiliar with the ways of Panama. They had underestimated Dykers. After reading the bill again carefully, he slowly and deliberately put his glasses away in a safe spot inside his jacket.

"We're gonna fight our way out of this dive—the hell with these robbers. Come on," he waved to all of us.

Here we had a new side of our aristocratic and elegant skipper. This was a call to battle from our commanding officer. How could we ignore it? I put my wallet in a safer place and began to look for the bouncer and to estimate his fighting ability.

Fortunately, Beetle had different counsel. "Wait a minute, Skipper. This place is loaded with police and shore patrol. We'll be under arrest and on our way to the hoosegow before we can ever get a cab. How is that going to look in the papers in the morning?" he warned.

"I agree," said the usually taciturn Refo.

Faced with these sober words from two respected shipmates who had recent experience in Panama, our captain reconsidered his fighting orders.

"I guess you're right—but it still burns my ass to be taken this way."

We divided up the bill and paid it, all the while grousing loudly to the waiter about highway robbery. Our waiter suddenly spoke no English, after having done pretty well all evening. His tip was very small, but there was no complaint.

We returned to the ship without incident, but I reflected on this new insight into our skipper's character. Some men are born with what the Navy calls "command presence" and what people in civilian life call "star quality." Dykers had it in spades. He looked, acted, and talked like a man accustomed to, and confident with, the authority and responsibility of command.

Beyond that, it now appeared that he had a tough side we had not seen before. But the toughness seemed to be balanced with good sense—after all, he had taken Beetle's advice on the fight.

The next morning we began our transit of the Panama Canal. We took the American pilot on board; he formally relieved the captain of his command for the passage, a move required by law. The pilot had taken several new American submarines through the canal and clearly knew his business. As First Lieutenant I was on deck supervising our line handlers as we went through the various locks that raised us to the level of Gatun Lake and then lowered us down again to the Pacific. It was a wonderful chance to see this magnificent American engineering accomplishment up close.

By afternoon we had arrived on the Pacific side, discharged our pilot, and without delay taken our departure for Pearl Harbor, a voyage of more than four thousand miles. We had fueled to capacity at the Submarine Base and had also taken on fresh water and supplies. We were ready to go.

The Isthmus of Panama twists to an east-west direction where the canal cuts across, so that the canal actually runs north and south. In fact, the Atlantic entrance at Colón is slightly west of the Pacific entrance at Balboa. As a result, one speaks of the northern (Atlantic) and southern (Pacific) rather than the eastern and western entrances to the canal.

On leaving the canal on the south side, to enter the Pacific, we went through the Perlas Islands. We had to be careful of fishing boats because, even in the middle of the war, sport fishermen were there to enjoy some of the finest big-game fishing in the world. Almost all of the fishermen, we were told, were wealthy South Americans, not Yankees, and that added to the language hazard if we had to talk to them by radio.

We had also been cautioned by the staff of Commander Submarine Squadron Three at Colón that, in addition to sport fishermen, we might meet U.S. Navy patrol boats on our first night out in the Pacific. They would be using the same two-letter recognition system we had used in the Atlantic. The staffers at Colón had warned, however, that we had to be careful, because the patrol boats weren't too sharp with the signals and frequently had the wrong ones.

Great, I thought. Here we go again.

Fortunately, a patrol boat doesn't provide quite as grave a threat as an antisubmarine airplane. There is usually a little more time to straighten out any misunderstanding.

Sure enough, on the midwatch that first night, after working our way around several fishermen, we encountered a patrol boat. He was up-moon, so we saw him from quite a distance. Not waiting, I challenged him with the two-letter signal then in force. Long delay . . . then, slowly, he came back with the wrong response. What to do? I called the quartermaster to the bridge, knowing that he was much faster and more accurate with the signal gun.

"Send him," I said, "'This is an American submarine. You have the wrong response.'"

The quartermaster repeated the message back and then sent it quickly and correctly. Too quickly, perhaps, because the patrol boat asked for a repeat. Then, haltingly, "Roger, roger," from the patrol boat. By this time he was drawing well astern, so I just logged the incident, informed the skipper, and went on.

It didn't, however, do much to strengthen my confidence in the two-letter system.

After a few days of quiet cruising in moderate or smooth seas, the Pacific showed us that it is not always like its name. A dropping barometer had forecast some foul weather, but this proved to be more than I had ever seen before. The northwest wind gradually built up to thirty-five or forty knots, with gusts above that. The huge waves were marked with long streaks of foam. The heavily overcast skies gave the ocean a mean, sullen look.

The bow of the *Jack* would plunge down, sending up a great cloud of spray, much of which would be thrown all over the bridge. Next we would get a heavy dose of green water on the bridge, some of it even going down the conning tower hatch, eventually making its way into the control room. Dykers slowed to two-engine, then one-engine speed to ease the jarring and to prevent water from coming down the main induction and into the engine rooms, where it could cause electrical shorts and worse.

Even at the lower speed the seas were brutal. We had the lookouts tie themselves to their platforms to avoid being swept over the side. The officer of the deck also put on a life belt. Finally, as the storm intensified, we brought the lookouts down for safety.

After a time there was nothing to do but bring the OOD down and shut the conning tower hatch. Only the main induction valve was supplying air to the diesels now, and even in its protected position under the cigarette deck, we got occasional heavy slugs of green water in the engine rooms.

The bridge was unmanned now, so we kept the watch on one of the periscopes, raised as though we were submerged. We all took turns on the scope—OOD, assistant OOD, quartermaster, lookouts—everyone.

It was not a job anyone cherished. Hanging on to that scope and trying to see anything as it swayed drunkenly through the sky was not for the weak of stomach. Still, most of the lookouts liked it better than trying to hang on to a lookout perch on the bridge with one hand while using binoculars with the other, with green water slamming into you every few minutes like a Mack truck.

Most of our men were pretty good sailors, but this storm proved too much for many of them. They were skipping meals, and a few were so seasick they couldn't stand their watches.

Of course, there is always the old hand who loves this sort of thing and literally revels in it. Our first-class gunner's mate, Frank Lynes, had a constitution that was impervious to seasickness and, so far as I could see, any other kind of physical punishment.

"Lotsa chow tonight! No competition. Lotsa chow!" he shouted as he walked through the heaving and pitching boat, rubbing his hands and laughing at his weaker shipmates. Most of them just groaned and turned away from him in their bunks.

Nor were the officers immune from this problem. Neptune is no respecter of rank. But as the new boy on the block, trying to prove that the Navy had made no mistake in sending these green '43 Ensigns straight to submarines, I was determined not to miss a meal. I appeared for evening meal on the first night of the big storm right on time. To my mild surprise, the only other person in the wardroom was Miles Refo. His surprise at seeing me was more than mild.

"Sure you feel like eating?" he asked with a grin.

"Absolutely—why not?" I shot back with more enthusiasm than I really felt.

That first meal of the big storm was roast pork and mashed potatoes. I can see it still. The stewards had soaked the white linen tablecloth and its soft underpad with water so that the plates and half-filled glasses would not slide. Bracing myself with one hand, I did my best to eat with the other. It was slow going, but I was making it.

Miles finished up quickly and immediately lit up one of his stogies. These were old, crooked, rum-soaked cigars that generated a dreadful odor. Even in the best of times, they were not very welcome in the wardroom, and I had noticed that Miles never lit one when the captain was present. Tonight, however, his stogie was going like Vesuvius. Before long the smoke was so thick that I could barely see across the little room.

Miles finished his apple pie while taking frequent puffs on his stogie. I was damned if I was going to let him chase me out of there with that cigar, so I grimly held on and finished my piece of pork roast. But I passed on the apple pie and repaired to my bunk—"to get ready for the midwatch," as I said.

That meal seemed a sort of watershed in my relationship with Miles. After that I think Miles decided that, for better or for worse, I was there to stay, despite my Yankee background and lack of sea experience. In the long run, I had no better friend on the *Jack*.

It was another rite of passage.

Day after day the storm went on. Our speed of advance was now well below plan; we were going to be at least a day late getting to Pearl. Slowly but surely, however, our seasick casualties were getting their sea legs and returning to their watches, despite the continuing storm. I have always been blessed with a strong stomach, and seasickness has not been one of my problems. But there is such a thing as sea-weariness. You're not sick, but you are so tired of hanging on, so tired of being unable to sleep without being tossed out, or nearly out, of your bunk that you wonder if the storm will ever abate—and if you will ever feel normal and energetic again. I remember getting out my Bible and reading from the 107th Psalm:

They that go down to the sea in ships, that do business in great waters;
These see the works of the Lord and his wonders in the deep.

For he commandeth and raiseth the stormy wind, which lifteth up the waves
thereof.
They mount up to the heaven, they go down again to the depths: their soul is
melted because of trouble.
They reel to and fro, and stagger like a drunken man, and are at their wit's
end.

The psalmist could have written that passage after a walk
through the *Jack* that afternoon. It was strangely comforting for me
to read those words, for they reminded me that men of the sea have
been going through such storms for centuries—and most of them
have survived in ships not nearly as sturdy as ours. When I put the
book away, I felt considerably better.

Finally, as with all storms, this one began to subside. The gray
skies, which seemed to have been there forever, began to break and
show patches of blue; the wind swung around to the east (a good
sign in that part of the Pacific) and eased to a pleasant ten or twelve
knots. Even though the northwest swells from the great storm were
still there, they were being calmed by the east wind. Dykers went to
two-engine speed, then to three. Before long we were zipping along
at about sixteen knots in relatively calm seas with sunny, warm
skies. Even the flying fish were attempting their long, skimming
flights again. Their silver sides, flashing in the new sunlight, seemed
a kind of celebration of the end of our ordeal.

Life at sea is not filled with diversions comparable to those
ashore. Any break in the daily routine is welcome—even a storm.
But there is nothing, absolutely nothing, so wonderful as the feeling
of having weathered a truly bad storm and come out the other side
with the ship in good condition, all hands surviving without injury,
and normal routine reestablished. Things are made shipshape once
again below. Wet clothes are dried out and restowed. Best of all, the
platform under your feet once again is nearly stable.

If that experience does not lift your spirits, then they are not
liftable—at least not at sea, so you had better try a different calling.
There are those who call it "hitting yourself on the head with a
hammer" because it feels so good when you stop—but I guess they
just don't understand.

It was mid-May, and we were looking forward to another landfall,
this time on the Hawaiian Islands. Here again blackout conditions
prevailed, so we planned for a daytime landfall, albeit one day late

because of the storm. This time we saw the high peak of Mauna Loa, on Hawaii, on my afternoon twelve to four. We had had lots of good stars for the week preceding, so this was not so much of a kick for Beetle. During that afternoon and night, we plowed along with the islands in sight on one hand or the other. Having been told that the Kaiwi Channel was always rough, I was not surprised as we moved through it on my night watch. Morning saw us entering the Pearl Harbor channel, with Diamond Head and Honolulu visible off to the right.

Pearl Harbor is shaped roughly like a three-leaf clover and is some five miles long, measuring from the main entrance (the stem of the clover) to the top of the harbor. The three leaves of the clover are called *lochs*. In the middle of the center loch lies Ford Island, a Naval Air Station and the location of the battleship moorings that had been the main targets of the Japanese that fateful Sunday morning of December 7, just a little more than a year before our arrival.

Seven of our battleships, then the heart of the Pacific Fleet, had been moored that morning at huge quays located along the southeast side of Ford Island when the Japanese struck. *Nevada* and *Arizona* were moored singly to the north, then *Tennessee* and *West Virginia* alongside each other, then *Oklahoma* and *Maryland* in another pair, and finally *California* alone in the southern position. *Pennsylvania*, the last of the fleet's battleships present, was in the dry dock across the way in the Navy Yard.

A half dozen or so cruisers and some twenty-five destroyers were scattered around the lochs in various places. It was a tremendous fighting force—but it thought our nation was at peace.

Admiral Yamamoto had, in great secrecy, assembled a mighty fleet consisting of six aircraft carriers carrying over four hundred combat aircraft. He had brought them, along with a powerful supporting force, undetected to within five hundred miles of Pearl Harbor on the evening of December 6. The next morning, by 6 A.M., Admiral Nagumo had brought his striking force of Japan's top six aircraft carriers to the launch point, about 275 miles north of Pearl Harbor.

A strike force of more than 180 combat planes—torpedo bombers, high-level bombers, dive bombers, and fighters—was launched, and they circled while they waited for their leader's "Tora! . . . Tora! . . . Tora!"

Then they struck. The carnage was fearful. It was like hitting a sleeping man on his head with a sledge hammer.

When it was over, all of the battleships except the *Pennsylvania* were put out of the war for at least a year, and even she had received a severe bomb hit. Cruisers and destroyers had been hit, and the Army airfields at Hickam, Wheeler, and Bellows Fields had been severely struck. The Army had lost two-thirds of its planes, while the Navy and Marine Corps had only 54 left out of some 250.

The Navy alone had over two thousand officers and men killed and over seven hundred wounded. Army and Marine Corps personnel losses were less numerous but were still severe.

In about two hours the Japanese had given the United States the worst one-day disaster in its history.

The *Jack* entered Pearl Harbor on May 21, 1943—some sixteen months after the strike on Pearl Harbor. It was a solemn moment for all of us as we went past Ford Island and saw the place where our battle fleet had been destroyed. Work was still under way on some of the sunken battleships, and the mainmast of the *Arizona*, still serving as a coffin for the more than one thousand officers and men trapped in her, could be seen in the distance.

Looking at the actual scenes of this disaster, I felt as though something very sacred to my country had been raped and pillaged—not in the fair give-and-take of war, but without warning on a calm and peaceful Sunday morning, while men slept in their bunks.

I do not consider myself a vengeful person, but that morning I felt a deep, burning desire to show these people they could not do that to the United States without paying a dreadful price. To my young mind, the day those red-ball-marked planes winged in from the north was one that indeed would live in infamy and change the world forever.

Fortunately and miraculously, the Japanese had ignored the submarine base at Pearl. When we tied up to those strong, well-built piers, we were in the midst of the largest and best-equipped submarine base in the world.

While the submarine base at Pearl was huge, it was also overloaded with work. New submarines going out on patrol, submarines returning from patrol with battle damage, and submarines needing modifications—all of this added up to more work than the base could handle alone. Even manned to capacity and working seven days a week, twenty-four hours a day, it still could not keep up.

Fortunately, the *Griffin*, the submarine tender assigned to Squadron Twelve, was at Pearl.

A submarine tender is a large ship, usually of ten thousand tons or so, equipped to be a floating submarine base. Torpedo shops, foundries, machine shops, electrical shops, medical and dental facilities, spare parts bins, paint shops, food stores—everything needed to keep a submarine and her crew well and happy—are on board. It was lucky for us that she was there, for despite the enormous priority the *Jack* had in our minds, the submarine base was simply too busy to take us on. We needed new piston rings on two of the HOR engines (too much oil consumption—a mildly ominous symptom), and we needed to have one of the new SJ surface search radars installed. The *Griffin* did it all and did it well.

We had our final prepatrol training at Pearl under our new Division Commander, Frederick B. Warder. This was an experience to remember. We thought we had a pretty hot attack party, but we certainly learned some new tricks from this old salt. There are some men who simply look at home on a ship, just as there are some who look like they belong on a horse. Warder looked as though he had been born to be on a submarine. It was as natural to him as breathing, and the crew members *loved* him. Not that he was any popularity jack (the sailor's name for an officer who tries to curry favor with them). But they *knew* he knew exactly what he was doing around a submarine, and they all felt infinitely better that he was the one giving us our prepatrol training.

And they were doubly pleased that he took the time before we departed to tell the whole crew, at quarters, that he thought we were well trained and ready to go to war.

Happy and productive as this prepatrol training was, one of its periscope daytime attacks produced a somewhat embarrassing incident. We were making approaches on a World War I four-stacked destroyer named the *Allen*. It was a sturdy ship but too old for the Pacific war, so it was being used as a target for practice submarine attacks.

On this occasion Dykers worked us into a good firing position; we were shooting our exercise torpedo from about half a mile away. We calculated that the track of our torpedo would be just about perpendicular to the track of the target, with a very small gyro angle—a perfect shot.

I barked out "Fire!" and we all felt the submarine lurch as the fish went out. I was pretty confident we had a good solution. Dykers put the scope back up to see if the target had zigged just as we fired. This inevitably occurs from time to time and may or may not cause a miss. It was one of the reasons that spreads of two, three, or four torpedoes (depending on the size and importance of the target) were used in actual warfare. In this case the sonar bearings were tracking on with the target—usually a good sign. I was confident that we were going to get a hit—but not of the sort we actually got.

"Holy suh-*moly!*" exclaimed the skipper.

"We've got a surface run!" was the next word from the periscope.

The torpedoes of the time had a mechanism that enabled them to sense the pressure, and thus the depth, of the surrounding water. The mechanism then sent signals to the horizontal rudders of the torpedo, which kept it at the depth set by the TDC before the fish was launched. An exercise shot was normally set to run safely underneath the target, its bubbles showing the target the accuracy of the shot.

But something was wrong with the depth-keeping mechanism of this fish. It was running on the surface, porpoising up and down as it traveled toward the *Allen*.

Surely the *Allen* will see it and avoid, I thought.

"I don't think he sees it!" said Dykers.

Just as the fish reached her, the *Allen* turned, but too late—the torpedo hit her right at the waterline and amidships. Like an old, fat man hit unexpectedly in the stomach, the destroyer burped a large cloud of black smoke from her stacks.

"Surface!" barked Dykers. Three blasts on the Klaxon followed. In a minute or two we were blinking over to the *Allen*.

"Are you damaged?"

"Checking," came the answer? There was no sign of the exercise torpedo. Was it inside the *Allen*? Or had it sunk? The destroyer seemed to stay on an even keel as we watched her anxiously.

"We have a large dent in the engineering spaces but only a small split. Taking water, but we can control it. The fish is not on board. Returning to port," came from the *Allen* by voice radio.

After a careful search, we concluded that the exercise torpedo had sunk.

Commander Warder joined us on the bridge and laughed, "Tommy, I think that fish had a transportation screw that didn't get removed."

He was referring to the small screw that held an internal pendulum in place while the fish was being transported from the base or tender to the submarine. Failure to remove it before loading the fish into the tube was a notorious cause of surface runs.

"I'll bet I know a couple of torpedomen who are glad that torpedo is lost and gone forever so we won't have a chance to check it." This was all that Dykers would say. He hadn't thought it was as funny as Warder had.

Wisely, no one on the bridge added anything to this conversation.

Before we left on patrol, Warder arranged for a sister ship of the *Allen* to give us a bit of a return wallop. The *Jack* had never received a depth charging, and we were about to lose our virginity in this department.

For this final part of our prepatrol training, we went to periscope depth and paralleled the course of the accompanying destroyer. We had plenty of periscope out of the water, so our location was plain.

"Rig for depth charge!" went out over the 1MC announcing system. Watertight doors slammed shut, other sea valves were closed, and we were ready.

"Ready when you are," Dykers told the destroyer on the underwater telephone.

"There it goes," said the skipper as he watched the depth charge roll off the stern of the destroyer.

Click . . . BANG! The *Jack* received her first taste of the real thing. Since we were a decent distance away, there was no damage to the *Jack*. But the sound effects were very real, and some of us realized a little more vividly what a dangerous game we were going to be playing.

I had to admit, it was a lot louder than I had thought it would be.

June 5 saw us under way for the island of Midway, eleven hundred sea miles or so to the west-northwest and a convenient stop for fueling and small repairs. We had good weather, and the passage to Midway was uneventful except for a few efficiently exchanged two-letter recognition signals with patrol aircraft from Pearl. We made good time and before daylight on the ninth, rendezvoused with a Midway-based patrol plane, who escorted us in. By 8 A.M. or so, we were moored at the small base and were beginning to take on fuel.

It was almost exactly a year since the famous carrier battle that had taken place as a result of the Japanese effort to take the little island.

The assault on Midway had been central to Admiral Yamamoto's plan to dominate the Pacific. Having severely diminished the United States' power at Pearl Harbor, he now wanted to lure that weakened fleet out to defend Midway and thus to attain his hoped-for sea Armageddon.

Two of his first-line carriers had been tied up in the Battle of the Coral Sea, but he took Admiral Nagumo and the four remaining top carriers, *Akagi, Kaga, Horyu,* and *Soryu,* not only for a strike on Midway but for the great sea battle Yamamoto hoped to invoke in the general vicinity of Midway. Nagumo and these four ships represented the cream of Japan's naval-aviation strike capability. They were all veterans of the Pearl Harbor strike just six months earlier. During these six months, Nagumo and his carriers had—to use their own words—"run wild" in the Western Pacific, wreaking havoc wherever they went.

Nagumo and his ace pilots were indeed a formidable force. Along with them, Yamamoto had brought a Midway-occupation force of some five thousand men, in twelve transports. All of this was protected by a huge surface force of more than 160 ships. It was essentially the bulk of Japan's combatant Navy.

Against this powerful force U.S. Admiral Chester W. Nimitz had only about one-third as many ships. He had only three carriers, the *Enterprise, Hornet,* and *Yorktown,* the latter of which had just received two days of emergency repairs at the Pearl Harbor Navy Yard from severe damage suffered at the Battle of the Coral Sea just a month earlier. The odds against Nimitz were long indeed.

But he had a powerful ally in the code breakers. Admirals Nimitz and Spruance (his tactical at-sea commander for this battle) had a pretty good idea of Nagumo's location and intentions. Nagumo had none about the Americans, and his supposition that they were not within striking distance proved critical.

Nagumo wisely kept half his planes armed with bombs and torpedoes to strike enemy ships should they appear—contrary to his expectations. Nevertheless, when his Midway strike-force commander returned to the flagship and said the island would need more softening up before troops could land, Nagumo ordered the ship-strike weapons to be taken below and the waiting planes to be armed with incendiary and fragmentation bombs.

While this change in armament was taking place, Spruance's dive bombers spotted the Japanese carriers and commenced their deadly attacks. Although Nagumo received some late warning of the nearness of the American carriers and attempted to change his deck load back to ship-strike weapons, it was too late. The Japanese carriers had what aviators called a "locked deck," and they could not get their strike planes off. To make it worse for Nagumo, his fighter cap was down too low to take on the dive bombers (they had been fighting off, successfully, a torpedo bomber attack that had suddenly begun).

Starting at fourteen thousand feet, the American dive bombers tipped over and roared down out of the cloud-flecked sky with the flight decks of the Japanese carriers in the crosshairs of their dive-bombing telescopes. The bombers scored hit after deadly hit. The Japanese carriers dodged wildly, their wakes looking like curlicues on the surface of the blue Pacific. But it was of no avail.

The bombs being transferred on deck detonated with devastating damage to the Japanese carriers. Their high-octane aviation fuel caught on fire, and in less than ten minutes, three of Japan's first-line carriers were sunk or sinking.

Akagi, Nagumo's flagship, was the first to be abandoned, and the Admiral had to transfer to a nearby cruiser, carrying the emperor's portrait with him. Before the day was out, the fourth Japanese carrier, *Hiryu*, was gone. The Americans lost the *Yorktown* in the fray, but the back of the Japanese striking force had been broken. In believing their code breakers (by no means all their superiors in Washington had felt that they should) and in launching their air strikes at exactly the right moment, Nimitz and Spruance had made some of the great command decisions of the war and had won the most important carrier battle in history.

During our visit to Midway, we felt we were on sacred historic ground. If the Japanese had won that battle and secured Midway for their use, they could have made land-based strikes against Hawaii at their leisure. In all probability they would have forced the evacuation of all civilians from these strategically vital U.S. islands.

More important from a military point of view would have been the continual threat to the Navy Yard and Submarine Base at Pearl Harbor. Midway itself was highly important to the submarines, since this advanced fueling base enabled us to stay on station in our patrol areas days longer than would otherwise have been the case.

A year after the great battle, we still felt a deep sense of gratitude to those brave airmen for what they had done. Almost surely they had changed the course of the war, and indeed of world history, in their few golden moments over the wrinkled blue surface of the ocean near Midway.

As the sun lowered in the west on a clear evening, we set the maneuvering watch to get under way. We left all of our mooring lines at Midway; otherwise, they could be depth-charged out of their deck lockers and betray our presence or foul our propellers. Leaving those lines, which we had guarded and maintained so well since commissioning, seemed somehow symbolic. We were cutting the umbilical cord now. From here on, the *Jack* would be on her own, alone in enemy waters.

As dark came, we steamed slowly out of the Midway channel, joined up with another submarine departing for patrol, and set our courses westward. After leaving the thirty-mile security circle, we wished each other "good luck" by blinker and set our courses for our patrol areas. Our companion was headed for an area near the Philippines.

We were headed for Tokyo Bay.

3

Patterns of War
in the Deep

During the weeks spent en route from New London to Pearl Harbor, I had learned from long conversations with both Dykers and Roach much more about how powerful fleet submarines like the *Jack* had been developed. It had not been easy. In the twenty-three years between the world wars, American submariners had fought a long and often discouraging battle for resources and recognition.

Despite the successes of German U-boats in World War I, American submarines of the early 1920s were looked on as faintly humorous upstarts, vainly aspiring for a place in the mighty fleets of the U.S. Navy. To make matters worse, the early American submarines were small, unseaworthy, and unreliable in performance.

A major problem surrounded the engines. World War I had made it clear that only diesel engines were safe and reliable enough to do the job in a submarine. Since they had originally developed the diesel, the Germans dominated this area, and their engines (mainly the MANs) were taken as the principal model by all navies interested in submarines.

The American submarines built during the 1920s and early 1930s were equipped with engines based on MAN designs. (This was before the introduction of the HOR MANs—these early engines were built on older MAN concepts.) They were less than successful and soon developed a well-deserved reputation for poor reliability.

Another problem was torpedoes. The Bureau of Ordnance and its Torpedo Station at Newport, Rhode Island, were responsible for the development of these weapons, but between the wars the Bureau had become a kind of exclusive club (more than a little surface-ship oriented) that was very slow in developing truly reliable submarine torpedoes.

Finally, by the late 1930s, the Bureau's Torpedo Station had developed the Mark XIV torpedo. This was a forty-five-knot, alcohol-and-compressed-air torpedo that, after a number of alterations that had to be undertaken during the war, became the submarine workhorse of World War II. The Bureau had, however, not been so successful in other areas. Along with its Torpedo Station, it had spent a huge amount of time and money on the development of a secret magnetic exploder for use with the Mark XIV torpedo.

This device was conceived to counter the increasingly heavy belts of armor coming into use in the warships built between the wars. The new exploders were designed to be set off by the magnetic field of the target ship and to explode underneath its keel (where there was no armor) rather than against its side. This required a delicately balanced exploder that would not be set off by the earth's magnetic field or that of the firing submarine but would be triggered only by that of the target ship. The heavy secrecy surrounding the magnetic exploder resulted in an absence of at-sea testing before the war—with dire results, as we shall see.

Despite all of these impediments, the submariners continued to attempt to get themselves and their ships accepted for broader roles in the Navy's planning. They wanted to move beyond their assigned roles as coastal defense units and develop submarines with true oceangoing capabilities. They wanted to be part of the big team.

By the early 1930s, the Navy planners had no choice but to assume that a war with Japan would occur in the Pacific within a decade or two. The responsibility of the planners is always to examine the *capabilities* of a potential enemy, not his *intentions*. Witnessing the rapid buildup of the Japanese Navy to world-scale size, the planners could see that it had the capability of waging war with the U.S. Navy on a fairly equal basis. It would have been irresponsible for them to fail to prepare for the possibility of such a conflict.

While the major emphasis of the planners was on the buildup of the U.S. surface fleet, the American submariners believed they themselves could also play a significant role in this effort. They believed they could develop submarines that would have the capability of making patrols in Japanese waters that could not only yield valuable intelligence information but also do real harm to the Japanese Navy. In addition, they felt the Japanese merchant marine, upon which this small island nation depended so heavily, was particularly vulnerable to properly conducted submarine warfare.

To most of the senior naval officers of the interwar period, the submarines were about as welcome in this expanded role as ladies of the evening at a debutante ball. The planners could see that not nearly enough money was available to construct the surface ships required. To these men the thought of wasting any of their precious resources on the dinky, unreliable submarines of the day was out of the question.

The submariners themselves, however, were the best thing the submarine force had going for it. They were tough, persistent, and persuasive. They insisted that submarines had real potential to help the U.S. cause if war came in the Pacific. The U-boats had demonstrated in World War I what submarines could do in areas that were totally under the control of a powerful surface navy. Needless to say, the battleship admirals were able to restrain their enthusiasm for this view of naval warfare.

Nevertheless, when President Franklin D. Roosevelt and his pro-Navy administration came into power in early 1933, more naval construction money became available, and finally some American submarines of real promise were built. Twenty-six of a significantly improved design were launched and designated, somewhat optimistically, as fleet submarines.

These boats had the best engines by far of any American submarines yet built. I have already discussed the evolution of the GM Winton and Fairbanks-Morse engines. They were stellar. The engine picture was clouded only, as I have said, by the poor performance of the HORs. (Eight of the twenty-six had these ill-fated engines.)

These new fleet submarines of the 1930s had a surface speed of about eighteen knots and a cruising radius of well over ten thousand miles—big enough to go to Japan, report its major fleet movements, and return back to Pearl safely. Once in Japanese waters, they could certainly sink some *marus* (as Japanese merchant ships are called) and, with good fortune, even some Japanese naval units. The American possession of Midway Island, a potential fueling station more than a thousand sea miles west of Hawaii, helped to buttress this concept. The Pacific submarine war patrol pattern was beginning to take shape—at least in outline.

It was clear from my discussions with Dykers and Roach that these differences between the surface and submarine officers in the developmental years of the 1920s and 1930s were very serious indeed. Feelings on both sides ran deeply.

We were all in the same Navy, with the same long-term aims

for the welfare of our nation. But dominant weapons make dominant groups of officers, and by its very nature, the submarine was a threat to the dominance of the surface navy. Dykers and Roach had cast their lots with the submarines and, quite understandably, they wanted their point of view to be heard. I was their willing audience for many a long evening.

In these intramural struggles between the wars, two names, in particular, had become known to every submariner, and to most senior surface officers—Charles Andrews Lockwood, Jr., and Ralph Waldo Christie. Both were dedicated submarine officers, and each played an important role between the wars as well as later in World War II itself.

During the 1930s Lockwood was the most articulate and effective of the submarine spokesmen. He held the submarine desk in the Office of the Chief of Naval Operations in the late 1930s. In this position he argued long and hard for a fleet submarine to be built that would have a surface speed of twenty knots, a cruising range of at least fourteen thousand miles, a submerged speed of eight knots (if only for half an hour), six tubes forward and four aft with a total capacity of twenty-four torpedoes.

This submarine was also to have an improved TDC for fire control, air conditioning, and reasonably comfortable living quarters for officers and crew. It was to be able to stay at sea for at least sixty days—seventy or more when needed—and to be capable of operating safely in any part of the world's oceans. This was a big order, and it required a big submarine. It would have to be over three hundred feet long and displace some fifteen hundred tons.

In addition to their arguments with the rest of the Navy, the submariners also had some intramural warfare. All during the interwar period there were, among the submarine officers themselves, advocates not only of the large submarine of the type that Lockwood, among many others, touted but also, equally persuasive, boosters of a smaller, simpler submarine. The small-submarine disciples argued that their ships would cost less and thus more of them would be available in the intense struggle for money of that period. Lockwood had a strong big-submarine ally in Ralph Christie, the most prominent submarine member of the Bureau of Ordnance's gun club. (He was a leader in the development of both the Mark XIV torpedo and the magnetic exploder.)

The small-submarine group, however, had a respected and senior advocate in Admiral Thomas C. Hart, who, to make matters worse for Lockwood and Christie, was Chairman of the powerful General Board that was, at least in theory, responsible for the characteristics of new ships to be built for the Navy. Hart wanted a ship of some eight hundred tons, similar to some of the U-boats of World War I and to those then being built, in contravention of the Versailles treaty, by Nazi Germany.

Despite the power and prestige of Admiral Hart, Lockwood and Christie, in a series of critical meetings in 1938, won most of their points; the resultant Tambor class was pretty much what they (and most younger submarine officers) wanted built. Each was 310 feet long, displaced about fifteen hundred tons, and was equipped with a much-improved TDC. Only six were authorized, however—a pitiably small number considering the ever more apparent threat then facing the United States in the Pacific. To the senior Naval officers of that time, it was not a question of whether there would be a war with Japan but only of when.

Three of these first six truly fleet-type submarines were equipped with GM Winton engines and three with Fairbanks-Morse. The Tambor class was a success from the start. It became the prototype for every fleet submarine built subsequently for World War II. There were minor changes, but the Lockwood-Christie concept proved to be what was needed for the Pacific submarine war.

Dykers and Roach made it clear that while it was the line officers (Lockwood and Christie, in this case) who laid out what was needed militarily, it was the officer and civilian engineers of the Navy's Bureau of Ships and their cohorts at Electric Boat and the two submarine-building Navy Yards (Portsmouth, New Hampshire, and Mare Island, California) who actually designed the submarines to meet these operational requirements. They also ensured that these submarines could be built in a reasonably short time and would have the reliability and toughness to make them effective warships. It was a fine example of effective line-staff cooperation.

For reasons unknown to either Dykers or Roach, the policy had developed that all submarines built at Electric Boat were to be equipped with GM engines and that all those constructed at the Navy Yards were to be equipped with FMs. Unfortunately for our Squadron Twelve, the decision was also made to equip its twelve boats, all being built at Electric Boat, with the already infamous HOR engines.

No one could explain to me why this decision was made. The only answer that made sense at all was that the GM Winton and FM manufacturing plants were overloaded from the heavy submarine building program. I noted, however, that GM engines were still being made available for new railroad locomotives. Where were our priorities?

When Pearl Harbor was attacked, there were twenty-nine boats in the Asiatic submarine force, based at Manila under the broad command of Admiral Hart. Six of them, however, were the relatively ancient and very limited S-boats,* while the remaining twenty-three were all pre-Tambor-class fleet submarines (one of which was Commander Freddy Warder's *Seawolf*).

There were only twenty-one submarines assigned at Pearl but twelve of them were of the new Tambor class, the pride of the submarine fleet. Of the twenty-one, however, in early December of 1941, eleven were in the States in overhaul or just shaking down on their way from the building yards. When the Japanese struck on December 7, only four submarines were actually at the Pearl Harbor Submarine Base, and only one, the Tambor-class *Tautog*, was a modern fleet submarine. As I have said, the Japanese ignored the Submarine Base and did no damage to it. They did fly over it, however, and the *Tautog* was credited with downing one Japanese plane with its fifty-caliber machine guns.

Later in the war, the *Tautog* gave the Japanese abundant reason to wish that they had targeted her on December 7.

When the war broke in the Philippines, Admiral Hart had had more warning than that given to Admiral Husband E. Kimmel at Pearl— most of the war alert messages in late November 1941 indicated that when the Japanese struck, it would almost surely be at the Philippines. It also was clear that any defense of the Philippines themselves would have to come mainly from the submarines. Almost all of the U.S. strike force was at Pearl, and Hart had no surface assets capable of taking on the Japanese. After Pearl Harbor he promptly deployed his available submarines around the Philippine area in an attempt to stop the expected southbound invasion forces.

Unfortunately, these submarines were largely unsuccessful in this mission.

The patrol reports of the submarines involved revealed some of

---

*The S-boats were built in the 1920s and were not really war-capable by 1941.

the reasons for this failure. The submarine force of late 1941 had many serious problems.

The scorekeeping in the prewar fleet exercises had placed such heavy emphasis on nondetection that many of the submarine skippers attempted to develop a method of shooting that depended altogether, or almost altogether, on sonar bearings. When the target or its escorts got at all close, these skippers would go to one hundred feet or so and finish the approach using only bearings given them by passive (listening-only) sonar. If no periscope ever broke the surface, they reasoned, how could they be detected?

Opinions on this tactic were divided, however. Tommy Dykers, commanding the old S-35 at Pearl Harbor in the 1930s, would have none of the sonar approach idea. He was a skilled periscope handler and was almost never detected before firing. In addition, the relatively precise information he had from the periscope at firing resulted in a large percentage of hits. He soon got the well-deserved reputation of being a torpedo hotshot. Still, the so-called sonar approach was favored by a lot of the fleet-boat skippers—perhaps because they were older men and inherently more cautious.

In any case, many of the first attacks of the war were conducted as sonar approaches, and practically every one was a failure. The use of the sonar attack by so many of its skippers was one of several reasons that the submarines of the Asiatic Fleet did so little to stop the invasion of the Philippines.

An even more important reason for the poor performance of our Asiatic submarines was that they had serious torpedo troubles. Some torpedos would sink shortly after leaving the submarine; others would run erratically, a few even circling back toward the firing submarine.

Even worse than the problems with the Mark XIV torpedoes themselves were the obvious defects in the much-vaunted magnetic exploders. Expert captains like Warder in the *Seawolf*, making periscope attacks where they could see clearly what was going on (one on an anchored ship), saw their torpedoes pass directly under the targets with no explosion. Worse yet, the delicate exploders would sometimes cause the warhead to detonate before reaching the target, doing no damage but giving away the presence of the submarine and often subjecting it to a gratuitous depth charging.

The submarine force was paying dearly for the total absence of any live peacetime firings with the magnetic exploder and for the inadequacy of exercise firings with the Mark XIV torpedo. Making matters worse, the Bureau of Ordnance tried to defend its work. They asked if the submariners were sure they were aiming the torpedoes correctly, whether torpedoes had been maintained and made ready properly. It was a bad example of staff-line relations, in contrast with the fruitful one between Lockwood-Christie and the Bureau of Ships.

All of us had to remember, however, that these early patrols were the Kitty Hawks of submarining in the Pacific war. The skippers had no patrol reports to read, no wartime experience to draw on, and no knowledge of just what capabilities the Japanese anti-submarine forces actually had. Not knowing, they had to assume the worst. To make their attacks, they had to work into position against opposition, real and imagined. It was nerve-racking and exhausting work. And then, having gotten into position and fired their torpedoes, to find them malfunctioning or blowing up in their faces was more than some skippers could stand.

In the early months of the war, it became apparent that some of the captains were just not wartime skippers. Command had been given, principally on the basis of seniority, to men who had not tried to force new ideas on their seniors, who had behaved themselves ashore, had kept their submarines clean and their sailors out of trouble. Commendable as at least some of these characteristics may be, they do not always belong to young men who will take their submarines in harm's way in wartime.

One had only to read a few of the early patrol reports to see that some, though by no means all, of the skippers had not only been less than aggressive but had actually evaded opportunities to attack when it appeared at all dangerous to do so. Other skippers tried to do the job bravely but simply could not take the burden of responsibility for other men's lives in such harrowing circumstances. Some even had to be relieved on patrol by their executive officers. Without doubt, the unreliability of the torpedoes, and particularly the magnetic exploders, played a major role in these failures of command.

On top of all these problems, there was a serious shortage of Mark XIV torpedoes. The Bureau of Ordnance had simply not foreseen the number of submarines that would be built, the number of torpedoes that would be fired, and the logistic problems of supplying these torpedoes in adequate numbers to Pearl Harbor, Midway, and the Far East.

The Squadron and Force Commanders were understandably

tense about this situation. They could visualize a time when they would not be able to send their submarines on patrol because the forces' torpedo supplies were exhausted. As a result, they hammered on their skippers to shoot only one, or at most two, torpedoes per target. They were confident that the magnetic exploders could do the job even if only one hit were obtained. Undoubtedly this pressure to economize on torpedoes was another contributing factor in the very large number of failed attacks among the early patrols.

As the war progressed through 1942 and into 1943, it became apparent that the endorsements attached to war patrol reports as they passed up the chain of command Navy fashion—from Division Commander to Squadron Commander and, finally, to the Force Commander himself—were becoming important policy-making instruments. These endorsements were as carefully read by all the submariners as the patrol reports themselves. The sonar approach became an early casualty along with periscope attacks made from too cautious a distance. In their endorsements the three levels of command often gave frank criticisms of the way in which the patrol had been conducted. They also, on occasion, gave bitter criticisms of the Bureau of Ordnance and its torpedoes and exploders. A few choice words were also included about the HOR engines and their failures on the firing line.

It became clear that U-boat tactics being observed in the Atlantic by British and American antisubmarine commanders were becoming known to the Pacific submarine squadron and force commanders. Some of their endorsements began urging night surface attacks, a tactic being widely used by the U-boats. Here the submarine was being used more as a torpedo boat than as a traditional periscope shooter.

It was apparent to all of us, as we studied the shape of the submarine war in early 1943, that we owed much to the mental toughness of these senior commanders. They had the moxie to call them as they saw them in their endorsements, even though they themselves had not been out there on the firing line. Men are instinctively reluctant to second-guess those who have actually been in battle.

It was also clear that the courage to make these policy-shaping endorsements was bolstered by the backing given by the Force Commanders. Rear Admiral Robert English had taken over the Pearl Harbor command in the spring of 1942 but had been killed in a tragic airplane crash in January 1943. Shortly thereafter, the man who had done so much to shape the fleet submarines that were carrying the brunt of the war, Charles A. Lockwood, was named Commander Submarines, Pacific Fleet. Admiral Lockwood encouraged frank criticisms by his division and squadron commanders and, indeed, often used his own endorsements to advocate new policy and attack doctrine.

I have gone on at some length about these endorsements because they provide insight into how the submarine force operated. To my knowledge, with the exception of the controversy surrounding the magnetic exploder (about which I'll say more later), no attack doctrine or policy was ever dictated to a skipper before he left on patrol. The submarine tradition of trusting the man on the firing line continued. Nonetheless, submarine skippers were quick to see what the most advanced and useful ideas were, whether they came from new tactics described by other skippers on patrol or from recommendations in the endorsements. Most of the new ideas were accepted on the spot by many, if not all, of the skippers. Once they departed on patrol, the skippers decided on what tactics they would use. That was left up to them.

I can remember a conversation with Dykers back in New London, when we were undergoing training. Although I cannot recall his exact words, their gist was that a submarine is an extremely complex device in which many things can go wrong at the worst possible time. Unless the skipper and his officers can rise above the complexity of this weapon and remember that it has only one purpose—to sink ships—they will never be successful.

Frequently, when reading reports of early patrols in which there had been a failure of command, I also thought about those words. In the last analysis, three things usually got to those skippers who could not handle the challenge: first, the complexity of the weapon system (the submarine and the torpedoes combined); second, the proneness of that weapon system to failure, often at the most critical moment; and third, the dangerous and nerve-racking environment in which that weapon system had to be used.

It took a good man with a tough mind—one who did not have an oversupply of imagination. There were enough real problems in the throes of combat to leave no place for a man who saw shadows. A sort of dogged, imperturbable stolidity was preferable to brilliance and imagination. But there had to be at least some of the latter, combined sometimes with an almost reckless aggressiveness, to get the best results.

It was a complex and somewhat rare combination of qualities. But those skippers who had them were beginning to rise above the pack by early 1943.

So here was the *Jack,* on the verge of entering its first real combat, steeped in the vicarious experience of dozens of patrol reports and endorsements, trained as well as hard work and Dykers's experience could make it. But the *Jack* depended on main engines of bad repute and stowed, deep in her torpedo rooms, twenty-four Mark XIV torpedoes still equipped with magnetic exploders.

I did not spend too much time thinking about the exploders. Surely Admiral Lockwood, with all of his experience, would not send us out with them unless he was convinced that the troubles had been corrected.

Still, I could remember the dark expression that always came across Commander Warder's face during our training periods whenever these exploders were mentioned. After all, he had been out there with them.

4

At the Gates
of Tokyo

The sea area around Tokyo looks like a fat, slightly recumbent, two-part snowman being viewed from the side. The head of the snow-man is some forty miles long and twenty to twenty-five miles wide. Roughly speaking, Tokyo is where the eye of the snowman would be, Yokohama at the nose, and Yokosuka at the chin. This is Tokyo Bay proper.

The neck of the snowman is a five-mile-wide channel known as Uraga-suido, or just Uraga Strait. It leads south to the fat body of our snowman, which is a large, deep bay called Sagami-nada. This bay, more than sixty miles long on its western side, shortens to less than twenty miles on its eastern side as it drops down from the Uraga Strait. It is more than fifty miles wide and thousands of feet deep. There is no way for a ship to reach Tokyo Bay and its three big cities except by going through Sagami-nada.

Tokyo Bay itself is not deep enough to permit the submerged operation of a submarine, and despite all press stories and movies to the contrary, no American submarine operated inside Tokyo Bay itself during World War II. However, Sagami-nada, where patrol-ling actually took place, rather quickly came to be called "Tokyo Bay" by submarine sailors and officers although, correctly speaking, it was not. Sagami-nada was, however, close enough to Tokyo to give pause. Several Japanese airfields and the naval base at Yoko-suka were located only a few miles away. A submarine, which must surface every night for a battery charge, had to watch its step in Sagami-nada.

Standing like a watchdog in the center of the nearly fifty-mile-wide entrance to Sagami-nada is the rocky island of O-Shima. Run-ning nearly ten miles from north to south and perhaps six miles wide, the island rises in some parts to more than two thousand feet. Shipping coming out of Tokyo Bay and its heavy industrial ports must go through either a fifteen-mile wide pass west of O-Shima or a twenty-five-mile pass east of it to reach the open sea.

On June 19, 1943, our first day in the patrol area, Dykers submerged the *Jack* about twenty miles southeast of O-Shima and began working up to the north to the bottleneck between O-Shima and the southern tip of the peninsula that forms the eastern edge of Sagami-nada. The tip is a cape known as Nojima-saki.

About an hour before dark, we sighted a southbound convoy of three marus (Japanese merchant ships) with a single destroyer escort. They were to the west of us, in the direction of O-Shima. This was the first contact of the war for the *Jack*—and on the first day in the area. Anyone who believed in omens had to feel that this was a good one. Unfortunately, we were new at periscope patrolling, and the ships had gotten well beyond us before we sighted them. They were going away from us rapidly.

But we were not about to give up. We set the ships up on the TDC as well as we could and, at dark, surfaced to chase them. Dykers planned to work ahead of them during the night, then submerge on their track and make a periscope attack about dawn. Using the TDC as a reference, and plotting estimated tracks on charts of the area, we pursued the ships to the south at four-engine speed. We didn't see how they could evade us.

An encounter was not, however, to be. Although we chased the convoy until the next morning, we never regained contact. A string of islands hangs south from O-Shima for many miles, and apparently our convoy had given us the slip by going westward between two of them. Whether or not the convoy knew it was being pursued, we'll never know. I doubt it very much; I think the course change had been planned all along, perhaps as a precautionary measure.

It was our first experience at being up all night in a fruitless chase.

We soon developed a routine for patrolling in Sagami-nada. We remained at periscope depth all day and watched for ships or for telltale smoke on the horizon. The OOD, not Dykers, manned the periscope. The skipper usually waited in his room or in the wardroom, or used some of the time to take his daily walk through the boat. We could, of course, call him at an instant's notice.

Periscope watching was tedious business. To start with, we

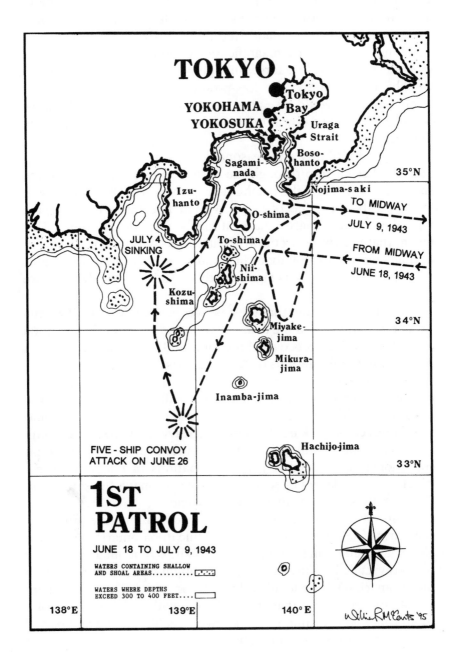

would put up the scope and take one sweep fairly quickly in low power, to be sure that no one had sneaked up on us. Then we would make a long, slow, careful scan of the horizon in high power, in an attempt to see a distant ship. The scope was shifted from low to high power by twisting one of its two handles like the throttle on a motorcycle. Low power made everything look roughly normal size, while high power gave a magnification of about seven diameters. It was easy to miss a close target in high power because it went by so quickly; consequently, the low-power sweep was an important safety factor. It would take about a minute to do all this. Then we would put the scope down for about three minutes before repeating the procedure.

In good visibility and reasonable seas, the distance at which one could see a ship through the periscope was a function of the size of the target and the height of scope exposed. Our routine was to expose about two feet of scope. With that height we could see the tops of an average maru's masts at maybe three or four miles. This meant that the circle of our observation was only six to eight miles in diameter, an area of about fifty square miles at best. Of course, rain or fog or rough seas significantly diminished the distance we could see.

When you consider that the passages east and west of O-Shima were much wider than the distance we could see, and that the total area of Sagami-nada is over three thousand square miles, you can understand the limitations of daytime periscope patrolling.

Fortunately, there was sonar. All the time that we were submerged the sonarmen were listening carefully for the sound of ship propellers. With everything quiet inside the submarine, the sonar sometimes could pick up the sound of heavy screw beats from Japanese ships several miles away. The distance depended on the sonar conditions, determined largely by variations in temperature between adjacent layers of seawater. In Sagami-nada the sonar conditions ranged from mediocre to really bad.

This cut both ways, however, since both submarines and antisubmarine (ASW) ships used sonar. While the submarine depended almost altogether on listening, the ASW ships sent out a short burst of energy, called a *ping,* that might, or might not, reflect back from the submarine with enough volume to be heard. This echo might be the first indication that the ASW ship had of the presence of a submarine. This technique was known as echo ranging and played a key part in antisubmarine warfare.

Variations in the temperature of the water layers make it much harder to use echo ranging successfully. The boundary between the layers acts as a barrier and deflects both the ping and its echo. Although the *Jack* was equipped with echo ranging equipment, we never used it since it would, without doubt, have given away our presence.

Reading patrol reports, we had learned that echo ranging by Japanese escorts, as they proceeded with their convoys, was frequently what had alerted the submarine to the presence of enemy ships. A pinging ship could be heard at ranges much greater than those at which it could hope to get an echo—and frequently at ranges greater than those at which a submarine's sonar could pick up the convoy's screw noises.

One other thing helped us with our submerged patrolling— smoke. Most of the marus put out black smoke as they moved along, and it could frequently be seen at a much greater distance than the ships themselves. Many of our daytime contacts were developed either by sonar or by smoke or by a combination of both, but confirmation by sighting through the scope was always essential.

Finally, the remaining thing the OOD had to be careful about with his periscope watch was the presence of aircraft. They were hard, but not impossible, to see through a periscope. The handle opposite the one used to shift power moved the line of sight up and down to a maximum height of about forty degrees above the horizon. Obviously, a plane that had gotten in close could not be seen. But a periscope properly handled was almost impossible to see from an airplane, so this was not too much of a worry—unless you tended to see shadows.

Such were the hard facts of periscope patrolling. Not the greatest way to cover an area, but in a place like Sagami-nada, a submarine that wanted to survive had no choice except to remain submerged during daylight hours.

About eight o'clock the next morning we sighted what appeared to be a trawler or perhaps an auxiliary ASW vessel. He was echo ranging and proceeding very slowly. He was of fairly good size, and Dykers estimated he was worth a torpedo attack. When we got within about a mile of him, he stopped echo ranging and also stopped his propellors. Was he listening to us with passive sonar?

His own screw noises would preclude his hearing us when he

was under way, but stopped he might be able to hear us and thus determine our possible location.

Putting all these questions behind us, we worked into an excellent position and fired three torpedoes—the *Jack*'s first war shots of her career. Short of the predicted torpedo run time, we heard a tremendous explosion. That should finish him, I thought.

"*Damn* those exploders . . . damn them all to *hell!*" said Dykers as he looked through the scope.

"The first torpedo prematured . . . just before it got to the MOT . . . and I don't know whether the other two passed under without exploding, or missed. Son of a bitch from *Baghdad!*" came the bitter exclamation from the skipper.

Our worst fears about the magnetic exploders were realized. After all this training, after coming halfway around the world to get here, our first shot was a premature. We had read volumes about the magnetic exploders, but here we were experiencing them at first hand.

Because our target was an ASW vessel equipped with both echo-ranging equipment and depth charges, Dykers went deep for a while. We heard some more pinging, but apparently this close brush with eternity had frightened off our friend. When we returned to periscope depth, he was hightailing it north for Tokyo Bay and safety.

We moved about fifteen miles to the east and resumed our periscope patrol.

We should have moved farther. In the late afternoon, we heard pinging to the north but could see nothing. Finally we thought we had pinging from two or three vessels, but in the gathering dusk, we could barely make out what we thought was an ASW vessel. Since it was too dark for a periscope attack, Dykers went to 250 feet and rigged for silent running.

During the next two hours, my throat was dry and my heart pounding as we maneuvered to avoid three pinging ASW ships that were clearly on our trail. At least twice they had us boxed in, with one ship in each direction and no way of escape.

Every once in a while, sonar would report, "He's shifted to short scale—he's coming in for an attack!"

Normally the pings in echo ranging were separated by several seconds, during which the pinging ship waited for an echo. But when they were sure they had something at close enough range, they shifted to short scale (usually about one ping per second) and stood in for the attack. Whenever this happened, we all braced, expecting the depth charge.

Whenever we heard the short-scale pinging commence, however, Dykers would start a slow, full-rudder turn without speeding up. This was meant to confuse the ASW ship, since he needed to drop his charges on our projected track far enough ahead of us so that they would have time to sink to the depth at which the hydrostatic fuses would cause them to explode.

Either Dykers's tactic worked or else the sonar conditions were so poor that our would-be attacker could not hang on to his contact. In any case, after each one of these attack runs, he would slow down and shift back to long scale without dropping a depth charge.

This was a nerve-racking ordeal. Each time one of the ASW ships would start another run and shift to short-scale pinging, I would be convinced that this would be the time we would get the depth charges. I could see some of my shipmates' faces grow paler as our attacker's screws passed overhead, and I'm sure that mine did also. I could only conclude that our Japanese friend wanted to be sure he had us absolutely dead to rights before he dropped those charges.

The experience of hearing the screws of an ASW ship passing directly overhead—you can hear it right through the hull—has to be experienced to be appreciated. The loud *whoosh-whoosh-whoosh* of those propellers passing right over your ship sounds like the impending approach of doom in the otherwise quiet-as-a-tomb submarine. If you don't see shadows then, you are just not susceptible to that weakness.

Frankly, I was scared to death and wondered, as I had a few times before, how in hell I had gotten myself into this mess. We were new at this game, and we weren't finding it much fun. The only cool-looking and relaxed person in the conning tower was Dykers.

As we were sweating out this ordeal (and we *were* sweating—at silent running there was no air conditioning, not even any air circulation), I had some very uncharitable and un-Christian thoughts about our engineers in the Bureau of Ordnance. There they were, back in Washington, sitting on their fat duffs in perfect safety while we were out here risking our necks with these lousy, prematuring torpedoes they had given us. This whole mess we were in had started with that damned premature. They had had twenty-three years between the wars to perfect these torpedoes and exploders—couldn't we have expected better?

After playing cat and mouse with us for more than two hours, the three ASW ships apparently were led astray by Dykers's slow but persistent evasion maneuvers, for at about this time they seemed to be fading off to the north. They were still pinging from time to time but were getting increasingly faint on the sonar. Had they stopped echo ranging and started listening, or were they really getting farther away?

We had secured from battle stations during this ordeal since there was no need for all those extra people to be up and about. We needed them now, however, because Dykers was going to go up and take a look. Still heedful of the need for quiet, we passed the word quietly on the phones to reset the battle stations. Dykers wanted to be ready for whatever might be there.

There was nothing in sight, and the ships had never dropped a depth charge.

Round one for the *Jack* . . . sort of.

Breathing a collective sigh of relief, we went off to the south on the surface and started a battery charge. Whatever had happened during the day, the night following was almost always more relaxed. The engines were running for the vital battery charge, and there was no need for quiet. Records were played, movies were watched, and games with occasional shouting took place in the crew's mess.

The cooks always made something special for the midwatch— oyster stew (obviously from canned oysters) was a favorite, and so were the cookies and brownies turned out by Delos Horney, our baker. Fresh bread was a nightly routine; its delicious aroma filled the whole boat during the night. Even the red lights to preserve night vision seemed more relaxing than the harsh glare of the white fluorescents used during the day. The nights were for laughing and scratching, as the sailors said. The daytimes were the tense times.

The batteries needed at least four hours of charging to be ready for the next day's submerged run, and actually a five- or six-hour charge was better for battery health. With the short nights of late June, it was difficult to get the full six hours, but we usually came close. The charge needed only one engine for the last two or three hours, and so, when we got to this point, the wonderful flexibility of our diesel-electric engineering plant permitted us to leave one engine on the charge and use the other three to speed up north* at seventeen knots or so to the location chosen by Dykers for the next day's periscope patrol.

Submerged, we were of course limited to battery power. Our electric motors were continually drawing down that reservoir of electric power. The amount of speed used was critically important. At eight knots, our top speed submerged, we would exhaust the battery in half an hour. At slower speeds we could last much longer. But when that battery was exhausted—whether in two or three bursts of high speed or after being nursed carefully for a long period—the submarine absolutely *had* to get to the surface to charge it.

This limitation imposed by the batteries governed much of the way in which our war patrols had to be conducted.

By June 26 we had been in the area for a week with nothing to show for it except one premature explosion. Close to the end of my midwatch, however, we started getting some intermittent radar contacts off to the northeast. We weren't sure whether they were real or not.

Finally, Charley Caw, the battle station radarman, who also stood regular watches on the radar, said, "Mr. Calvert, these are real. There are at least four ships—maybe five."

I called Dykers. While he was coming up, I put four engines on propulsion and started heading over in the direction of the estimated track Caw had given me. I tried to make out the ships in the direction that radar was indicating, but it was so dark I couldn't see anything. When Dykers got to the bridge, he put on the battle stations. I went to the TDC and set up the ships from the radar information.

We started to close the estimated track of the convoy at best speed. As the range closed, we could see clearly that there were four good-sized ships in line, following each other, with a smaller ship out on the wing away from us. We weren't sure whether he was an escort or another heavy. The convoy was zigzagging as a precaution, and after a few minutes we worked hard to see if we could determine his plan. We couldn't get anything definite, but it looked as though the whole formation were changing course at intervals of between three and six minutes.

As the morning approached, it became too light to stay up any

---

*We went south every night to be farther away from air search.

longer, and we continued the approach submerged. Light transmission in the attack periscope is not very good. Had it not been for the fact that the ships were silhouetted against the gradually lightening eastern sky, Dykers would not have been able to see them. As it was, he was able to make pretty good observations, and it was clear we were getting into good attack position on the second heavy in the column.

During an approach the skipper routinely gave the depth setting for the torpedoes to the TDC operator. It was put in at the TDC and, as explained earlier, electrically transmitted to the torpedo room, where it was automatically set on the fish.

As we got to this point in the approach, Dykers said, "Jim, set the depth at fifteen feet."

I could hardly believe my ears. If these ships were as large as Dykers was saying, they had to draw more than fifteen feet. The rule of thumb was to set the fish to run five or ten feet under the keel of the target so that the magnetic exploders would have the best chance of working. I had expected a depth setting of maybe twenty or twenty-five feet, but not fifteen.

I recalled that Dykers and Roach had had a long talk about exploders the afternoon of our fiasco with the premature on the trawler. At the time I thought nothing had been decided. Suddenly it began to look as though something had been decided after all. I knew that our magnetic exploders had not been inactivated, but I also knew that these torpedoes had an additional firing mechanism that worked on contact with the hull of the target. Dykers was not going to violate his orders to use the magnetic exploder—thus he accepted the chance of another premature—but he did not want these fish to run under the target with nothing happening. All of this went through my mind in the very short time before we were in firing position. Soon I had no more time to worry about it.

Just as it looked as though we had worked into a perfect position for shooting, the convoy zigged toward and headed almost directly for us. Not good, but we had to make the best of it. We were in there now, almost between the two lead ships—no turning back. Submerged, we had very little mobility. We had to keep our speed slow to avoid showing a periscope feather. We had no choice but to take what was being dealt at this point.

Then, just as we were turning toward the convoy ships to make a sharp track shot (from nearly dead ahead), they zigged again to the left and put us in perfect position for the broad track shot that submarines always want. That bad leg (bad for us) had lasted only three minutes, and the fortunate zig came at just the right time. Luck was with us. Dykers had wanted to shoot first at the second ship in the column because he looked like the best target. He had either army tanks or army trucks loaded all over his main deck and looked like a troop transport.

Dykers began giving me the final setup on this ship.

"Up periscope!" he snapped.

Roach threw the control handle over, and the glistening stainless-steel tube moved swiftly upward from its well in the conning tower deck. Dykers crouched low so that he could see the moment the periscope broke water. He had to be extremely careful—we were in very close on two of the heavies as well as the escort on our side. If we were spotted now, everyone would scatter and the opportunity would be lost.

"We're in good position . . . final bearing and shoot . . . mark!"

Beetle snapped out the bearing as he read it from the bronze ring at the top of the periscope.

"Set!" I called out from the TDC.

"Start shooting. Down scope!" from Dykers. The eyepiece and black handles quickly and silently disappeared down the well.

"Fire one!" I barked, and the young sailor standing on the port side of the conning tower pressed home the large red button that sent the first torpedo racing toward the transport. The *Jack* lurched slightly as the fish left the tube.

"Fire two!" and "Fire three!" came in close succession as we followed our well-drilled procedure.

"Torpedoes running hot, straight, and normal," came the report from the sonar operator, who could clearly hear our noisy Mark XIV torpedoes racing toward their targets. Were we going to have more prematures? Everyone in the conning tower had the same question in his mind and on his face.

We knew from the TDC that our torpedoes would take about forty seconds to reach their targets. The quartermaster had the stop watch in his hand, waiting.

Without delay Dykers ordered left full rudder, to swing the *Jack* around to shoot another of the heavies from our stern tubes. As the ship began to swing, we still had time to wait on the first shots. It seemed like an eternity. Our torpedoes, with their plainly visible exhaust bubble tracks, were streaking across the few hundred yards of open water between us and the targets. How could they, or the close escort, fail to see those tracks?

No one spoke. The only sound came from the large brass clock ticking on its bracket near my head. Had forty seconds ever taken so long to run out?

Then . . . *WHAM!* Almost exactly on schedule, the first torpedo hit, followed a few seconds later by another *WHAM!* Two hits out of three. Not bad, I thought to myself.

"Eee-*yah!* No longer virgin!" came a shout from Gunner Lynes in the control room. Too early for celebration, I thought to myself; but I was as happy as Lynes.

We had caught them totally by surprise, and neither the escort nor the heavies seemed to know where we were. The escort started off in the wrong direction, echo ranging wildly as he went.

The heavies were all changing course. It was going to be difficult to get a good setup on any of them. In a moment, however, Dykers gave me a bearing, a course estimate, and a range on another one of the heavies.

"Final bearing and shoot . . . mark!"

We fired three fish in this salvo, even though we weren't too confident of our solution.

This time we were closer, and there was only about a thirty-second wait. The time went by and no explosions. Then, when we had about given up . . . *WHAM!* and then ker-*WHOOM!* The last torpedo of the three had caught him. There must have been a secondary explosion on that ship, because a much heavier explosion followed the warhead detonation. By now we knew what an exploding warhead sounded like. This was a much bigger explosion, and it shook the *Jack* from stem to stern.

"Time for just one more shot . . . hurry up, Jim," as Dykers called out another quick setup. Three more torpedoes sped out of our forward torpedo room.

WHAM! One more hit. We had now fired eleven torpedoes and gotten four hits—and the four hits were on three different ships. Not bad for beginners, not bad at all.

There was exultation all through the ship. Backs were slapped, and men were yelling in glee. The crew outside the conning tower and the control room didn't know all the details for now, but they knew full well what those explosions meant.

Dykers gave the order to reload torpedoes both forward and aft. The torpedomen in both rooms opened the heavy, bronze inner doors on the tubes (there were interlocks to prevent any possibility of opening both the inner and outer doors at once—a mistake that could sink the ship) and attached the blocks and tackles to haul the massive weapons into their firing positions.

It was important to keep the ship on an even keel during this maneuver; any sizable angle could make it impossible to maintain control of the torpedoes while they were unlocked from their stowage skids but not yet secured in the tubes. This was doubly difficult since we were still at periscope depth, where precise depth control required at least some up- or down-angle on the ship from time to time.

Dykers put up the scope for a look around. A low whistle of exultation sounded from his lips. Then, leaving the scope up, he said, "Come take a look, Jim."

Quickly grasping the black handles of the scope, I saw the first ship sinking, almost vertically now. Dozens of men were scrambling down the sides of the ship, hanging onto lines, sliding, shouting, grasping at each other. Smoke was belching from the ship in several places. Her twin propellers were spinning aimlessly in the air. The red-and-white Japanese merchant colors fluttered from the stern. The sonar operator reported loud breaking-up noises from the direction of the transport.

I swung the scope around, and there, within twenty yards—so close that I could see the facial expressions clearly—was a lifeboat crowded with seamen and soldiers. Some of them ducked behind the gunnel of the lifeboat when they saw the periscope, instinctively fearing that it could do them some harm.

While some of the other officers and men in the attack party took a quick look around, I reflected on what I had just seen. Up until now everything had been just mechanical. Did we have the right target course and speed? Was the torpedo run short enough? Did we have a good firing position? We had drilled so long for this moment that it was almost rote.

Now I had a good chance to see what horrible damage our warheads could do.

I felt a quick flash of pity and anguish for these men. They had had no warning of this quick and devastating attack. They had had no chance to fight back. But then, I thought, what chance did our men at Pearl Harbor have on December 7? The anger returned that I had felt on the day we entered Pearl for the first time.

Admiral Halsey expressed it for all of us when he said, "When we get through with them, the Japanese language will be spoken only in hell."

I was snapped out of this reverie by Dykers's voice saying that we had one more shot—this time at the escort, which had now spotted us and was heading our way with a big bone in his teeth (that is, with a bow wake). We set him up quickly on the TDC and prepared to fire three torpedoes at him on a very sharp track—almost "down the throat," as submariners call it.

Dykers was just opening his mouth to tell me to commence shooting when all hell broke loose. There was an airplane escort overhead. He had not been there to begin with but had probably been called in by the convoy commodore during the attack from a military airfield close by on the perimeter of Tokyo Bay.

But we had not seen him, and . . . ker-*WHAM!* This one was for us. He must have seen our oft-exposed periscope; his bomb landed very close. It blew our stern completely out of the water. I distinctly saw red for a split second, and the splintering of a lightbulb behind my head convinced me that something drastic had happened to our ship. I saw that the radar set had broken loose from its brackets and crashed to the deck beside me.

The conning tower was shaken so severely that I almost lost my footing. Desperately Miles Refo, beneath us in the control room, attempted to get the submarine down to safety. Partially on the surface, we were in serious danger of being rammed by the onrushing escort. If that happened, we knew that would be the end of the *Jack*.

Refo flooded water into the variable tanks and ordered full speed in an attempt to drive us down. The conning tower tilted so steeply that everyone in it slid down to the forward end. Only the collapsed radar set blocked me from going with them. Charts, pencils, navigation equipment, and flashlights—everything loose—tumbled with us. It was chaos.

Suddenly Miles found that the electric power for the bow and stern planes had been knocked out. The concussion had popped their electric circuit breakers open. Quickly the operators shifted to hand operation, but this method was too slow to do any good in such a desperate situation.

We were out of control and heading for the bottom!

Now the shoe was on the other foot. Happy shouting was replaced by grim silence. We heard the order given to blow high pressure into the ballast tanks, but the downward momentum of the boat was so great that it seemed to do little to control our steep angle. Flushed faces became pale. I found sweat breaking out on my brow as I watched the depth gauge at the end of the conning tower spin far past our design depth of 312 feet.

We had never been down here before—we weren't ever supposed to go this deep. We realized we could be crushed by the rapidly increasing squeeze of the sea. The bottom was thousands of feet away.

I found myself thinking that this, our first attack, might also prove to be our last. I quietly formed a quick prayer that those New England craftsmen who had built our submarine just a year earlier did a good job—that, indeed, they built in a little extra strength.

Dykers said nothing. He knew that Miles was doing his best to regain control. One of the cardinal rules of submarining is not to shout when there is trouble. No one except Refo said a word.

Slowly . . . agonizingly . . . after reaching nearly four hundred feet, the ship began to respond. The angle came off, and we began to rise. I breathed a quiet sigh of relief. Then I saw that we were coming up too quickly. Were we going to break the surface and give the airplane another target? I heard the tanks being vented, releasing the huge bubbles of air trapped in them. I realized, along with everyone else, that those air bubbles would be visible from above. But they might be taken as evidence of a killed submarine—particularly if we could avoid broaching again.

Gradually and skillfully, Refo regained control of the submarine, and we stabilized at one hundred feet. We were well below periscope depth but comfortably safe—for the moment.

We began to assess our damage. Some of it was evident right in the conning tower. The radar set, about one-quarter the size of an upright piano, had broken loose from its moorings on the side of the conning tower and had landed on the deck, where it took up much of our limited space. Lightbulbs were broken, and emergency lights had come on. Cork insulation had been knocked off the sides of the conning tower. Water was spraying in fiercely through a fitting where a cable came through the hull.

Dykers nevertheless returned to periscope depth. He saw that two ships of the convoy had sunk. A third was severely damaged and sinking. Meanwhile, the escort was some distance away. He had doubtless veered off when he saw the aircraft bomb and may well have been convinced that the bomb had finished us.

As damage reports continued to come in from the rest of the ship, Dykers decided to withdraw from the scene of the action and make a more thorough inspection. We still weren't sure how badly we had been hurt. In addition, we were sure that there would soon be other ASW ships and aircraft out looking for us.

When we had the time to assess our damage more fully, we saw more of it than we had expected. One of our two periscopes was flooded and useless. The port propeller shaft had a bad squeak, which would reveal our presence to any listening ship. One of our high-pressure air banks was leaking, and we also had several serious hydraulic oil leaks. Finally, four of our ten torpedo tubes were damaged beyond our ability to repair them at sea.

Well, we thought, we had really gotten into the war *this* day, both on offense and on defense. Perhaps the *Jack* was beginning to prove that she was a lucky ship.

Without question she had been lucky to survive.

We spent most of the remainder of the day catching up on sleep and licking our wounds. There was nothing we could do about the howling port shaft, but we moved the number one periscope from the control room up to the conning tower to replace the flooded attack scope. We were able to repair most of the hydraulic leaks. We isolated the ruptured high-pressure air bank so that it was no longer bleeding air into the boat. We picked up the radar set from the deck, rebolted it to its position on the side of the conning tower, and began checking its circuitry.

We could do nothing about the damaged torpedo tubes. One up forward and three aft had been so badly damaged by the airplane bomb that they would require Navy Yard repair to be made usable. The same was true of our main sonar heads. We did have a remaining auxiliary sonar that was still usable, although reduced in efficiency.

We had nine torpedoes remaining, five forward and four aft. But two of the forward fish and three of those aft had been in open torpedo tubes at the time of the bomb, and their condition was suspect. We checked them carefully and put them in reserve.

There were also numerous smaller things damaged—gaskets blown out, and tubes in electronic equipment broken. Hydraulic leaks were everywhere. The way in which the crew, under the leadership of the chiefs, pitched in and got these smaller things cleaned up and repaired was amazing for me to see. I realized that there was a certain amount of self-interest in this, but nevertheless it greatly increased my confidence in the *Jack* and what punishment she could take and still survive.

It was almost as though the men were saying to the officers, "All right, you've shown us you can get some torpedo hits—now let us clean up at least some of the mess you got us into with that bomb."

That night we had a conference in the wardroom to which we invited the three senior chief petty officers who were the most familiar with our battle damage. Each of us carefully listed the status of everything in his cognizance that had been damaged. Then each officer made a final report, giving his opinion on the overall capability of his department to continue fighting.

No one made a recommendation as to whether we should stay on station or head for the barn. We knew that this was Dykers's call.

After a considerable pause, he said, "All right . . . we'll stay— and fight."

That ended the conference.

5

Fighting Wounded

It took us several days to realize fully just how badly our ship had been damaged. The howling port shaft made it doubtful we could work in as close to a convoy as we had on June 26 without being detected. We would have to operate mostly on just the starboard shaft, which would make depth control difficult. Also, having lost the slender (one-and-one-quarter-inch thick) attack periscope, we were now left with only the number one periscope, more than twice as thick. It would be far more susceptible to detection on an attack.

In addition, we were becoming increasingly concerned about our most effective detection equipment, the SJ surface search radar. It had taken a terrible beating from the aircraft bomb. When it had been dumped out on the conning tower deck, many of its parts either jarred loose from their moorings or broke in place.

Charley Caw, our battle station radarman, and his men worked for a couple of days repairing—almost rebuilding—the SJ. After it was reassembled and repaired as well as they could do it, we tried it out against some of the rocky islands in Izu-shoto, the chain south of O-Shima. The radar's response was discouragingly feeble. Caw estimated it was working at less than one-fifth of its normal efficiency.

That soon cost us. About two nights later, again on the mid-watch, we made a radar contact about five thousand yards astern—about one-quarter or one-fifth of the range at which we should have detected him. Soon afterward I could see him . . . clearly a big ship.

We set the battle stations, and it was soon apparent we were going to get a shot at a Tenryu-class cruiser! He was unescorted—a real break for us.

Just as we were about to submerge, he seemed to see us because

74

he turned away about ninety degrees and increased speed. The torpedo runs were too long to make even a desperation shot worthwhile. He evaded us to the west and then took off for the Tokyo area at high speed. We chased him at twenty knots, but he was slowly opening up the range on us. He was making twenty-two or twenty-three—the chase was hopeless.

Had we been able to pick him up at, say, twenty-five thousand yards—a reasonable range for a ship of his size—we might have been able to submerge, get him up-moon, and make a very important kill.

We tried all day and into the next night to revive the SJ, but it was clearly dying. By June 30 we had to admit that our best detection device and best protection at night was gone for the rest of the patrol. The SJ was dead.

With the squealing shaft, the loss of our attack periscope, and now the loss of our surface search radar, our military effectiveness was being gravely reduced.

On the Fourth of July, we were patrolling at periscope depth near the peninsula that forms the western shore of Sagami-nada. All day there had been intermittent rain squalls that seriously interfered with visibility. But in a clearing spell about three in the afternoon, we sighted smoke and, later, a good-sized maru. The sea was fairly rough—we needed both shafts to assure depth control. Just as we had begun to get a good TDC track on him, the maru disappeared into a dense rain squall.

Sonar, however, kept track of him and reported that he apparently had an escort with him that we had not seen in the rain: the fast, light screws of the escort were mixed in with the heavy churning of the big maru's propeller. In a bit the rain lifted a little, and Dykers sighted the heavy again. He was zigzagging and was a little too far away to shoot. Then he zigged toward us. The range was OK, but the track was too sharp.

Just as we were about to give up and shoot on the sharp track anyway, he obligingly zigged away and gave us a beautiful shot, about an eleven-hundred-yard torpedo run on an eighty-seven-degree port track. The torpedo would intersect almost at right angles, giving it the maximum chance to hit. There had been no discussion of the depth set on our torpedoes on the attack of June 26—we all knew what a delicate subject it was, and who can argue with such success? Once again came the order for the fifteen-foot depth setting.

We were getting in awfully close. Would they hear our port shaft squealing?

Almost as though he were reading our minds, Dykers said, "Port stop."

We were going to continue the approach on one shaft. This was bound to be hard on Miles and the planesmen—the force of the wash from the propellers against the stern planes is one of the main factors in controlling the angle, and thus the depth, of the submarine. By stopping the port shaft, Dykers was giving up half of that force. In this increasingly rough sea, it was going to be tough to hold our proper depth.

We were in so close that any broaching would be fatal. Less than a thousand yards lay between us and the closest escort. We could hear the sound of his pinging right through the hull.

I'll admit I was terribly apprehensive. Here we were, with a badly wounded submarine, able to use only one shaft, right in the midst of a convoy with escorts. Were we pressing our luck too far?

The rain was still coming down in torrents, but we were in so close now that Dykers could see our target pretty clearly.

"Final bearing and shoot . . . mark!"

I had already been told we would shoot four torpedoes.

"Fire one!" I barked. The next two went out at about six-second intervals.

Just as the torpedo run time was expiring on the quartermaster's stopwatch:

WHAM! . . . WHAM! . . . WHAM! Three hits!

"Boy, did we sock him," came the satisfied murmur from the skipper.

"That's our Fourth of July celebration—way to do it, skipper," said Beetle Roach with a big grin.

But our revelry was short-lived. Dykers saw the escort heading right for us at high speed. We started down.

"All ahead full," came the order from Dykers. No point worrying about howling shafts now.

As we passed about 150 feet, two ear-splitting CR-R-R-ASHes sounded. These were not torpedoes exploding; these were depth charges—for us. And they were close enough to break some light-bulbs in the conning tower. We rigged for depth charge and braced for more of these calling cards from Tōjō.

In the meantime, our target was submerging about as fast as we were. The crunching, sucking, and breaking-up noises were so loud that they could be heard through the hull. No need for sonar to report that information. It was not a pretty sound to hear—no matter which side you were on.

While we braced for more depth charges, sonar reported the escort fading away in the direction of the other heavies. Apparently he didn't want to stay and fight; he was going to stick with the rest of the convoy.

This had been a beautiful approach. It may sound as though Dykers always got the lucky zigs, but I was beginning to see that there was more to it than luck. He had the knack of working in close and then taking advantage of the zig plan to get just what he wanted. Of course, there had to be some luck to it. But I noticed that in both attacks we got in very close with a sharp track. Then, no matter which way our targets zigged, we would probably get a decent shot—better on one side than on the other, but actually OK either way. And if he happened to be on an extra-long leg . . . well, that hadn't happened yet.

There seemed no doubt that the escort had gone off with the convoy, but Dykers elected to stay deep for a while as a precaution. Things were pretty quiet so I hopped up on the plotting table on the other side of the conning tower to relax and began to shoot the breeze with Leyton Goodman and Billy Coleman. Dykers came over and slapped me on the knee.

"Jim, we've got a hell of a team here. We're really beginning to shape up!"

Submarine skippers are not famous for giving out lots of praise, and Dykers was no exception, so this little gesture meant a lot to me. It's something I have never forgotten.

It is hard to reconstruct what that successful attack meant to us in terms of confidence. The attack on the troop transport convoy had been great, but it hadn't really put us in the big leagues. This one did. We were building up a patrol total that could stand comparison with the best of them. We weren't trying to win any blue ribbons, but we desperately wanted to avoid being one of those submarines that went out on patrol and time after time came home with nothing.

Sad to say, some of these "still virgin" submarines, as the sailors called them, had skippers who had been considered hotshots in peacetime. These men could shoot torpedoes, all right. But in wartime conditions they lacked the nerve to work their submarines in close, where they could get a really good shot. It was becoming apparent to all of us that Dykers did not have that problem. He could work the *Jack* in tight, and torpedoes permitting, he could get the hits.

New-construction wartime submarines went through two phases in shaping up to be successful fighting machines. We had gone through the first phase in New London. By the time our training there was over, we had shaped ourselves into a smooth working team. We could handle the submarine. We knew how to dive it rapidly and safely. We had our routines and emergency drills down cold. We were proud of our ship and our teamwork—but always . . . always we knew that the real test would come in the Pacific. Were we just for show, or could we put Japanese ships on the bottom when the chips were down?

Now this second phase of our development was beginning to come into place satisfactorily. We *weren't* just for show. We had gone out green and untried to one of the toughest areas and had shown we did not swallow our cud when things got tough.

It was a good feeling.

The next days, July 5, 6, and 7, were plagued with heavy and almost continuous rain. At night visibility was severely limited; I don't think we could see five hundred yards. Sonar was essentially useless with the submarine on the surface, and so, without the radar, we were really blind. It was a continuing worry at night.

Up until now we had been relying mainly on Izu-shoto, the island chain south of O-Shima, to keep us oriented navigationally. We could either get periscope bearings during the day or radar bearings and ranges during the night. Now we had nothing. It was too dark and rainy to see the islands. For days the sky had been overcast and given us no chance to get any stars. We were not sure *where* we were.

A good many times on this patrol, when we had been out of sight of land, and even beyond radar contact on land, celestial (star) navigation was our only means of knowing where we were. A major problem with celestial navigation was that, for safety reasons, we couldn't surface until after that short time when both the stars and the horizon are clearly visible—what the navigators called "evening star time." Then we usually had to submerge before morning star time. In the dark of night, it was impossible to see the horizon well enough to get a sight.

Earlier in the war, the submariners had come up with at least a partial solution to this problem. A sextant was normally used either with no magnification or with a nearly useless little telescope provided with it. Most navigators, working in normal hours, put the telescope away and forgot it.

But the submariners, working on dark nights where they couldn't see the horizon well enough to bring the star down to it with any accuracy, had developed a new idea. They took half of a binocular and mounted it on the sextant's line of sight to the horizon. Then, even on the darkest nights, unless the stars were obscured by clouds, the binocular made it possible to see the horizon well enough to get a reasonable sight.

These middle-of-the-night observations varied in quality. Sometimes the lines crossed in a pattern of the desired BB size, and sometimes they made a pattern more the size of a nickel. But even that was far better than nothing. Knowing where you were within, say, five miles could mean the difference between safety and disaster.

In any case, for the nights of June 5, 6, and 7, we had no stars, no radar, and no sight contact with the land. We couldn't even use our fathometer to check the water depth because of the need for security. Fathometers were as easy to hear as echo ranging.

Making matters worse, the Sagami-nada and its approaches had heavy currents—sometimes as much as two or three knots. In the course of a day, they could wash you into positions far distant from where you thought you were. Because of all these factors, we felt it safer to pull out from Izu-shoto and well clear of Sagami-nada.

On the eighth, however, the rain cleared. We had good visibility, and we moved north. We were at periscope depth, still patrolling farther east of Izu-shoto than we had normally been. At about ten in the morning, we sighted heavy smoke on the horizon to the north. Soon the sonar had contact, but we could still see nothing of them through the scope. Finally we were able to observe the tops of three marus, southbound and apparently on a course that would enable us to close for an attack. Later we could see they had a single escort, a destroyer type. He was pinging.

You have to realize that a World War II submarine on periscope patrol was something like an intelligent but only somewhat mobile minefield. The maximum speed submerged was eight knots, and, as we have seen, that speed could be held for only a short time without dangerously compromising the staying power of the submarine, should it later be held down by ASW vessels. Three or four knots was more like it. And if the contact with potential targets was made before noon, let's say, and if they were not coming right at you, or nearly so, there was not much hope for an effective torpedo attack. If it was late afternoon, the submarine might be able to surface after dark and give chase. But, you'll remember, our one experience with this tactic had not been too encouraging.

In this case, however, we were in luck. The marus were heading roughly in our direction, and Dykers put on about four knots to enable us to close their projected track. They were zigzagging on very short legs, so it was hard to get any feeling for their plan—if they had one. With the TDC and the plot working together, however, we soon had a fairly good idea of what they were doing.

All the time we were maneuvering for position, all of us worried about the health of our torpedoes. Despite the fact that three of the four torpedoes remaining aft had been exposed to the airplane bomb—they had been in ready tubes, with the outer doors open at the time of the blast—the torpedomen said they were in better shape than the two remaining forward. The gyro spindles on the after tubes had been bent and somewhat egg-shaped, but the men had worked on them and thought they would be OK.

Because of all these considerations, Dykers decided to get a stern shot if possible. This was never as easy as a bow shot, and it was particularly difficult to get in as tight with the stern tubes. But we had only two fish left forward, and they were both highly suspect.

Clearly we had a prize target here. The lead ship in the convoy was a passenger-freighter type with very nice lines. He looked new but not exceptionally large—maybe five thousand tons, Dykers estimated. I waited for the depth setting, thinking it would probably be twelve feet or less due to the smaller size of the target.

"Set torpedo depth at eighteen feet."

What was going on? I'll never know, but I think Dykers decided to give the magnetics one more chance.

We were in with Dykers's usual good position, with very small gyros (that is, torpedoes going directly out our stern, so that the gyros had to turn the fish only a short amount after launching) and a nice broad track to give the best chance of hitting. The only thing less than ideal was the range, about seventeen hundred yards. We had not fired a torpedo on this patrol at a range greater than twelve hundred yards.

"How good is your solution, Jim?" Dykers asked.

"Right on. I think we have him dead to rights," I replied.

"Stand by to shoot."

"Final bearing . . . mark!"

"Fire seven!" I snapped.

Tubes eight and nine followed in rapid sequence.

"Torpedoes running hot, straight, and normal," from sonar.

This run was going to take longer than we had been used to waiting—well over a minute.

"Down scope."

We waited, and waited . . . and waited.

"Torpedoes should be hitting now," said the quartermaster.

Nothing.

It was clear, however, that the ships in the convoy had seen the fish. They were scattering in all directions, and the escort was heading right for us at high speed. We went deep and listened for the end-of-run explosions: torpedoes that missed were set to detonate after running well beyond any possible target range (so that they could not be recovered for intelligence purposes). None ever came.

Whether it was the depth setting, the failure of the torpedoes for some other reason, or just a plain miss, we'll never know for certain. Dykers and I, however, were certain we had him right, and we hadn't had any misses yet. The absence of end-of-run explosions made it appear that the already suspect torpedoes had not performed properly.

Click . . . *BANG!*

That was no end-of-run explosion. That was a depth charge and close enough to shake the boat.

Click . . . *BANG!* Click . . . *BANG!*

Two more in rapid succession and much closer than the first.

This is serious, I thought. Sonar conditions are relatively good and this guy seems to have a bead on us.

We were at silent running and rigged for depth charge. The battle stations were still on. There was nothing more we could do now except to work on quiet evasion. We tried to move away from his bearing at two knots. He appeared to be listening as well as pinging. We shut down absolutely everything except the one shaft being used for propulsion. The boat was eerily quiet and hot as an oven. Shirts came off, and men were either in skivvy shirts or bare from the waist up. Everyone's body glistened with sweat, some from the heat and some from just raw fear.

Click . . . *BANG!* Click . . . *BANG!*

Two more, still very close. A couple of lightbulbs shattered. Nothing serious, but not good for the nerves.

I have been asked a hundred times what it is like to be depth charged. Hollywood has not been much help; the movies are only partly accurate. The lights do not dim and then return to normal brightness as though the generators were slowly regaining speed after that terrible jolt. That doesn't happen because no generators are running. All electric power, including that for lights, comes from the battery.

But it is hot, insufferably hot. And you're scared. At least I always was. There are always so many unknowns. Maybe the next charge will be right on, and that will be all she wrote. After all, we had already had one close call with death. Who could say this might not be another?

We were all scared. Being in a small metal capsule deep in the ocean while presumably well-trained Japanese sailors were up there trying to kill you—that was not apt to bring on a sense of mental ease and repose.

The *Jack* had shown she could dish it out; now we were going to see how good we were at taking it. I wasn't pleased with how I was taking it. During attacks I was always so busy with the mental exercise provided by the TDC, and so caught up in the excitement of the attack, that I never felt much fear. But this was different. I had absolutely nothing to do. Dykers relied on a plot to keep track of where we had gone and what the ASW ship was doing. Besides, the TDC made too much noise. Not a lot, but any noise at all was too much in that situation.

I had to face the fact that I was afraid. I would have died before letting anyone else know it, but I was deeply, seriously scared. Had I made a mistake coming into submarines? Wouldn't it be better to be up there in the sunshine, dropping the depth charges, than down here getting the hell jarred out of me?

Click . . . *BANG!* Click . . . *BANG!* Click . . . *BANG!*

Three more, and closer than any yet.

Each time we got the report from sonar, "He's shifting to short scale—coming in for the attack," we all braced ourselves for the shocks we knew were coming. How was he keeping such good track of us? Had we developed an oil leak? I thought back on all the calm analyses I had made, sitting in the safe comfort of New London, of failed skippers and how they had seen shadows. Now that I was out here on the firing line, I was seeing shadows myself—and lots of them.

In warfare it is always so much easier to sit back and analyze than it is to get out there and do the fighting.

I was aware, however, that I was better off than most of my shipmates. Certainly, if one of those depth charges hit, or was close enough to crush us, we would all die together. But at least I was in the conning tower with Dykers and could see the logic in his evasion moves. I was 100 percent up-to-date as far as the *Jack* was concerned. The people I felt sorry for were the men in the engine rooms, in the torpedo rooms, and even in the control room, where they couldn't really tell what was going on. All they knew was that every once in a while we would receive a terrific jolt, with no warning.

The next two depth charges were the closest we had had since the airplane bomb. Right after we were shaken, urgent word came from one engine room that they had a serious leak they couldn't stop. Chief Archer came to the conning tower and gave us a direct report.

"We've apparently got a leak in the main induction piping. It isn't flooded, but it will be if we don't do something about it. I think I can crawl in there and fix it."

I could hardly believe my ears. This was a long tube, maybe two feet in diameter, with no lights, with water coursing down it from the leak, and with depth charges rattling all around. And Archer wants to crawl *in there* and fix the leak? Is he out of his mind?

"Tell Mr. Refo I want to see him," said Dykers.

Miles poked his head up the hatch from the control room and said, "Archer wants to do it and says he's not worried about getting caught in there. He's sure he can fix it. I recommend we let him do it."

"Very well—but be sure there is someone standing by to communicate for him and to help if needed," replied Dykers.

Here I was, standing around in a well-lit conning tower with plenty of room—and *I* was scared? What was wrong with me? I had to admit that if anyone had suggested *I* go in that main induction pipe, I would have told them they had to be out of their *minds*.

The word was all over the boat like a flash.

"Chief Archer is gonna crawl in the main induction pipe and fix a leak!"

"Jee-*zus*. He's gotta be crazy!"

But he wasn't. He got the necessary tools together, found two flashlights, tied one to his belt in the back, and went in. He had no more than started when:

Click . . . *BANG!* Click . . . *BANG!*

The leak started getting worse. Water was streaming down the pipe and all around Archer. The men in the engine room could see his flashlight getting farther and farther away in the blackness of the long pipe.

"He says he's pretty sure he knows just where the joint is that's causing the trouble," reported Refo to the skipper over the phones. Miles had turned the dive over to Obie and had gone back to the engine room to stand by Archer.

Click . . . *BANG!* Click . . . *BANG!* Click . . . *BANG!*

Three more. What would these sound like in the cramped, black pipe? It must be deafening, I thought.

After it seemed that Archer had been in there for an hour (it was more like ten minutes), Refo reported, "The water's stopped— he must have gotten it!"

About five minutes later, from Miles again, "He's back out. He scraped his arms a couple of places, but he's OK."

"Thank *God*" was Dykers's heartfelt reply. He spoke for all of us.

Throughout this ordeal we had tried to pass the word over the telephones to each compartment so they would have at least some idea of what was going on. But naturally they all wanted to know more.

"Billy, you take a walk through the boat, and try to tell the men as much as you can about what happened with Archer and how things are going in general," said Dykers.

What a good idea, I thought. Not only can Coleman give them some info, but his sunny disposition and bright face will cheer up all but the most desperately worried.

Click . . . *BANG!* Click . . . *BANG!* Click . . . *BANG!*

Lots of lightbulbs shattered on these three—but no vital machinery, as far as we could tell, had been damaged. Almost everything on the boat was shut down, however, making it hard to tell just how much damage we were sustaining. In one sense, the airplane bomb had served us well: we knew what happened when an explosion was *really* close—and we had had none that bad so far.

The radar set had not yet come loose from its brackets on the side of the conning tower.

Although I have never smoked, I have noticed that men under tension like to smoke. It seems to have a calming effect. Our men were under tension all right. But we could not tell how long we would be held down, and we had to preserve the freshness of the air inside the submarine as much as possible. So Dykers had put the smoking lamp out as soon as we went deep and were running silent. Watching men fidget and ache for a cigarette convinced me that this was a habit I could do without. This was long before all the medical evidence of the harm that comes from cigarette smoking was around, but I didn't need it. Watching those men desperately craving a cigarette during that depth-charge attack was enough for me. I didn't want to go through that for anything. It was bad enough as it was.

We all wondered why the click came before the depth-charge explosion. The sailors said it was the detonator pistol inside the depth charge. I suspect that it was more likely a preliminary shock wave, but I don't know enough about underwater dynamics to say anything more than that. To this day I don't know for sure why the click always preceded the bang, but I am certain it did. It was always there, and the time interval between the click and the bang did not seem to have anything to do with how far the depth charge was from us. Shattered lightbulbs were a better indication of that—and the radar still hanging on its brackets.

Through all of this, Dykers was solid as a rock. If he felt any fear or had any doubts about our survival, he never let them show. The only signs of his emotions appeared when Archer was in the induction piping and when word came that the chief was safely out.

Dykers carefully maneuvered the *Jack* to give the attacker as little target as possible. And in the ASW ship's long periods of just listening (we could hear his screws stop), Dykers would also come to all stop and just let Miles Refo keep our balance, hovering with no motion. Of course, while doing this Miles would occasionally have to run the trim pump to keep our balance. When he did, it sounded like a cataclysm of noise in the silence.

All told, our Japanese friend dropped thirty-nine depth charges over a period of about five hours. That is, the clock said five hours. It seemed more like five days to me.

Along toward evening, the destroyer appeared to have lost contact. As we crept silently away to the southeast, he seemed to be heading north and getting farther away all the time. Then, after a long period of listening, we heard him pinging again, on a regular search scale. It was clear from the fainter sound of his pinging that he was much farther away.

With no radar we did not want to wait until dark before coming back to periscope depth. So at about dusk, with the battle stations still set, still running silent, and with the smoking lamp still out, the *Jack* came back to periscope depth. Dykers took a long, careful look around. "Nothing in sight. He's gone."

Those were the sweetest words I had heard in a long time.

"Secure from silent running, secure from rig for depth charge."

Still no word about the smoking lamp.

"Prepare to surface."

"Put four engines on propulsion."

OO-gah, OO-gah, OO-gah, went the surface alarm.

"Blow all ballast," from Refo. The sound of high-pressure air rushing into the tanks sounded like thunder after all the silence.

"Open the hatch," from Dykers. The quartermaster quickly spun it open and threw it back on its latch. Dykers went up.

"Light the smoking lamp." Dykers had not forgotten.

The four engines lit off without delay. And as the clean, sweet, fresh ocean air swept through the boat, down through the conning tower hatch, down through the induction piping, purging all the foul air of the day, life came back to our crew. It was like that experiment in high school where we sealed a burning candle inside a bell jar and watched it gutter nearly to extinction, then opened the little glass valve at the top to admit air and saw the flame revive with brightness and cheer. Color came back to our cheeks, brightness to our eyes, and more clarity to our thought processes. I said a short prayer of thanksgiving, and I'm sure I was not alone.

Watching the smokers (three-quarters or so of the people on board) light up their cigarettes, some with trembling hands, and seeing color come back to their complexions and repose to their faces, I was reminded of how, in the *Ring*, the gods of Valhalla magically return to health and vigor when Freia returns from captivity and gives them the golden apples of eternal youth.

Comforting as it looked to light up, I once again vowed I would not become part of *that* magic circle.

We sped to the southeast and the comparative safety we knew lay in that direction. After an hour or so, Dykers slowed to two-engine speed and put the other two engines on battery charge. After a much-needed meal (we had had no lunch), Dykers called another meeting in the wardroom to assess our situation more carefully.

We went over our problems, one by one, writing them all down on a yellow pad. During the depth charge attack, Refo had noticed that the boat was getting slightly lighter and that he had to flood water to keep us at neutral buoyancy. Checking the pressures on all of our high pressure tanks, he had seen that one of the banks, located inside a ballast tank and therefore not available for repair at sea, was slowly losing pressure. He had isolated the bank from our others, but it was continuing to leak inside the ballast tank. Sooner or later it would cause real trouble.

After the depth charge attack, we discovered that the howling on the port propeller shaft had clearly gotten worse. We could not use that shaft now at any speed—even dead slow—without unacceptable noise. In addition, we had no radar, and all three of our remaining torpedoes were seriously suspect from the damage they had received.

"We don't have enough effectiveness left to justify staying out here. We're going to head for the barn," said the skipper. Once again, that ended the conference.

That night Dykers sent the first radio message of our patrol. It was *Jack* serial number one, addressed to Commander Submarines Pacific Fleet (ComSubPac), giving him the results of our patrol, our decision to return to base, and the reasons for that decision.

We said goodbye to Sagami-nada and set our great circle course for Midway, more than two thousand miles to the east. It was July 9; we had been in the area, on station, for twenty-two days and had shot twenty-one torpedoes for nine hits. But six of those misses had occurred with torpedoes that were either known or strongly suspected to have been faulty.

We had obtained hits on five ships and were certain that four of them had sunk.

On the way out to our patrol area from Midway in June, several members of the crew had asked me if we could have church services on Sunday when time permitted. There was, of course, no chaplain on board, and since none of the other officers volunteered, I took on the job. We didn't have much material, but I did have a copy of the Book of Common Prayer, and I used the form for Morning Prayer on occasion, for Evening Prayer other times. Since we didn't have the list of appointed scriptures and psalms, we chose our own.

The Sunday after our depth-charge attack, we were on our way home and traveling on the surface at high speed in smooth weather. That bright Sunday morning, our attendance was up a good bit—maybe to twenty. Billy Coleman, who had been a regular attendee and who usually read the psalm, suggested that Psalm 91 might be appropriate. He read:

> He that dwelleth in the secret place of the most High shall abide under the shadow of the Almighty.
> I will say of the Lord, He is my refuge and my fortress: my God; in him will I trust.
> Surely he shall deliver thee from the snare of the fowler, and from the noisome pestilence.
> He shall cover thee with his feathers, and under his wings shalt thou trust: his truth shall be thy shield and buckler.
> Thou shalt not be afraid for the terror by night; nor for the arrow that flieth by day;
> Nor for the pestilence that walketh in darkness; nor for the destruction that wasteth at noonday.
> A thousand shall fall at thy side, and ten thousand at thy right hand; but it shall not come nigh thee.

This psalm seemed just right for the occasion, and after the service I thanked Billy for suggesting it and for reading it so well. True to his Sewanee traditions, he smiled and reminded me that it had been one of Stonewall Jackson's favorites.

I could not escape the Civil War—not even in Sagami-nada.

Our stop at Midway was brief—just long enough to unload the three torpedoes for overhaul in the Midway shops. We took departure for Pearl the same day we arrived.

Our return to Pearl Harbor on July 19, forty-four days after our departure, was memorable. Our Division Commander, Freddy Warder, was there to meet us, as was Admiral Lockwood himself. That was a surprise and a further indication that our patrol must have been looked on as a real success.

Further proof of that came directly from Admiral Lockwood, when he informed us that some of the Hawaiian Islands' most important families had invited the wardroom of the *Jack* to spend two weeks with them on the island of Maui. The Admiral told us that for this privilege these families had asked him to recommend, from time to time, a submarine that had had an unusually successful patrol.

We were certainly honored to have been so recommended.

The men of the *Jack* were all going to the Royal Hawaiian—all except one who was married to a Hawaiian girl. Understandably, he skipped the Royal Hawaiian.

Naturally all of us in the wardroom were looking forward to Maui. But more important than the trip itself was the indication of the esteem in which our patrol was held by Admiral Lockwood.

We felt the *Jack* had arrived.

6

A Taste
of Defeat

Many people consider Maui to be the most beautiful of the eight Hawaiian Islands. About one hundred miles east-southeast of Oahu, Maui is some fifty miles long and nearly thirty miles wide. As we flew into the island's lone airport, we could see plainly the dominant feature of the island, the extinct volcano of Haleakala, soaring more than three thousand feet above the eastern part of the island. On its slopes are found some of the most desirable and beautiful places to live on Maui.

The descendants of the original missionaries to the islands formed into five major families, known for many years as the Big Five. At the time of our visit to Maui, in 1943, they were still a powerful and prestigious force in the islands. Although their businesses were mainly in Oahu, at least three of the families had homes on the slopes of Haleakala. Some were vacation homes, others were permanent residences.

These were the families that had invited us to visit them during our rest period. It was a generous and patriotic thing for them to do, and we were determined not to get into the social and political controversies that even then surrounded the Big Five.

The seven officers of the *Jack* were divided among three families: the Rices, the Baldwins, and the Von Tempskys. The last family was not one of the Big Five but was very much involved with them through friendship. Billy Coleman and I were assigned to the Von Tempskys. We were met at the plane by a driver who took us to their home on the slopes of Haleakala.

As we drove up the mountain, we could feel the climate changing. The air became cooler, the humidity lower, and the trees and shrubbery more like those belonging to a temperate clime. As we approached the Von Tempsky ranch, we began to see cattle and horses grazing in meadows that could easily have been in New England.

It was a different world.

Before leaving for Maui, we had turned over all responsibility for the *Jack* to the relief crew at the Pearl Harbor Submarine Base. The relief crew consisted of a group of officers and men capable of taking over the *Jack* during its rest period and caring for it as if it were their own. There was a commanding officer, an exec, an engineer, and so on. Each of these officers had a group of men qualified to do the necessary maintenance work. They were also to carry on the liaison with the submarine base or tender responsible for the refit.

There was a written change of command between the relief crew and regular skippers. If anything happened to the submarine, such as a fire or a battery explosion, the relief crew's commanding officer was responsible. The idea was to have the ship's regular officers as free as possible from the burdens of the ship during their rest period.

At the end of the rest period, there was to be a formal inspection of the submarine when it was turned back over to its regular officers and crew. The relief crews took pride in presenting a submarine that was clean and ready to start its training period for the next patrol. Since the relief crew officers and men were mainly people hoping to be assigned to an active submarine, they had plenty of incentive to do a good job.

As we turned the *Jack* over to our relief crew, it had been apparent to all concerned that the refit was going to take more than two weeks. The Bureau of Ships had decided to change the HOR engine gearing once more. This would require major disassembly of the engines and by itself would take more than two weeks. In addition, all of our battle damage had to be repaired. The propeller shaft and torpedo tube repairs would require long periods in a dry dock, and we might have to wait our turn for one of these over-scheduled facilities.

It had finally been decided that the job was too big for either the already overburdened *Griffin* or the Submarine Base and that the *Jack* would have her work done at the Pearl Harbor Navy Yard. This was a most unusual move. The Navy Yard, across the loch from the Submarine Base, had been going all out repairing battle-damaged surface ships and was not exactly looking for more work. They had realized, however, that ours was an unusual case, and they had taken us on.

We all had known that the work could not be done in anything like two weeks, but we had still been entitled to our two weeks of rest. So we had turned everything over to the relief crew with the clear understanding that there would still be much to do after we returned.

Then, after checking once again that all the arrangements had been made for our men at the Royal Hawaiian, all seven of us had taken the plane for Maui.

The Von Tempsky home was large and comfortable but not pretentious. Mrs. Von Tempsky, a strikingly attractive woman in perhaps her late forties, said, "It's just a ranch house, but we love it."

You can imagine how it looked to us after all those months in the cramped quarters of the *Jack*. Billy and I were each given a separate bedroom, large and airy with its own bathroom. For several months now, the two of us had been sharing a tiny room in the *Jack*, about the size of the closet in one of our Von Tempsky rooms. We knew these luxurious surroundings would last for only two weeks, but we weren't going to let that bother us for now.

There were already two guests in residence when we arrived—Captain Jim Flatley and his young naval aide. Flatley had distinguished himself in several Pacific air actions, including the Battle of the Coral Sea. He was a fine-looking man who had already won a Navy Cross, and we were honored to have his company. In addition, he had a wonderful sense of humor and added a lot to the group.

Even though there were four guests at each meal, we were made to feel like members of the family. The conversations were always interesting. The Von Tempskys were a very literary family. Many of the dinner conversations involved books, current and past, and I was grateful for Billy with his good Sewanee background in literature. He made the submarine contingent look better than it otherwise would have.

For us, Maui seemed like paradise. Aside from the delightful climate, there were so many things to do. Colonel Von Tempsky, a tall, handsome man with a military bearing, was very much in charge of the ranch and spent a good bit of time out of the house checking on cattle, barns, and the considerable amount of help the ranch used.

The Colonel loved to ride, and since there were plenty of horses, we were occasionally asked to join him on his inspection tours of the ranch. He told me I truly looked like a sailor on horseback . . . somehow just not cut out for it. Nevertheless, I enjoyed riding and even got over the saddle soreness after a couple of days. The Colonel was not very talkative, but he went out of his way to take us by some particularly pretty views he wanted us to see.

Besides horses to ride, there were long walks to take and endless bull sessions to be joined on the broad veranda, with its sweeping views. Also on the veranda, there was a sort of continual bridge game, never with the same four contestants for long since it proceeded with the understanding that after a couple of rubbers at least one participant would change. Our two aviator friends were sharks.

Flatley said, "We don't have much else to do when we're not flying."

I doubted that, but somehow they had both gotten to be whizzes.

Despite the many diversions, I had time during our stay in Maui to do a good bit of thinking about the *Jack* and its war adventures. The close calls of our first patrol stuck in my mind more than I had thought they would. The hell and terror of that patrol made such a contrast with the tranquil and beautiful life on Maui that I could not get it out of my mind. The memory of those frantic men scrambling down the side of the troop transport was as vivid in my mind as though it had happened yesterday.

When one is primarily concerned with survival, there is little time and even less inclination to think about anything other than the business at hand. But here in these halcyon surroundings, there was time for philosophy.

Which was the real world? The hard-bitten, kill-or-be-killed life we led in the *Jack*—or the luxurious, leisurely dinners we had at the Von Tempsky ranch with their long philosophical discussions? The relentless search for semi-defenseless merchant ships to kill—or the half-sleepy picnics we enjoyed, talking lazily of Proust? (The allergy-ridden Frenchman was a favorite of our hostess.)

I found myself aching for a better understanding of just what we were doing and why we were doing it.

I spilled all of this out to Jim Flatley as we sat on the veranda one afternoon, looking out over the peaceful meadows of the ranch. His answer was quick and memorable.

"Look, Jim, why do you think these people have asked us over here to share their homes? Because they like the way we part our hair? We're here so they can express some of their gratitude for what we are doing for them. These islands are not just their homes, they're the source of their wealth.

"They aren't out there risking their necks, *we* are. And don't think they forget it. If we had not won the Battle of Midway so decisively and practically destroyed Japan's first-line air power, the Japanese would have had a fine base for bombing the Hawaiian Islands. There would have been no recourse for our government except to vacate all civilians from these islands. Where would the Big Five have been then? What would have happened to their businesses?

"No, Jim, don't feel guilty about what we are doing in this war. I, too, feel sorry for those oil-soaked seamen, just as I do for the aviators we shoot down. But don't ever forget that the Japanese asked for this war, and unless we go after them hammer and tongs, the opportunity for this peaceful life on Maui and the long, philosophical talks at dinner will be gone. Gone probably forever. You and I live in the real world, all right. It isn't for the faint of heart or the weak, but it is absolutely necesssary.

"Take my advice and stop worrying about it."

Clearly, after so many years, those aren't his exact words, but they are certainly the thrust of what he had to say. I needed them, and I have always been grateful for them.

After fond goodbyes to the Von Tempskys and promises to write (which we did for many years—at least at Christmas), we left Maui. It had been a wonderful and refreshing experience. But the conversation with Jim Flatley was the most important part of it for me.

The return to Pearl Harbor on August 2 was a return to reality, all right. We found our engines strewn all over the dock and the gear work not nearly done. We were still scheduled to go into the dry dock to correct the port-shaft howl.

Our two weeks in paradise were up, and we moved back on board the *Jack*. For a day or two it seemed as though we had moved into a cigar box. But fortunately, young men are resilient, and despite the contrast with our luxurious surroundings on Maui, we soon felt at home and were back in full swing.

Dealing with a Navy Yard is never easy, and the next few weeks were filled with struggles to convince this one that the *Jack* was the most important thing on its schedule. We weren't entirely successful, but in due time everything got done. Our torpedo tubes were totally overhauled; we were given an entirely new SJ radar; our port shaft was pulled out, realigned in the shop, reinstalled, and satisfactorily sound tested; our damaged attack periscope was replaced with a new one; our high-pressure tanks were made whole again; and we were finally ready for sea.

But the shadow of those HOR engines hung continually in the backs of our minds. The *Jack* had been repaired as well as possible— but was she still "rotten to the core," as Dykers had once put it?

Having arrived back from patrol on July 19, we stayed through September 5 to ready our ship for sea and complete our prepatrol training. We said goodbye to Pearl and were at Midway to top off our fuel on the ninth. We were alongside taking fuel by midmorning and at about five that afternoon were taking departure for our new patrol area.

Our area was close to where we had been assigned for our first patrol. We would be patrolling along the Izu-shoto, the string of islands hanging down to the south from Sagami-nada, a bit farther south than we had been before.

After transiting the more than two thousand miles between Midway and the Izu-shoto without incident (except for an occasional dive to avoid being sighted by an enemy patrol plane), we submerged in our assigned area on September 18.

We were almost a month later than we should have been in returning to the war zone.

While we had been refitting the *Jack* and living in lotusland on Maui, a lot had been happening on the torpedo and magnetic-exploder front. Admiral Lockwood had taken the final decision to order all his submarines to deactivate the magnetic exploders. But it was becoming clear from attacks made without the magnetic exploders that something was still wrong. One submarine had fired fifteen torpedoes in one day and had clear proof that eleven of them were duds. The contact exploders were not working right, either.

Admiral Lockwood ordered three torpedoes to be fired, with warheads, against the cliffs of Kahoolawe, one of the Hawaiian Islands then being used for target practice by the aviators. The first two torpedoes exploded; the last was a dud. With a submarine rescue vessel standing by, a diver volunteered to go down and attach a line to the dud torpedo with its still-live warhead. It was pulled, with great care, up to and on board the rescue vessel.

The diver got, and deserved, a decoration.

Examination of the torpedo on board the rescue vessel showed that when the warhead struck the cliff, its exploder cavity had been deformed sufficiently to prevent the firing pin from reaching the fulminate caps designed to detonate the warhead. In short, there was a serious design defect in the contact exploder.

Admiral Lockwood then designated an ordnance postgraduate officer, Captain Herman Pieczentkowski, to conduct tests at the Pearl Harbor Submarine Base on dummy warheads made to have exactly the same weight and construction as a live warhead. These dummy warheads were raised to a height of ninety feet by a cherry picker crane, then dropped onto a firm steel plate. Those that hit the plate head-on deformed the exploder cavity so much that the firing pin never went home. The pin was too heavy—and consequently too slow—to strike home before its cavity was deformed by the impact.

Next Pieczentkowski dropped dummy warheads on a steel plate set at a forty-five-degree angle. These exploders functioned normally, thus showing that the best torpedo shots—those hitting the target ship at a ninety-degree angle—were the ones most apt to be duds.

While work went forward at the Base torpedo shop on a new firing pin, a famous message went out to the submarines at sea recommending they try to hit their targets "on the turn of the bilge," so that the exploder could have the desired glancing blow. Without doubt, this message caused some blue language in the wardrooms of the submarine force. With no sure way of estimating the draft of targets and with all the other problems an attacking submarine has, asking for hits on the turn of the bilge seemed a bit much, to put it mildly. It was a message, I am sure, that Admiral Lockwood and his staff would rather forget.

Fortunately, better news came quickly. The Submarine Base torpedo shop, on its own, developed a modified firing pin that was lighter and faster, yet strong enough to do its job. Many more dummy warheads were dropped from the cherry picker with the new firing pin, and they all functioned properly. The detonators went off as designed regardless of the angle of striking. From that day of August 1943 forward, all submarines departing on patrol had the new firing pins in their warheads.

So by the beginning of September 1943, the operating submariners had detected and solved three serious defects in the Mark

XIV torpedo: its faulty depth setting, skittish magnetic exploder, and sluggish firing pin. All three problems had been solved by the operating forces in their tenders and bases, without help from Newport or Washington.

So much for Bureau support.

Thus, when the *Jack* departed for patrol on September 5, she was equipped with warheads lacking magnetic exploders and with firing pins cut down to the new weight.

Armed with this new confidence and knowing we had been assigned a good area, we looked forward to another outstanding patrol. We conducted our daily periscope watches diligently and searched the area carefully at night with the SJ radar. Yet we made no contacts whatsoever—no smoke, no sonar contact . . . nothing.

In the wardroom we several times discussed patrolling on the surface during daylight to get the much wider circle of vision that would provide. But the large number of patrol planes we kept seeing through the periscope made Dykers decide against it.

I still had the midwatches. On the night of September 24, the only thing going on was our usual battery charge. As the battery charge progressed, the load could be carried with fewer engines. Accordingly, when I heard one of the engines shut down, I expected a routine report that they no longer needed two engines on the charge and that I could have the other engine for propulsion, if needed. Instead of sending a report, the chief engineman, Earl Archer, came to the bridge. From the look on his face, I could tell that something serious was wrong.

"We have a casualty on number two engine," he said. "I'm not sure what it is, but it could be a broken crankshaft."

"Very well," I replied, trying to sound as undisturbed as possible. "Will you go and tell Mr. Refo and the captain now?"

"Better tell the exec, also," I added.

I wasn't anxious to be the Chinese messenger on this piece of news.

About a half hour later, we had the verdict. It was a broken crankshaft. No possible chance of a repair at sea. We were a three-engine submarine.

I spent the next half hour silently cursing the men in our Bureau of Ships who had decided, after all the bad results in the earlier fleet submarines, to put these damned HOR engines in a new squadron of ships being built right at the time the nation needed them most.

I knew there was no better trained submarine out here than the *Jack* and not many skippers as aggressive and competent as Dykers. We were, without doubt, one of the finest ships in the submarine force—but without good engines, we could do nothing.

The next day, while submerged, Archer and his men inspected the other engines and found many loose locknuts on the large bolts that held the crankshaft main bearings in place. Loose locknuts probably had caused the casualty, but we had no way of knowing for certain.

While Dykers was debating what to do next, we received a message from ComSubPac telling us that another U.S. submarine, operating to the south of us, had crippled an auxiliary aircraft carrier. The cripple was heading north, probably for his base in Yokosuka, and could come close to us. He was escorted both with destroyers and aircraft. At dusk we surfaced and, forgetting engines for the moment, headed west at our best speed to intersect the projected track of the cripple.

The sea had picked up during the day from the west, and that night it continued to get worse. We were not making the speed we needed to get to the desired intercept point, and, with all three engines on propulsion, we were getting in no battery charge at all. At daybreak we wanted to stay up but were forced down by patrol planes. It looked as though the formation would pass west of us.

Then, about two hours after diving, we sighted an Akikaze-class destroyer. Was he an advance scout? Or was he away out on the east wing of the formation? If he was a scout, attacking him would alert the cripple, and he would divert away from us. If the Akikaze was the east wing escort, he would probably be our only chance for a shot at any of them.

Dykers took a good look around and could see nothing more coming up from the south.

After some more thought, he decided we would attack the Akikaze.

We began to work into position and could immediately see that the destroyer was making high speed. Our best estimate was seventeen knots. This meant it was very important for us to shoot him on a fairly sharp track angle so that we would have as short a torpedo run as possible.

Dykers ordered four torpedoes to be made ready forward, with

the depth set at eight feet. We would see how the new contact exploders worked.

The destroyer tracked well, and with the torpedo run about
fifteen hundred yards, we were preparing to shoot.

"Final bearing and shoot. Up scope," called Dykers. Then, "Hold
it—he's zigging away. Down scope."

The famous Dykers luck was deserting us here. We had been in
perfect firing position, but this was the wrong zig at the wrong time.

"Up scope. Angle on the bow, 95 starboard. Down scope." The
skipper glanced at me. "What kind of a track and torpedo run does
that give us, Jim?"

"About a three-thousand-yard run, with about 130 starboard
track."

"No damn good, but it's now or never. Final bearing and shoot.
Up scope."

With a seventeen-knot target, you don't have a long time to sit
around and ponder the situation.

We fired four bow tubes with a good spread—wide enough to
cover considerable errors in course or speed.

We waited the necessary time—almost two minutes in this case.
No explosions. I couldn't believe we had missed. We had too good
a setup for that. One thing the TDC operator knows is whether or
not he has a good setup. This one was good. Everything checked,
sonar bearings and all.

While I was pondering, we heard the end-of-run explosions and
received word from sonar that the destroyer had turned toward us
and speeded up.

Dykers took a quick look.

"Holy suh-*moly!* Here he comes like a bat outta hell! Down
scope." The Akikaze had seen the torpedo tracks, all right.

"All ahead full, go to three hundred feet. Rig for depth charge,
rig for silent running." Down we went. Then, only a few seconds
later:

Click . . . *BANG!* Click . . . *BANG!*

Here we go again, I thought. Only this time we couldn't blame
it on the Bureau of Ordnance. It had been my fault. We had just
plain missed him. The spread should have gotten him—but it
hadn't. This was a lesson in humility for Calvert.

We were at three hundred feet, and Dykers began his evasion
tactics without delay.

"Shifting to short scale—coming in for the attack," came the quiet but foreboding report from sonar. This time there was no reluctance on the part of our attacker to drop charges.

Click . . . *BANG!* Click . . . *BANG!* Click . . . *BANG!*

Closer this time.

No one said anything, but I think the word got around the boat rather quickly that this working over was courtesy of the TDC operator.

Click . . . *BANG!* Click . . . *BANG!* Click . . . *BANG!*

No doubt about it—these were getting closer and closer.

"Take her down to 350 feet, Miles."

Dykers had decided to go below test depth in an effort to take advantage of a thermal layer at just about 310 feet.

The *Jack* slowly and silently sank down to 350 feet, down to that part of the ocean where almost no sunlight penetrates. We were running silent in the black depths.

We sweated it out and continued our slow, quiet evasion. Everyone in the crew knew that Dykers had intentionally gone below our test depth, but I think most of them thought, Well, we've been to four hundred feet once and survived it—why not again? They had confidence in the skipper.

Click . . . *BANG!* Click . . . *BANG!*

Our friend was holding contact on us, even with the *Jack* at 350 feet.

After about four hours and a number of very close charges, the explosions seemed to be getting a little farther away—or was it just wishful thinking?

Click . . . *BANG!* Click . . . *BANG!* Click . . . *BANG!*

These sounded closer again.

"How many of those damned things is he carrying? This must be an ammunition ship," muttered Gunner Lynes in the control room.

More than five hours later, the explosions were definitely getting farther away. He was still dropping, but we heard no more of the rapid-fire pinging that always heralded another series of depth charges. Perhaps he had lost contact and was just dropping to keep us submerged. Was the carrier coming near us, after all?

Finally, after forty-two charges, we believed we had heard the last of his attacks. Either he was out of depth charges or he was giving up. Sonar said the Akikaze was fading out to the north.

Nevertheless, we stayed silent and deep. The smoking lamp stayed out. More sweating, more silent brooding. I thought to myself that this was a hell of an ordeal to have given this crew after all they had been through on the first patrol. The fact that the miss had been my fault hung over me like a black cloud. I had the feeling I was going to be the local pariah.

But as I stepped down into the control room after the battle stations were secured, one of the men said, "These depth charge attacks are a piece of cake—right, Mr. Calvert?"

That wasn't exactly how I felt about it, but it certainly made me feel better to hear it from him.

That night we got off a message to ComSubPac telling him of our engine situation and the results of our attack on the Akikaze. That same night we got a reply telling us to terminate our patrol and return to Pearl Harbor.

Were we sad? I think it is fair to say we all had mixed emotions. None of us wanted to be out here with only three engines and clear evidence that we were about to lose more. On the other hand, none of us wanted to lose valuable time in the war zone. Were we ever going to get the *Jack* bandwagon rolling?

We turned our bow homeward, and on October 10 we tied up at the Submarine Base in Pearl. We were met by Commander Warder, our Division Commander, and were told we would be returning to the Mare Island Navy Yard in San Francisco for the replacement of our HOR engines with GM Wintons.

There was to be no delay. The next day, the eleventh, we left for San Francisco. On the way back, we lost two more engines. We were going to come into port with one engine—if we were lucky. Talk about coming back on a wing and a prayer.

Finally, we chugged under the Golden Gate Bridge with our one engine still wheezing away. Although none of us felt happy about the reason for our return, there is no way one can pass under that beautiful bridge without experiencing a surge of emotion. It is so graceful, so distinctively American, so much a symbol not only of a great city but also of a great nation that one would be a cold fish indeed not to have a moist eye on passing under it after a long time at sea.

We stood up the bay to the north until we reached the Navy Yard, which is at the town of Vallejo. There were no formalities. We were met by the Commander of the Yard and the officer who would be in charge of the re-engining project as well as the other work to be done during this yard period. Within a half hour of our arrival, workmen were using torches to burn off the superstructure over our engine rooms. They clearly had been coached ahead of time and knew exactly what they were doing on this particular submarine. We were to be worked on three eight-hour shifts a day, seven days a week.

All of the officers and men were moved off the *Jack* and onto a wooden barge built for this purpose. We had small rooms for the officers, a makeshift wardroom, a crew's berthing compartment, a crew's mess, and a galley. It was crude but adequate.

As we moved off, the yard workmen swarmed on. I had never seen so many men on board a submarine in my life. There wasn't a square foot to move around in. I wondered if she might sink from their sheer weight.

The time to complete the entire job was estimated at an unbelievably short seven weeks. In peacetime a job like this would have taken more than a year to complete. Seven weeks, however, was long enough for our families to come out, and they all did.

It had been only six months since Nancy and I had said goodbye on that cold April day in New London. But what a six months it had been. It is hard now to convey the intensity of the experiences we had had. It seemed more like two years than six months. There was no question that I had changed over that short period. I was harder and tougher than the young man who had sailed out of New London. But my love for Nancy had not changed, and our reunion was sweet and warm.

How could I explain to her what stability and courage she had given me during this six months? How could I explain what we had been through, how much the knowledge of her steady and faithful presence in Annapolis had meant? How could I tell her that she had become the symbol of what we were fighting for? How could I say any of these things without sounding maudlin?

The waiting had not been easy. As the old saying goes, we on the *Jack* knew *we* were all right, but she did not. Nancy was living in Annapolis, where a submarine wife was widowed almost every other week. In those long periods of waiting between letters, it took real courage to hang on and keep the faith. Our letters from the *Jack* were heavily censored, and in effect, we could say little except that we were well and missed our families. Now was the time to talk, but I don't think I—or any of us for that matter—did a very good job of telling our wives what they had meant to us while we had been away.

The Navy provided Quonset huts (long, tunnel-like structures built of corrugated iron sheeting) for all the married officers and married crew. They were adequate for temporary living but could not, by any stretch of the imagination, be called comfortable or cozy. We were young, however, and love overcomes many inconveniences.

Naturally all of the officers were busy during the day, seven days a week, with the overhaul. While the Yard workmen did the actual work, we were a sort of quality control force, making sure that jobs were done as ordered. We were getting a brand-new, improved model of the SJ surface search radar—and we didn't need any more convincing as to how vital that equipment could be to us. In addition, our listening sonar was being replaced with a new and better model. The *Jack* was slowly but surely being reborn.

We weren't so busy, however, that we did not have time to read Commander Warder and Admiral Lockwood's endorsements on the report of our second patrol. We were sharply criticized on two points:

> The commanding officer erred in attacking the Akikaze-class destroyer with an unfavorable firing position in a daylight attack when other more important traffic could be expected. The net result was to immobilize the submarine for five hours while it underwent a depth charge attack.
>
> It is also considered an error to go intentionally to 350 feet for evasion.

This was our first taste of criticism from above. The first patrol had received nothing but praise. But here we were, getting it right in the teeth. My first reaction was to ask Dykers what the hell these fat staffers were doing second-guessing the decisions we had had to make on short notice in the heat of battle.

Dykers gently reminded me that one of these "fat staffers" was Commander Frederick B. Warder, who had made some of the finest patrols of the war and who knew exactly what he was talking about.

"We were wrong. We were criticized justly, and I intend to learn from it," said the skipper.

I was beginning to see how the Navy operated at what to me at that time were high command levels. And I had to admit that I liked what I saw.

The upgrading of the *Jack* that interested me most was the removal of those accursed HOR engines and their replacement with the new, shiny GM Wintons, model 278-As, waiting for us in their heavy wooden crates on the dock. As mentioned, the entire top of the engine rooms had to be removed together, of course, with the myriad pipes and wires under those tops. It was a huge job and took weeks, even with the seemingly limitless number of men working on it.

The thing I really wanted to see, however, was the last of those four HORs being lifted out of our ship. Fortunately, I had the duty that night and knew that the removal was scheduled to take place about three in the morning. I was out on the dock with about half a dozen of the *Jack* enginemen, who also had a special interest in this operation.

The entire after end of the ship was bathed in light from huge floodlights strung above the opening in the after engine room, where the last of this infamous four was still waiting, sullenly, to be removed. A dozen or more hard-hatted Yard workmen in heavy coveralls stood around the edges of the open engine room, looking expectantly down into the dark interior. The whole scene had a rather dramatic look, as though some great ceremony was about to be performed. In a sense, it was.

When the riggers finally had all the cables and chains attached, the signal was given to hoist away. The huge dockside crane puffed and strained and groaned like a beast in agony. Finally, like a diseased tooth that had defied all the dentist's previous efforts to extract it, the last HOR came out from the dark cavern of the engine room. There was a small but heartfelt cheer from the *Jack* contingent watching at the dockside as this monstrous source of trouble and heartache, some twenty feet long and ten feet high, came swinging away from the ship and onto a waiting railroad flatcar.

"Off to the scrap heap!" exulted one of our enginemen.

"She'll be razor blades in a month."

"I wouldn't shave with any razor blade made from that son of a bitch," was another comment. "The first thing it'd do is cut your throat."

"Especially if it knew you were an American. I'll always believe the Heinies sent those things over here to sabotage us."

Sailors habitually say that any scrapped Navy ship or heavy machinery will be "made into razor blades," and I suppose they are not always wrong.

And so went our heartfelt good-byes to our HOR engines. When that last one came out of the *Jack,* I felt that something rotten and contemptible had been removed from our beloved ship and that her rebirth had taken a major step forward.

In late December of 1943, as we neared the end of our time in the Yard, we learned that the re-engined boats in Squadron Twelve would all be transferred to the Southwest Pacific and based in Fremantle, Western Australia.

That was earth-shaking news. Our new boss would be Admiral Ralph Christie, who was a quite different man from Admiral Lockwood. Although they had worked together effectively to develop and push through the fleet submarine in the 1930s, they had distinctly different ideas on some important matters and were known not to be the warmest of friends, now that they had somewhat competitive responsibilities.

"Christie is a very smart man, and he knows the submarine business backward and forward," was Dykers's comment to the wardroom officers when he heard the news.

Equally important to all of us was the fact that we would be based in Fremantle, the seaport for Perth. Our rest periods would not be spent on some gooney-bird-infested island but in a large city with all that can mean. Probably every officer and man in the *Jack* received the news of our new base in a different way—but our response was overwhelmingly favorable. We were young and strong, and this was adventure.

We were going halfway around the world to our new base and would make a war patrol en route. We had new engines and a powerful new radar. As the ship began to take shape and we were able to clear out all the debris from the Yard work, our spirits began to soar, despite the coming parting from our families. This was what we had been trained to do, and we were going to have another good crack at it.

When we went out on our postoverhaul sea trials with the glistening new Wintons in the engine rooms, I could feel the different spirit in the ship. As we passed under the Golden Gate Bridge and the *Jack* began to move and weave with the seas coming in from the Pacific, she felt like a fighter getting ready for the bouts that lay ahead.

Soon we were back at Mare Island for the final adjustments.

After a farewell Christmas dinner with our families, we sailed under the Golden Gate, heading for Australia with some important business to do on the way.

The *Jack* had, in truth, been reborn, and it had a brave new adventure ahead of it.

7

The Tanker Sweep

We had some important changes in the wardroom during our time at Mare Island. Beetle Roach was detached to get command of his own submarine, and Miles Refo moved up to be our new exec. Leyton Goodman and my good friend Billy Coleman were both detached to go to new construction. Two reserve officers, Alec Nading and Kent Lukingbeal, reported on board as replacements.

Before we had left on our first patrol, in June, Chief Archer had been recommended for officer rank. After his successful crawl into the induction piping during our depth charge attack, we had all felt even more strongly that he deserved special recognition. Dykers had made some phone calls to Washington about Archer's promotion while we were in the Pearl Harbor Navy Yard being repaired, in July. The Navy Department finally came through in November, while we were at Mare Island: Earl was promoted to the rank of Ensign. Citing the very successful example of Jack O'Brien, we asked to keep Earl on board, and Ensign Archer soon received orders to the USS *Jack*.

Thus we had three new faces in the wardroom as we left Mare Island. Such changes do not come easily—the old wardroom had become a very close club. We had been through a lot together—some victories and some defeats—and we had known and trusted each other. We had relieved each other on watch. We had shared meals together in smooth weather and in storms so rough that we had to hang on with one hand and eat with the other. We had proved ourselves in battle in Sagami-nada and had experienced the heartbreak of the all-too-short and unsuccessful second patrol. In the wardroom after dinners, we had fought most of the battles of the Civil War, from Fort Sumter to Appomattox, without striking any blows or having any really hard feelings. Our continuing bridge games had left some of us richer by pennies, others poorer by the same amount, but all still good friends.

How could we just casually say goodbye after all that, as though we were going to the corner drugstore? In truth, we couldn't. We were realistic enough to know that we might never see each other again, but we also knew that we would never forget each other. Beetle Roach had been a good friend and adviser to me when I was green and in need of help. It was hard seeing him go. His wife, Ann, had been a warm friend and helper for Nancy while the *Jack* was being built at Electric Boat and again while we were together at Mare Island. Billy Coleman had been an especially good friend, and I was going to miss his cheerful face and irrepressible high spirits. There were a lot of tough good-byes for all of us.

Alec Nading was a dark, slightly balding man of average size who seemed quiet and somewhat reserved. In a wardroom where there were not many introverts, he had a hard time getting a word in edgewise; but we all realized we had a solid and dependable new shipmate.

Kent Lukingbeal was an unforgettable character. Somewhat shorter than average and chunky of build, Kent had a perpetually cheerful face and jovial manner. He was also extremely bright. He had stood number one in his law school class and had volunteered for active duty almost as soon as he graduated. Although no Civil War expert, he could hold his end up in this area, and the Yankee contingent received some welcome reinforcement. Kent also knew a good bit about music, and the quality of our very limited record collection took a definite turn for the better with his arrival.

Naturally this new cast of characters meant a significant change in our attack party. Alec took over the plotting position, with Kent as his assistant. Miles was the new assistant approach officer, and Obie took over as battle station diving officer.

The changes in the wardroom were not the only ones on board. About a quarter of the crew was detached and sent back to new construction, including Chief Hunt, our Chief of the Boat. This was a blow because, as I have said before, it was difficult to find just the right man for this job.

The natural leader among the crew members seemed to be young Frank Lynes, the gunner's mate. While we were at Mare Island, he had won his promotion to chief petty officer at the age of twenty-five—about the youngest man any of us had seen reach that cherished and respected level. He was young to be a chief but especially young to be a Chief of the Boat. Still, we all believed he deserved careful consideration.

Frank's father was a dentist in the Navy who, naturally enough, had wanted Frank to go to Annapolis. Frank was certainly bright enough, but somehow I had trouble visualizing this robust and somewhat rambunctious young man buckling down to the routines of Bancroft Hall and putting up with Plebe Year. In any case, he had joined the Navy as an enlisted man, and we were indeed fortunate to have him. He combined the elements of a strong body, a tough, nimble mind, and an irrepressible spirit.

After considerable thought and discussion in the wardroom, we gave the job to Frank Lynes. He was a success from the beginning. I had worried about how the older chiefs (some were in their forties) would feel about such a young man holding the Chief of the Boat job. I need not have worried. Lynes could hold his own with any of them—and then some.

During our stay at Mare Island, we had plenty of time to read and reflect on the latest patrol reports. With so many new submarines in the Pacific, the mail brought fresh reports almost every day. One thing was clear from reading them—our submarines were using more and more the German U-boat tactic of the night surface attack. Our superior radar and twenty knots of surface speed made a powerful combination for attacking Japanese convoys in the broad Pacific. The night surface attack was a natural for American submarines.

There was an attack teacher of sorts at Mare Island. We spent many hours attacking mock convoys while giving ourselves the surface speed and maneuverability of which we were capable. We placed imaginary escorts out on either wing at distances ranging from a half mile to two or three miles. It was a new tactic to us, but even on the attack teacher, we could see that it could be devastatingly effective if done correctly. A surface attack could also be highly dangerous because the traditional protection of the submarine, the water in which it was submerged, would not be there. A submarine attacking on the surface was as fragile as an eggshell. One well-placed shot from an escort's gun could finish her.

The day after Christmas, we took our final departure from Mare Island and got under way for Pearl. We all took one long, last, fond look at the Golden Gate Bridge as we nosed out into rougher-than-usual seas. We arrived at the Submarine Base at Pearl on January 2, 1944. New Year's Eve and New Year's Day passed en route without much celebration because of another one of those Eastern Pacific storms with which we were becoming all too familiar. At Pearl Harbor we were met by Commander Warder, who was to be our training officer for the upcoming third patrol. Dykers had written him from Mare Island asking if we could have some training in night surface attacks before departing on patrol.

Not only had Warder gotten us some night surface attack training, he had even been able to arrange for us to make some practice attacks on a U.S. convoy leaving Pearl Harbor. It would be a five-ship convoy with two escorts, bound with supplies for Western Pacific bases. Clearly this sort of training for our submarines was being given high priority—or else Warder had been unusually persuasive in his request. Probably some of both.

One other thing showed us the new emphasis being placed on night surface attacks. At the beginning of the training period, the *Jack* was painted a ghostly gray color from stem to stern. Gone was the familiar black; it had proved too easy to see at night. The exact shade of gray being used was carefully chosen to make us hard to see either in moonlight or in complete darkness.

One night during the training period, we worked with another submarine that had also been painted with the new camouflage. We tried spotting each other at various distances, up-moon and down-moon. It was amazing how well the new paint worked. Several times we knew from radar exactly where our friend was, but we couldn't see him. We were talking by VHF radio, so we were able to compare notes continually. It was clear to both of us that the white splashes of our bow wave and wake were the easiest things to see. The slower we went, the harder we were to see. Slow speed was not, of course, what we wanted in a night surface attack. But all in all, what we learned was very reassuring.

During our practice attacks on the outgoing U.S. convoy, the escorts were told to use their radar on some runs and not on others. We were not told which was which, simulating the fact that some Japanese convoy escorts we met would have radar while some would not.

We were not long in finding out how much tougher it was when the escorts were using their radar. There was no doubt that the *Jack* was hard for either the escorts or the heavies to see, and on each nonradar approach we got into excellent firing position without being detected. On each radar-equipped approach, however, we were detected early and got the big, bright spotlight of the escort shining in our direction, simulating gunfire.

The best intelligence we had was that most of the Japanese escorts did not have reliable radar. Well, we would see.

Warder made our training period an unusually long six days, partly because we had so many new officers but mainly because we had so few submarine-qualified officers on board. Only Dykers and Refo wore the gold submarine pins. Obie and Earl Archer were, of course, qualified in submarines as enlisted men, but the requirements for officer qualification were significantly different, particularly in the torpedo-shooting area. They were working on it but had a long way to go. Nading and Lukingbeal were just getting started.

Qualification in submarines is, as the saying goes, a big deal. The young officer who aspires to it has to learn the boat thoroughly, be able to sketch every system from memory and to operate every piece of machinery, including the main engines and the electric controls. He must also qualify as officer of the deck, make a satisfactory torpedo approach and firing (as substitute skipper), and be able to send and receive messages by blinker light in Morse code. It usually takes about a year to qualify.

Those who qualify are rewarded by the authority to wear the gold submarine pin. About three inches wide, this consists of a rather antiquated-looking submarine supporting the chins of two classic-design dolphins on each bowplane. The dolphins' tails fan out on each side to complete the design. Under the submarine and the dolphins ripples a fair representation of seawater. The pin was, and is, worn with pride by every submarine officer. It is the symbol of the profession. But in December 1944 I had not yet earned the right to wear it.

By the time we were into the prepatrol training for our third patrol, however, I had completed all the requirements for qualification except my torpedo approach and firing. Commander Warder arranged for me to shoot my torpedo toward the end of our prepatrol period, after he was pretty well satisfied with the *Jack*'s new attack party. I was all set to go with the approach—but who would take the TDC? No one else ever had.

"I want you to have the best, Jim—I'll take the TDC," said our skipper.

This was a brave move since to my knowledge Dykers had never touched the machine before; more important, it left me in sole charge of seeing that the approach was safely made. A common mistake of beginning approach officers is to get so close that there is danger of collision. On my qualifying approach, then, there was no safety officer, although I noticed that Warder took a quick look around at one point and winked reassuringly at Dykers.

I suppose I wouldn't be telling the story if the torpedo shot had not been a hit, but it was. The practice torpedo ran right under the middle of the target—an MOT.

"We've got a new TDC ace here—you better watch out for your job, Jim," grinned Warder as we recovered the practice torpedo.

Two nights later, at the end of the training period, Dykers arranged a dinner at the Base Officer's Club, at which my gold pin was presented. Commander Warder was there too, which gave it extra meaning for me. There were no speeches, just a few nice words; but, at least up to that time, I had never had an award that meant more. The *Jack* now had three qualified officers in a wardroom of seven.

I was, however, to receive one more award during our brief stay in Pearl. Tommy Dykers was being awarded a Navy Cross, the Navy's second highest combat decoration, junior only to the Congressional Medal of Honor, for the first patrol. The skipper had recommended me for a Silver Star medal for my part in that patrol. When Admiral Lockwood pinned that Silver Star on me during the same ceremony at which our skipper received his Navy Cross, my cup was really running over. To make the day complete, Miles Refo also received a Silver Star for his part in the first patrol, and Earl Archer received a Bronze Star for his bravery in repairing the induction pipe leak. So, all in all, we had been given occasion for another festive dinner at the O Club. We took it.

I was now the fourth officer in seniority in the *Jack* (Alec Nading was senior to me by a few weeks), qualified in submarines and wearing the Silver Star. In addition, I was the new torpedo and gunnery officer, having relieved Leyton Goodman while we were at Mare Island. I had happily turned the communications and first lieutenant jobs over to Kent Lukingbeal. I was moving up in the submarine world.

Unfortunately however, we had only two qualified top watch standers, Miles and myself. On the way out to Pearl, Miles and I stood watch-and-watch (four on and four off) and conducted one of the all-time most intensive training sessions for new OODs to get

Nading and Lukingbeal ready to take a top watch. We put on what would later be known as the full-court press.

Nading had been a qualified top watch stander in surface ships, so he did not have far to go except to be sure he had the diving routine down pat. By the time we reached Pearl, both he and Lukingbeal were qualified. Miles came off the watch list (normal for the exec) and, voilà, I was the senior watch stander. (I got this job despite being junior to Alec Nading because he was not yet qualified in submarines.) I happily turned the midwatches over to Kent and took the luxurious eight to twelves for myself. Nading took the four to eights.

Perhaps because he felt we were still thin on experience, Commander Warder assigned us a prospective commanding officer, Commander Frederick Laing, to ride us for the upcoming patrol. This had become common practice by this stage of the war, particularly with older submarine officers who were senior enough to get command but were coming from shore duty and needed to have the experience of at least one patrol under their belts before taking over a boat.

This worked out well for us. Laing took on the navigation duties, leaving Miles free to get the new job of being exec under control. In addition, Freddy, as he was called, became assistant approach officer so that he could experience being in on our attacks. Miles moved back to the battle station diving officer job with Jack O'Brien as his assistant, giving Obie that much more time to work into this key job.

Freddy Laing was a short, balding man of very cheerful disposition who proved to be a good shipmate. He realized that he was fortunate to be making a patrol with someone as respected as Dykers, and he also realized that if all went well and he got a good writeup from Dykers (which was by no means a foregone conclusion), he would probably get command of a submarine based in West Australia. All in all, these were good prospects, and Freddy worked hard to carry his weight on board.

On January 16, 1944, we departed Pearl Harbor for our patrol area, which we were told would probably be in the South China Sea but would be confirmed for us when we reported to Commander Submarines Southwest Pacific. That would happen about the time we crossed the international date line.

We had more foul weather on the eleven-hundred-mile passage

to Midway, and when we arrived on the twentieth, it was too rough for us to enter. This was not left up to us: the Base commander told us to lay off the entrance at a safe distance until told we could enter.

Our new engines were running like Swiss watches. It is hard for me to tell you what this confidence in our ability to stay at sea without engineering disasters meant to us. It was a whole new ball game.

Finally, on the morning of the twenty-first, we were cleared to enter. Not long after leaving Pearl, we had developed difficulty with the new SJ radar training mechanism, the motorized device that made the radar antenna search around automatically rather than by hand (as the old set had made us do). The repairs took longer than expected, and it was the twenty-fourth before we could leave.

Even then, luck was not with us. We had more radar trouble. In addition to the surface search SJ, we were equipped with an air search radar—by and large, relatively primitive—designated the *SD;* it didn't orient you to the direction of the airplane, but it told you how far away it was. About eight hours out of Midway, the SD's main transformer shorted out. This was not a spare we carried; we had no choice except to go back to Midway. On the way back, the SJ training mechanism jammed again. What kind of a start was this?

The next morning, January 25, we were again told that it was too rough to enter. So once more here we were laying off Midway Island, impatient to get in, get repaired, and get going. This was getting to be a habit. On the morning of the twenty-sixth, the sea calmed a bit, and we were able to reenter Midway.

The repair folks at Midway put in a new SD transformer and an entirely new gear train for the SJ training mechanism. Satisfied that we finally had everything right, we departed again on January 28, eight days later than we had hoped to say good-bye to this desolate home of the gooney birds.

About a week later, the SD earned its salt. It was a heavily overcast day with many low-lying clouds. We were passing Marcus Island, a known base for Japanese patrol planes. We had an SD contact at four miles and did not wait to try to see him. As we passed about sixty feet, *WHAM!*

The SD had seen something, all right, and the patrol plane must have seen us diving. We leveled off at 150 feet.

WHAM! . . . *WHAM!* Two more bombs, much closer.

"Let's hope that three is all he carries," said Dykers, who by now had come to the conning tower. Apparently it was, for we heard no more. About a half hour later, we surfaced. Although visibility was still poor, we had no sign of anyone on the SD. This all-around primitive radar had until then been looked on as a sort of poor cousin of the SJ, not really needed with our faultless lookout system. Suddenly the SD took on a new status. No lookout had seen that plane, and if we had stayed up until we *had* seen him, I might not be writing this now.

All day that day, February 5, we were plagued with aircraft from Marcus obviously looking for the submarine that had been bombed. They combed the area pretty thoroughly. We had to dive four times. Each time the airplane was detected by the SD. Twice the lookouts sighted the planes about the same time; they were proud of the fact that even in such thick weather they could match the SD in performance.

On the eighth we reached the boundary between ComSubPac's area of responsibility and that of Commander Submarines Southwest Pacific (ComSubSouWesPac) and reported by radio to Admiral Christie for operational control. We were given a large area in the South China Sea covering much of the route used by the tankers going between the Empire (the name we used for Japan all through the war) and the oil fields in southeast Asia (formerly the Dutch East Indies).

The South China Sea is big. It stretches some fifteen hundred miles, more or less north and south, from Formosa (Taiwan) at its northern end to Singapore at its southern. Its western side is bounded by China in the north, Vietnam in the central part, and Malaysia in the south. Its eastern boundary is formed by the Philippines on the north and Borneo on the south. The sea narrows to about five hundred miles between Vietnam and the northern tip of Borneo. This, coupled with the fact that much of the oil for the Empire was coming from huge refineries along the north coast of Borneo, made the South China Sea a good hunting ground.

In early 1944 the Pacific war was reaching the point where the supply of petroleum for the Japanese homeland was becoming critical. Just before we reached our area, Admiral Christie changed the top priority for submarine targets from Japanese combatant ships to oil tankers. We were primed to look for tankers.

After a few days of trying to patrol this huge sea area by periscope during the day, we realized this was a vain effort. By running on the surface and setting a watch on the high periscope, we achieved a significant increase in our coverage. In this condition we had an effective height of eye of about fifty feet. This meant that in the clear weather characteristic of the South China Sea, we could see the top of a ship at fifteen miles, her smoke maybe even farther. Thus we were covering an area of more than seven hundred square miles with the high periscope watch, as compared to a maximum of fifty square miles with the submerged periscope watch.

Of course, patrolling on the surface in the daytime made us vulnerable to detection and bombing by patrol aircraft, but we had to take that risk. Although we were not far from the major Japanese base at Cam Ranh Bay, we believed our lookouts were up to the job of spotting its patrol planes before they saw us.

Even with this new patrolling technique (which resulted in at least two or three dives a day to avoid aircraft), we were not spotting any tanker traffic. The crew was beginning to wonder if the South China Sea was just plain empty of everything except Japanese patrol aircraft. Where were these tankers we had heard so much about?

Then, about 3:30 in the morning on February 19, Charley Caw, our battle stations radar operator, picked up a group of ships at about thirteen miles. They were northbound. We were about half-way between Cam Ranh Bay and Manila, a little north of the narrowest point of the Vietnam-Borneo passage. Caw reported the contact to Kent, who had the deck.

GONG-GONG-GONG went the incessant call of the battle stations alarm. I woke up and, after a moment of wondering what was going on, crawled hastily out of my bunk and padded to the conning tower in a pair of khaki trousers, an undershirt, and bare feet. Speed was more important than formality at this point. When I got there, Alec and Kent already had the plot going and were trying to figure out the formation.

Before long they had it doped out pretty well. To the east of us and up-moon were four large ships. They looked like tankers in the dim light, moving in a column with three other, smaller ships on the side of the formation away from us. At least two of the smaller ships looked as though they might be escorts, but we couldn't be sure. The convoy was running a fairly standard zig plan, turning the formation twenty to thirty-five degrees about every five minutes, on the average. There did not seem to be any escort ships on our side. This seemed hard to believe, but we could not see any on the radar or visually from the bridge.

Before long we could see for certain that these were tankers, and we realized we were going to get a crack at these top-priority targets. All of us felt that the big chance the *Jack* had been looking for ever since she had been built was right here, staring us in the face. All the hard work in training, all the disappointments, all the worry over HOR engines and torpedoes that didn't work—all of these could be put in the background forever if we could just do properly the work that was sitting before us. Our training on night surface attack procedures was also going to pay off, for this was a situation made to order for that tactic.

The night surface attack required the skipper to be on the bridge, where he could make the tough decisions about just how to come in on the convoy, how close to come to escorts, when to dive if necessary, and when to shoot. Dykers wanted to have Freddy Laing on the bridge with him because there Laing could learn the most about night surface attacks. So Miles Refo and I were joined in the conning tower only by Kent and Alec on the plot and Charley Caw on the radar. It was a bit of a lonely feeling.

I also worried about Dykers being on the bridge with no TDC or plot to help him get the picture. He was used to standing about three feet from the TDC, where he could easily see, continuously updated, the target's range and bearing, course and speed—everything he needed to know, there at a glance. Up on the bridge, he had nothing on the tactical picture other than what he could visualize in his head. We did have a talkback system between the TDC and the bridge, so I could keep him posted on how the situation looked on the TDC; but it wasn't easy. In our drills at Pearl Harbor, we had worked over and over on this new arrangement, and we had slowly gotten more used to it. Now it was going to get a real test.

We had a senior signalman, Stacey Bennett, whose night vision was extraordinarily good, and Dykers wanted him on the bridge at battle stations. Bennett could see at night, all right, but he had another habit that gave the whole bridge gang, from Dykers down to the lookouts, the willies. He had a good singing voice, and when a situation got tight—as it certainly was now, as we closed in on the near column of tankers—he would start to sing. Bennett's favorite, "Nearer, My God, to Thee," may have been great for him, but it had a distinctly unsettling effect on everyone else.

"Dammit, Bennett, can't you sing something else?" from the skipper.

"I guess so, Captain, but this just seems to be so comforting."

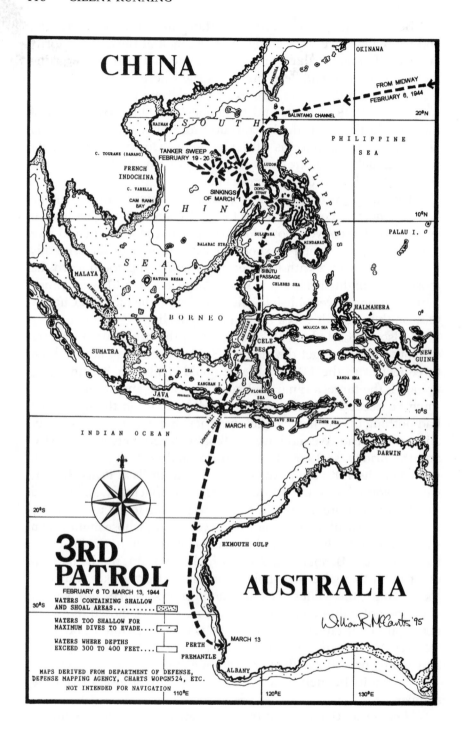

Moments later Bennett saw and reported something about the formation that no one else had seen. Even when specifically pointed out by Bennett, it remained invisible to others. This was priceless information, so the skipper just shrugged. "Nearer, My God, to Thee" kept on—at a slightly lower volume.

We were getting in close enough so that when they zigged the next time, we should get a good shot.

"We'll shoot six torpedoes. Make ready all six tubes forward. Set depth ten feet," came from Dykers. "Jim, we'll shoot at the second and third tankers on this side of the formation."

"Aye aye, sir, but they're about due to zig."

"OK, I can hold off a bit longer, but they're getting pretty close."

Conscious of how visible our bow wake could be, Dykers decided to slow: "All ahead one-third."

"There comes the zig—they're going away," I reported on the intercom.

"Yeah, I can see it from up here. Dammit, they're going farther away than I wanted. Let me know when they've settled down."

It turned out to be a forty-degree zig away, the biggest one they had made since we started tracking them. This made the torpedo runs longer than we wanted, but there was nothing to do but shoot now. It would only get worse. The memory of that miss on the Akikaze was still plaguing me.

One of the key things in shooting torpedoes was to get the exact bearing of the target set in the TDC just before you shot. With the periscope three feet away from the TDC in a daytime periscope attack, this was no problem. At night it was a different matter. Someone had to look over the gyro repeater on the bridge with a thing called a *pelorus* and while looking at the target read the bearing from the illuminated dial underneath. Freddy Laing had been assigned this job.

"Jim, as soon as you get the bearing from us, shoot the first three. We'll give you a new bearing on the second target for the next three."

"Aye aye, sir."

"Bearing two four," from Laing.

"Fire one!" I said as our first surface-fired torpedo lurched from the bow of the submarine.

"Fire two! . . . Fire three!" The next two went out at eight-second intervals.

"First three are gone," I reported to Dykers.

"Here's the second ship—bearing one three," from Laing.

"Fire four! . . . Fire five! . . . Fire six!" The last three went out as scheduled.

Just as I turned to the quartermaster with the stopwatch to ask how much more time was left for the first fish: Ker-*WHOOM!*

This was no torpedo explosion. I had never heard any explosion so loud or so paralyzing. Then two *WHAM*s as the second and third torpedoes hit.

"Holy suh-*moly*," from the bridge. "After the first fish hit, flames ran back and forth across his deck, and then in about two seconds the whole ship exploded. He's gone—there's nothing left of him."

A moment later there were two more loud *WHAM*s as the second salvo began to hit. The bridge could see the flashes at the water line as these torpedoes hit a ship in the far column. No ship explosion there, however. No flames. But two unmistakable hits.

"Right full rudder, all ahead flank," from Dykers as he prepared to pull out.

"One of the ships in the far column is a well-decked destroyer, and he's shooting at us—I can see the big, orange flashes!" reported Dykers, still cool but obviously concerned.

"Pour it on, maneuvering. Don't spare the horses," from the skipper as he simultaneously gave orders to the helm to start weaving twenty degrees either side of our course to make us a harder target.

I gave a short prayer of thanks that we had those sturdy Wintons back there instead of four HOR cripples. I also thought of Sandy Sanderlin and Bob Craig, our battle station controller operators, back there coaxing everything they could out of that propulsion plant without making the fatal mistake of tripping something out.

"He's got the range, all right. Some of these splashes are getting damn close," from Dykers.

From the bridge, down the hatch, I could now hear the strong, clear tones of "Nearer, My God, to Thee." Bennett was in full voice now, with no holding back.

We were all thinking the same thought—Is the skipper going to have to dive? Are we in for another five hours of depth charging?

No order was given for diving, but the skipper did send everyone down from the bridge except Bennett. As Freddy Laing came down to the conning tower, he said, "Either the skipper likes the singing, or he wants to keep that night vision up there." I think we all knew which it was.

"All stop. Steady as she goes. Make ready all four tubes aft," from Dykers.

What was up? I couldn't figure this one out.

"I think all he sees is our wake. If he continues to close, we'll try to shoot him before we dive. Get him set up on the TDC," from Dykers.

"He already is. We've got him locked in," I replied.

Then I remembered our night training experience with the other submarine at Pearl. The wake was all we could see. Dykers was trying to make us disappear. But if this Japanese destroyer had radar . . .

The next shot from the destroyer went way over. Then off to the right. We could hear Bennett and the skipper talking about it on the bridge, their voices drifting down through the conning tower hatch. We didn't need the intercom.

I was getting continual ranges and bearings from Charley Caw on the radar. "He's slowing down and turning to his right," I reported.

"I don't think he can see us any more—most of these shots are going wild out to starboard," from Dykers.

A minute or two passed uneventfully.

"I think he has stopped shooting. No shots for quite a while now," from the bridge.

"The destroyer is echo ranging now," came the report from the sonar room. "And he has slowed down."

Good! I thought. He thinks we've submerged.

The ruse had worked.

I reported all this to the bridge. "Great, but we can't see him any more. I don't know what he's doing," from Dykers.

Then, distantly, one of the sweetest sounds I had ever heard: click . . . *bang!* . . . click . . . *bang!* Depth charges. But not the bone-rattling noise that we had gotten to know all too well. Instead, this was a sort of benevolent, distant confirmation of the fact that we had given him the slip.

We were still up, and he thought we were down.

"Come right twenty degrees. All ahead two-thirds," from the bridge. We were slipping away.

Little by little, Dykers eased away from the destroyer and came to the same course as the convoy, which had now reformed and was fleeing to the north. We slowly worked up to flank speed, twenty knots.

Dykers came down from the bridge, looked at the TDC and plot, and said, "I'm going to pull out far enough from them so that when it gets light, they won't see us. We'll make an end-around and then dive on their track so we can get another shot at them."

By daylight on the twentieth, we had pulled out so far that we could no longer see the convoy except through the high periscope. It was a clear, calm day, and from time to time we would check the convoy on the radar. We were just seeing their tops at a range of more than fifteen miles. There was little or no chance they could see us since all we had above the horizon, as they saw it, was our high, thin attack periscope. Not much to see.

During the day Dykers secured the battle stations so people could get some rest, but he asked me to stay on the TDC. Nading and Lukingbeal took turns keeping the plot up-to-date. I was still dressed only in my undershirt, so I asked Domingo, our senior steward, to bring me a regular shirt, a sandwich, and some coffee.

During the morning Dykers and Laing came up for a bit of a postmortem with me.

"The tanker must have been loaded with high octane gasoline. When he exploded, the flames shot hundreds of feet in the air. Within less than a minute, he was gone. We could see clearly because the sea was covered with burning gasoline," explained Dykers.

"I don't see how anyone on board could have lived more than a few seconds. It was an enormous explosion," added Laing.

"How come you gave us a bearing on a ship in the far column for the second salvo? I thought we were going to take two of the tankers in the close column," I asked. "I know we had their course and speed nailed right to the mast."

"My fault," said Laing. "In the excitement I gave you the bearing on one of the ships in the far column. We were so close I got them mixed up."

"I don't think he was a tanker. I still don't know why only one destroyer came after us. Maybe we hit an escort of some kind in the far column," said Dykers. "Whatever he was, you sure had the dope on these guys. Five hits out of six isn't bad."

"You really had us guessing when you came to all stop and got those after tubes ready," I said.

"There was no way we could outrun him. We were making twenty knots, and he was still closing us. I decided to find out if he could see us—or just our wake."

"It sure worked," I grinned.

"Yeah, but not everyone on the bridge thought it was a great idea. When I came to all stop, Bennett groaned and muttered under his breath, 'Oh, *no* . . . oh, *no.*' He's a real morale booster, that boy. But he can see like a nighthawk. I'll take him any day," said Dykers.

"He's a great singer, too," added Freddy Laing.

All that day we worked ahead of the convoy. Twice we had to dive for patrol planes. But we stayed down only about twenty minutes, then were back up again. After last night's action, we couldn't see why there were not more planes out, but we just accepted what was happening without worrying too much about the shortcomings of the Japanese ASW effort. The convoy was zigging much more radically than the night before, and all this back-and-forth made their advance substantially slower. Of course, it also made it easier for us to pull ahead of them.

The performance of the new SJ radar was superb, but we didn't want to use it unless we had to. There was a chance the convoy had a radar detector on board, and we were just as happy to have them think we were still back at the scene of last night's attack. So we tracked the convoy on the high periscope, staying at the extreme range we could see them, playing it as safe as possible. Every once in a while, they would zig far away and we would lose them on the periscope. Cutting in the radar, we could hold them out as far as eighteen miles and thus had no trouble closing enough to get their tops in sight once again.

What a difference this all was from our first two patrols, when we had been struggling with a balky radar set and worrying continually about those undependable HORs. The *Jack* was really flexing her muscles now.

I could not help but think, also, about how much the Pacific submarines had progressed since those early days of the war when some skippers were so fearful of being detected that they tried to shoot on sonar bearings alone. The night surface attack was a far cry from that.

In the afternoon we began to close their track to get dead ahead of them. By about three o'clock, we submerged on what we estimated from the daylong plot was their intended track.

There was a considerable period after we dove when we could not see them, had no sonar contact, and of course lacked radar information. We were betting on the accuracy of our plot and the hope that the convoy commodore would not decide to make a significant change of base course. We knew we would find ourselves hopelessly out in left field if he did.

Somehow, though, I believed this was our day. We had been training this ship more than a year to be ready for just this kind of opportunity, and I could not believe it was going to get away from us. All of our equipment was working beautifully, and all of our people were right at the top of their game. Whether on the surface or at periscope depth, we were, I believed, going to get some more shots at these guys.

About an hour after submerging, sonar reported faint echo ranging dead ahead. Once again that practice of echo ranging as they proceeded was betraying them.

Before long Dykers had their tops in sight through the periscope. Alec Nading and Kent Lukingbeal had worked out an overall speed of advance for the convoy based on its zig plan, and I had just set that in the TDC rather than trying to estimate the convoy's many zigs and zags.

As the ships got closer, Dykers was able to get a periscope range; it was only five hundred yards out from the estimate we had from the plot and the TDC. We were really hitting on all cylinders.

"There are still four tankers left, two in each column. One escort far out on the other side," from the skipper.

Because they were west of us, proceeding north, they were silhouetted against the lowering sun. We were working in close. Dykers had to be very careful of the scope since the sea was almost mirror smooth.

"Make ready all six bow tubes. Set depth ten feet."

The echo ranging from the escorts was loud now. But sonar kept reporting that they were on the long search scale—no sign of their having detected us.

We were in very tight, waiting for the zig. It came, but it was small. We were too tight for a bow shot.

"Left full rudder. Make ready all four stern tubes," snapped the skipper.

Once again the part-luck, part-skill Dykers formula worked. We were going to be in beautiful position for a stern shot.

"We'll shoot two at the first and two at the second . . . stand by."

"Bearing, mark."

"One six five," from Laing.

"Fire seven! . . . Fire eight! . . . Fire nine! . . . Fire ten!"

All four torpedoes went out on time and spread just as planned.

WHAM! . . . WHAM! . . . WHAM! Three hits, all right on time.

Then, a few seconds later, Ker-*WHOOM! . . .* and then, Ker-*WHOOM!* These ships were exploding!

"Up scope."

"They must all be high-octane gasoline tankers. Our targets are almost gone, and the sea is covered with burning gasoline. What a sight." After our near-disaster on the first patrol, however, we had agreed there would be no more sight-seeing through the periscope.

Apparently the escort on the far side was confused since he started off in the wrong direction, dropping depth charges as he went. They were too far away to be dangerous, but still, I liked the sound of them better when we were on the surface.

It looked as though the convoy commodore, whichever ship he was in, did not want his escort to stay around looking for submarines while he went north without any protection. All the remaining ships took off in a northerly direction without much delay. When the generated range on the TDC made it look as though it would be safe to surface, we came up and started to chase them at flank speed.

On the word "Prepare to surface," we got a question from the forward torpedo room: "Shall we blow down the forward tubes?" In the excitement of the attack, we had all forgotten that those tubes were being left flooded a long time. Not good for the torpedoes, but probably OK.

When we got to the surface and got the radar going, we could see that the Japanese commodore had split his convoy. There now remained two tankers and apparently only one escort. One tanker was going to the north alone while the other was diverging to the north-northwest with the escort.

We prepared for another night surface attack, this time on the unescorted tanker. We made our end-around on him, and as we tracked him, it became apparent that he had taken the wildest zig plan in the book. He was zigging every two or three minutes, with course changes up to fifty degrees each time.

We made ready the bow tubes as we completed our end-around and began to close in for the attack. We were in good position and were firing from about eighteen hundred yards. I didn't see how he could fail to see us, but there was no sign that he had.

We used our regular procedure of Freddy giving me a bearing from the pelorus on the bridge.

"One six," from Laing.

"Fire one! . . . Fire two! . . . Fire three!" I snapped. Everything went as arranged.

"No noise from the first torpedo, sir. Sounds like a cold run," came from the sonar room.

Oh no, I thought, remembering that these fish had been flooded a long time on the late-afternoon periscope attack.

"The second fish sounds OK, but I think it's running too far ahead of the target," from sonar.

I reported all this to the bridge as Dykers gave the orders to turn and pull away from the target.

"I never saw any torpedo tracks from up here," said the skipper. This was unusual for a night surface attack.

"The last torpedo is erratic. It is running away off to the right and doesn't sound right," came the next depressing report from sonar.

Our lone tanker friend had dodged the bullet.

"I'm afraid we've missed him," I said to the bridge.

"That's OK. We'll get him yet. He's shooting at us now. From the flash it looks like a pretty big gun. Five-incher, I would guess. Big orange flashes," came the calm report from the bridge. Bennett will be singing now, I thought.

"Tell the forward torpedo room to pull those other three fish that were flooded so long and load fresh ones. We'll check the flooded ones later."

Suddenly we felt the whole ship shudder as though from a collision. Had we been hit?

"Wow! That shot was close," said the skipper. "It passed right over the forward deck below the bridge level. It sounded like a freight train going by. The splash from it was close as hell!"

If it had been three feet lower, that would have been the end of the *Jack*.

We started weaving again and went to twenty knots. We knew we had the speed advantage on this guy in a big way. The highest speed at which we had tracked him was ten knots.

There were a couple more shudders from close shots, but none as close as the one that crossed over below the bridge level. The sounds of "Nearer, My God, to Thee" were coming down the conning tower hatch loud and clear now.

But as we pulled away from our slow target, we all began to breathe a little easier and to make plans for the next attack.

The tanker continued his frantic zigging, and although we had no trouble catching him, it was extremely difficult to get into a good position. We did not want to give him another chance to use that five-inch gun on us.

Finally, at about eleven at night, we got into the right spot and fired four torpedoes from up forward.

WHAM! . . . *WHAM!* . . . *WHAM!* Three hits!

The tanker disappeared in a burst of high-octane white flame. Tōjō was losing a lot of valuable aviation gasoline in this series of attacks.

It had taken so long to finish off this lone wolf that we had lost the other tanker and escort on the radar. We took off after them at flank speed, but long after midnight, we had to admit defeat. We broke off the chase.

I had been at the TDC for nearly twenty-four hours and now noticed for the first time that I was still in my bare feet. I had been out of the conning tower only a couple of times, to go to the head, and I had had nothing to eat but that one sandwich. I suddenly realized that I was ravenously hungry and awfully tired.

Alec had the watch on the bridge, but the rest of us convened in the wardroom for a review.

We had fired seventeen torpedoes for eleven hits—and two of those torpedoes had malfunctioned because of the long flooding. If we counted just the good torpedoes, we had eleven hits out of fifteen. That was good in any league.

We had sunk four tankers loaded with gasoline and clearly had sunk a fifth ship in the first night attack. We could not be certain whether the fifth was a tanker or an escort, but we were sure the other four were tankers. Not many submariners had seen such spectacular fireworks from each target. Every one had been a high-octane bomb.

After about four ham sandwiches and three cups of hot cocoa, I was beginning to feel revived.

"Shouldn't we say something to the crew?" asked Freddy Laing.

"Good idea," said Dykers.

All fleet submarines had an announcing system that led to each compartment and was loud enough to be heard even over the noise in the engine rooms.

"This is the captain speaking. We have lost contact with the convoy, but we have sunk four of the five tankers and probably one of the two escorts. It has been quite a day's work—one that any submarine in this Navy could be proud of.

"This was a team effort. We all worked together, and I am proud of every one of you."

I had the eight-to-twelve watch coming up in the morning, now only about three hours away. They were three of the soundest hours of sleep I ever had. I was exhausted.

After pulling about sixty miles south from the scene of the attacks, the morning of February 21, we spent the next week patrolling on the surface with the high periscope—without results. Many dives for patrol planes, but no ship contacts.

By this point in the war, American submarines were getting extremely valuable help from the code breakers at Pearl. These were the same men who had given Admiral Nimitz the information that helped win the Battle of Midway against such tremendous odds.

As the months went by after Midway, it became more and more apparent, even to the nonbelievers in Washington, that the code breakers were consistently getting good, solid information.* It also became apparent that much of this information could be of great value to submarines on patrol.

Very important in the development of this information for submarines was a former submarine skipper named Jasper Holmes, who had been retired because of a physical disability. After retirement he became well-known as the author of submarine adventure stories for the *Saturday Evening Post,* written under the pen name Alec Hudson.

When the war came, he asked to come back to active duty. He was assigned to duty with the ultra-top-secret code-breaking group at Pearl Harbor. Naturally he had no trouble putting himself in the place of the submarine skippers on patrol, and he realized how valuable to them some of the intercepted information on Japanese ship movements could be.

Holmes had been a good friend of Tommy Dykers during their S-boat days. Dykers had had the S-35, Jasper the S-30. After Holmes retired, they had remained in touch. Dykers was a big fan of the Alec Hudson stories in the *Saturday Evening Post.* So was I. They were great.

Working with ComSubPac staff, Holmes was able to develop a

---

*The first significant tactical use of code-break information had been at the Battle of the Coral Sea, about one month before Midway. Its use there, however, had not been as decisive as at Midway.

series of messages, called *Ultras*, that gave submarines good information on the projected tracks both of convoys and of combatant ships.

Needless to say, the security surrounding these Ultra messages was severe. We would have lost a priceless advantage in the war had the Japanese gotten any clear indication that we were reading their mail. Messages containing such information had a special symbol indicating that they could be decoded only by an officer cleared for Ultra.

The Ultra messages did not yield any concrete results for us on the first two patrols, but the five-tanker convoy contact had been developed with the help of an Ultra. Then on February 29, ten days after our tanker sweep, we received an Ultra telling us of the approach of a Nachi-class heavy cruiser. He was believed to be unescorted and traveling north at high speed.

We closed the projected track at high speed on the surface. After a few hours, his tops came plainly into view, and we dove. If he had sighted us, he would have diverted and our opportunity would have been lost.

We had not had any stars that morning and thus were not absolutely sure of our position. Either our navigation or his was a bit off, for we were never able to close him to less than nine thousand yards, far too great for even a desperation torpedo shot. He was making twenty-five knots, so it was all over in a hurry.

The tremendous handicaps under which a submerged submarine operates were driven home to us vividly by this experience. Once again I realized that a battery-powered submarine operating submerged was no more than a slightly mobile minefield. With the submarine on the surface . . . well, that was different.

The big cruiser was a tough one to lose. Things had been going so well that we believed we could do anything. This showed us that we could not. If we could have gotten him, this would have been the best patrol of the war to date.

We had seven torpedoes left, four aft and three forward. The forward torpedoes were suspect since they had been in flooded tubes for so long during the tanker convoy attack. They had, however, been worked over carefully, and the torpedomen were confident they were OK.

That evening (February 29) we received another Ultra giving us information on a southbound convoy that would pass fairly close. We cranked up our faithful Wintons and got over to the projected track. About one in the morning on March 1, we had radar contact with a convoy of four large ships, in a box formation, and two escorts, each out on the forward wing about a thousand yards. Because we had four torpedoes aft and only three forward, we tried hard to get into position for a stern shot. This is much harder to do on the surface than submerged.

We tried for more than an hour to get a stern shot but could not do it. The moon had set and it was pitch dark, but those escorts seemed to know that something was up. Every time we tried to work into position for firing, one of them would start over in our direction. Did they have radar?

After another half hour or so, we were getting into final position. I was waiting for the pelorus bearing from Freddy.

"Uh-oh. Tracer fire coming in our direction—long yellow arcs," came the alarmed report from the skipper.

This was a new experience for us. We pulled out again, armed with the information that they almost certainly knew, or strongly suspected, that there was a surfaced submarine about.

We gave up the stern shot idea and began carefully to work in for a bow shot. We came in well abaft the escort on our side. This convoy was tracking at fourteen knots, making it much more difficult to work in and around it than had been the case with the tanker convoy at ten knots.

Try as we might, we could not get a torpedo run of much less than twenty-five hundred yards. This didn't leave much room for error, but I believed we had them about right and told Dykers so.

We fired the three remaining bow tube torpedoes at this long range and, right on time, *WHAM!* . . . *WHAM!* Two hits.

The target exploded violently and issued a lot of smoke amidships. He wasn't a tanker, but he was clearly carrying something explosive. He was sinking fast. The convoy was scattering in all directions, and the near escort was heading for us with a zero angle on the bow and a large bone in his teeth.

Dykers turned away at flank speed and gave him a small, weaving target. Two bursts of tracer fire came our way, but there was no large gunfire. It soon became clear that sixteen knots was the escort's top speed. Before long he gave up the chase and turned back to the convoy. So did we. We were determined to use those last four torpedoes on this convoy.

There were now three heavies left, along with the two escorts. Everyone was obviously fully alerted. The zig plan became even more frantic. But once again Dykers worked his way in astern of the close escort and then, in a quick maneuver at high speed, turned the submarine to bring the stern tubes to bear. Fortunately, this leg turned out to be long enough for us to complete the turn. We had a good setup, though once again the torpedo run was much longer than we wanted. Nevertheless, we fired four torpedoes at the regular intervals. As soon as Dykers heard the last torpedo go, he began to pour on the speed to get out of there. We were headed in the right direction—there was no delay.

WHAM! . . . *WHAM!* . . . *WHAM!* Three hits out of four!

There was no big explosion from the target this time, but it was apparent to all on the bridge that he was mortally wounded. He sagged in the middle, clearly broken in two. Shortly we saw him go under the waves.

The escort, however, was not out of action, and he came for us like a wolf in the fold. We poured on the coal and weaved.

"Here come the tracers again. Pretty close—he has us spotted," from the bridge. We could hear Bennett singing.

Once again Dykers got everyone off the bridge except himself and Bennett.

How fast was this escort? Could he catch us? Soon we knew that he could not; sixteen knots was his best speed. After a few more tracer bursts, the escort turned away and rejoined the convoy, which now had only two heavies remaining.

We were out of torpedoes. That was disappointing, but this was the *right* way to end a patrol instead of with howling propeller shafts or disabled engines as we had before.

We got off a message to Admiral Christie giving him the results of our patrol and telling him we were proceeding to Fremantle. We set our course for the Mindoro Strait to pass from the South China Sea into the Sulu Sea.

En route we picked up another convoy, consisting of two large ships and two escorts. They came right over us, but there was nothing we could do except go deep, let them pass over, and then watch them disappear over the horizon.

"We sit on station for days with twenty-four torpedoes and no targets, and then when the fish are all gone, we run into a convoy we can't avoid even when we try," said Dykers ruefully as we talked it over in the wardroom.

There were lots of planes out looking for us this time. We dove again and again but tried to come up each time so that we could make some time. In the afternoon one spotted us for sure and, as we passed one hundred feet on the way down, *BANG!* . . . *BANG!*

Two bombs—not too close, but they sure got our attention.

A half hour later, just as we were getting ready to come to periscope depth, *BANG!*

"Well," said Dykers, "I think we'll stay down a little longer."

We surfaced at dark and proceeded to pass through the Mindoro Strait. We couldn't forget about enemy submarines. These guys were probably not as tough as the U-boats, but they might well have been advised of our presence and be watching for us. We kept up a pretty vigorous zig plan as we traveled.

That evening as we cruised on the surface past the islands of Mindoro and Panay, I could see long strings of fire on the sides of the island mountains. Because I did not know what they were, I reported them to the captain.

"I'll come up and see them," he replied.

"Those are Filipinos burning out their sugarcane fields. They always do it about this time of the year." Dykers had served out here on the Asia station as a younger officer and had seen the burning fields many times.

This seemed totally strange to me. "You mean, these guys are out here farming their sugarcane as though nothing was going on?"

"Not everyone takes this war as seriously as we do. They are living in an occupied land, and they have to feed their families. So they work." With that, after a careful look around, Dykers went below.

But for the rest of the watch, I looked at those strings of golden lights and reflected on how differently war affects different nations. Here we were, twelve thousand miles from home, fighting a vicious war in the Filipino's backyards, and they were up in the hills, quietly burning their sugarcane. I concluded that this disparity was the price of power—at least, that was the best explanation I could come up with at the time.

It was quiet, but all through the night the breeze came slowly to us from the land, carrying with it the sweet scent of the burning cane.

Soon we passed through the Sibutu Passage, near the northeastern tip of Borneo, and entered the Celebes Sea. Each day brought more patrol planes and more emergency dives, but we had to stay up as much as we could during the day if we wanted to get to Australia within the month.

Next was the Makassar Strait, between Borneo and Celebes. This strait is wide, and we were able to make most of the passage on the surface, thus entering the Java Sea. As we spent day after day cruising through these huge islands, so rich in resources, we realized how much the Japanese had taken from the Dutch. The value of it all was staggering to contemplate.

The Lombok Strait, between the islands of Bali and Lombok, is only about ten miles wide; we knew it had given many of our submarines trouble in the past. The currents were so swift that we thought it risky to make the transit submerged. Dykers decided to do it on the surface.

Radar showed at least two patrol boats in the strait—maybe more. They were small and hard to see. The night was dark and the sea as smooth as a mirror. There was so much phosphorescence in the water that both our bow wave and our wake looked like neon signs. Should we use high speed and hang the phosphorescence or creep along and take much longer getting through? We decided to compromise by moving through at about ten knots, making some wake but not too much.

It was an eerie sight with the huge, cone-shaped mountain of Bali looming to the right and the more distant mountain of Lombok to the left. Choosing a time when the patrol boats were mostly to the east, we moved along the Bali shore at our sedate ten knots.

It worked. Within an hour or two, we were clear of the strait and going back to four-engine speed to put distance between ourselves and this southernmost boundary of Japanese control.

8

Australia and Admiral Jay

After clearing the Lombok Strait, we were still some seventeen hundred miles from our new home in Fremantle, Australia. Through day after day of balmy weather and smooth seas, we plowed southward, with the Southern Cross hanging high in the clear night skies. As we got into the part of the Indian Ocean bordering Western Australia, we knew that any patrol planes we saw would be friendly and well briefed on our presence. Still, we kept our two-letter recognition signals at hand. The sea began to take on a Caribbean blue look, and even the flying fish were back. We were more relaxed than we had been for weeks.

Our landfall on Fremantle was to be in the early morning, and although it was not my watch, I was on the bridge to catch the first glimpse of the huge light perched on Rottnest Island outside Fremantle harbor. We were told it would be burning, and since it would be the first navigational light we would have seen since leaving Midway, it was going to be a welcome sight in more ways than one.

We had had beautiful stars all the way down from Lombok; we knew just about when we would see the light. But even before it was due to appear over the horizon, we sighted the loom of the powerful light in the clear night sky. We checked its characteristics—it was Rottnest Light for certain. It is difficult to convey what seeing that light meant to me. It was safety; it was respite from the eternal vigilance for Japanese planes; it promised relaxation and letters from home; and it welcomed us to a place that would, we knew, be our home away from home for some time to come.

As dawn was breaking, we sighted and exchanged recognition signals with the Australian Navy ASW ship sent to escort us into Fremantle. It was March 13, 1944, a month and a half since we had left Midway on that stormy, gray afternoon. What a difference those six weeks had made. We had crossed the Western Pacific, spent almost a month in the South China Sea, then come home through the Celebes Sea, the Makassar Strait, the Lombok Strait, and the Indian Ocean, a total of more than twelve thousand miles—more than halfway around the world—without a single worry about our engines. The Wintons smoked a bit when suddenly loaded heavily, but that was a shortcoming we could easily forgive. The change in the whole outlook of the engine room team was phenomenal. They knew now that they had reliable horses.

More important, we had proved ourselves. The attack on the tanker convoy had been brilliantly conducted and was certainly one of the finest single-submarine actions of the war to that date. We were entering Fremantle with all of our torpedoes expended and all of our machinery working. What a contrast from our second patrol, when we came home having accomplished nothing and with our engines falling apart.

We came up the Swan River to the small submarine base at Fremantle with the welcome sight of our old tender, the *Griffin*, moored there. Appropriately, the weather was beautiful, a Navy band was playing on the dock, and Admiral Christie was there to meet us. As soon as the brow, or gangway, was in place, he came on board with a big grin on his face.

"Tommy, that was a *great* patrol. We're all proud of you and the *Jack*."

And with that he pinned a Navy Cross on our skipper's chest. This was most unusual. Combat awards had to be recommended, then approved by the Fleet Commander (Admiral Nimitz), a process that usually took at least two or three weeks, sometimes longer. We learned later that some of the higher-ups were not pleased with this short-circuiting of the regular procedures. For one thing, it seemed to reveal that Admiral Christie had used the code breaker's work, because he knew exactly the results of our patrol. At the time, however, none of that worried us. We were just proud of our ship and our skipper.

While Admiral Christie was not free to discuss code-break material with us, he was free to tell us that in the midst of our night-and-day attack on the tankers, the convoy commodore had sent an uncoded message to his superiors in Tokyo stating that he was under attack by a wolf pack of submarines. You can imagine how the crew felt about that. From then on we were *"Jack* the Pack" to all of them. It was truly frosting on the cake.

To top off the recognition that Dykers was receiving, all of the *Jack* officers were invited to have lunch at The Bend of the Road, Admiral Christie's handsome house on the outskirts of Perth. We knew that this was a privilege extended only to those submarines considered to have made a particularly outstanding patrol.

So here we were in Australia, the promised land. What adventures it would bring none of us knew, but we were anxious to get started. We had heard a lot about Perth and Fremantle from other submarine officers, and almost all of it was favorable.

Fremantle is the seaport for Perth, in Western Australia, and is separated from it by about ten miles of good road. In 1944 Perth was a bustling city, and despite the fact that every man between eighteen and fifty-five had gone overseas with the armed forces, it remained an active center of insurance and merchant banking for the extensive agricultural economy of Western Australia.

There was a certain frontier town atmosphere about both towns (Fremantle was much smaller) that was, at first, unfamiliar and strange to us Americans. The interior decoration in the homes reminded some of us of the 1920s. We also had to adjust to the seasons, which were, of course, reversed compared to North America. The climate of the area was superb, something like that of central California.

The rest period arrangements that had been made by Admiral Christie and his staff were all that anyone could desire. He had rented two large houses in suburban Perth for the use of the skippers in from patrol. Dykers was assigned to Lucknow, a beautiful house named after the Indian city in honor of its famous siege and capture by the British (with substantial help from the Australians) in the mid-nineteenth century.

Christie had also rented a small resort hotel, the Majestic, a few miles out of Perth; it was given over to the remaining submarine officers. The Majestic was very comfortable. There were single rooms available to each officer, some with a private bath and some sharing a bath down the hall. In true Navy fashion, rooms were assigned on the basis of rank, so I was using a bath down the hall. I couldn't have cared less. The bath had a huge shower with an unlimited amount of water. Who could ask for anything more?

In addition to all of this, we had a house mother. Valerie was from Adelaide, the wife of a physician there. Her husband, naturally enough, was overseas with the Australian Army. Since she was alone and wanted to do something to help the war effort, this seemed like a pleasant way to do it. Val was about fifty and quite attractive.

She had clearly been told that while boys will be boys, there were limits, and as a result, the Majestic had fairly strict rules about women. Otherwise we were pretty much on our own. The food was excellent, and although breakfast and lunch were catch-as-catch-can, we all sat down to dinner together, more or less as in a well-run fraternity house. Either you were on time for dinner, or you missed it. Val always presided.

The arrangements for the enlisted men of the submarines in from patrol were more varied than at most of our wartime bases. In downtown Perth they had the Wentworth Hotel, a comfortable place that, like the Majestic, came complete with house mother. The Navy had also taken over the Ocean Beach Hotel, another nice spot right on the beach, which was preferred by many of the men over the Wentworth.

Finally, enlisted men had the option of going some two or three hundred miles into the outback of Western Australia. Not many of our crew took advantage of this, but those who did had some great stories to tell—hunting kangaroos in jeeps, experiencing real frontier life, playing poker without restriction—and some pretty wild tales about the nightlife. Kalgoorlie was a far cry from the refinements of Perth. More important, the outback was far away from any naval officers, and thus there was no need to worry about uniforms or saluting or shore patrols or any of those other things that can spoil a well-earned rest period.

Within the first day or two, I was given a very special favor that affected all of my life in Australia deeply. Chester Nimitz, the son of the admiral, was a submarine officer who had been brought ashore for a brief period to work on a special task for Admiral Christie.

During his time ashore, Chester had gotten to know a family named Aberdeen, the head of which was a well-known physician at the main hospital in Perth. Chester gave me a short letter of introduction to the Aberdeens with an assurance that I would enjoy their company. This was a particularly nice thing for him to do, since we were only acquaintances and he was some seven years senior to me. The letter of introduction was a sort of gift from on high.

Chester stated, more or less incidentally, that the Aberdeens had a very attractive daughter named Kathie, who, among other things, was a driver for the Navy. There were a few cars assigned for the officers in from patrol to share. Each car had its own driver. Kathie was one of these drivers. Chester said, rather pointedly this time, that Kathie was a nice girl who had been reared rather strictly.

Probably with prompting from Chester, the Aberdeens asked me to come out for dinner one of the first evenings of our rest period. Kathie picked me up at the Majestic in one of the Navy cars. She was a tall, slender girl with dark hair, a beautiful complexion, and very pretty eyes. She had a smile that seemed to light up the whole car, and a pleasant, cheerful voice. Every once in a while you meet someone who is especially easy to talk to from the first. That was how it was with Kathie.

The Aberdeen homestead was a modest but well-maintained brick house with an air of order and hominess. Kathie took me into the living room to introduce me to her father. The room was warm and comfortable, with many well-filled bookcases. There was a lamp with a Tiffany-type glass shade that brought a swift pang of memory to me. My mother had had an almost identical lamp in our living room when I was growing up. That room reminded me of my boyhood home more than anything I had seen in years.

I liked it.

Dr. Aberdeen was a distinguished-looking man in his fifties. He was of medium height, with silvery hair and a strong but comfortable face. He greeted me warmly, asked me to sit down, and apologized for not being able to offer me a drink. All gone to the troops overseas, he said.

This led conveniently into something I had wanted to ask him about anyway.

When the Americans were driven out of their base at Subic Bay in the Philippines, after Pearl Harbor, Admiral Hart sent the submarine tender *Otus* to southeast Asia (the Dutch East Indies) to save her from destruction. She stayed for a time at Surabaya, the Dutch naval base in Java, supporting the rather ineffectual U.S. submarine effort being conducted from there. Finally, when she was driven out of Surabaya, she came to Fremantle.

Before the *Otus* had left Subic Bay, however, some practical-minded and farsighted officer had taken all of the liquor from the Officer's Club and stowed it in her hold. She had arrived in Fremantle with this precious store more or less intact. Faced with this enormous supply of booze, which was absolutely unavailable in Australia, Admiral Christie had made a wise (from our point of view, anyway) decision to award each submarine officer returning from patrol a fifth each of scotch, bourbon, and gin as well as one case of beer. The beer was from Australian supplies, and although very hard for civilians to get, was made available for purchase by the U.S. Navy.

We had been told about this delightful practice by other submarine officers, and indeed it had been confirmed in an informal message to Dykers from Admiral Christie as we were proceeding from Lombok to Fremantle. This intelligence had left me in something of a quandary. Here I was to be in possession of all this valuable hooch, and I did not drink. I had had an occasional beer, but that was pretty much it.

Kent Lukingbeal said, "I'd sure like more than one bottle of scotch. I'll swap you my beer for your scotch."

"Sounds good to me," I said. At this point Kent proved what a good and faithful friend he really was.

"That's not fair," he replied. "A bottle of scotch in Australia is worth more than one case of beer. I'll get someone else to share with me, and we'll give you two cases of beer for the scotch."

Before we arrived in Fremantle, I had exchanged all my liquor for beer. I was to be in possession of six cases of Australian beer.

When we arrived at the Majestic and our supplies were delivered in a Navy truck, I found out to my astonishment what a case of beer was in Australia—twenty-four quarts, all laid neck-to-neck like fine wine, in a heavy wooden case. I literally had enough beer to float a small rowboat. It was all piled in my room, and I had to decide what to do with it.

I told this whole story to Dr. Aberdeen, who knew about the liquor ration the submarine officers were getting but had never heard of anyone swapping it all for beer.

"Jim, do you like to play tennis?"

"I do."

"Well, you have been invited to be a guest of the Royal King's Park Tennis Club while you are here, and the club has a special problem. As you know, every man in Australia between the ages of eighteen and fifty or so has gone overseas—and all of our beer goes to them and to you folks here in the U.S. Navy. The old fuds at the Tennis Club are left without a drop. They are parched. If you would contribute your six cases of beer to the club, you would have more friends than you have ever dreamed of and a happy home for as long as you are here."

It was good advice, and I made arrangements for all six cases to be delivered to the club the next day. Dr. Aberdeen arranged a small get-together at the club in recognition of this gift; it was a happy occasion for all. I really didn't want any of the beer, so it was all gain for me—and I did enjoy the tennis and the companionship. I made several good friends among the older doctors, lawyers, and businessmen of Perth and Fremantle. I also got extremely astute advice from the lawyers on just how to make sure I could continue this swap arrangement on future patrols.

It was too good a thing for them to lose.

The fact that all of the men between eighteen and fifty in Australia had gone to war created either an opportunity or a problem, depending on your point of view. The great majority of the submariners enjoying their rest periods were married. That made the heavily female population of Perth and Fremantle a problem. On the other hand, the submariners were young, restless, and just in from a couple of months at sea. From this point of view, the women of Perth and Fremantle were an opportunity.

Among the submarine officers, there were several schools of thought about fidelity. One group felt that when you crossed both the international date line and the equator, which we all had, all bets were off and any pledges made on the other side of those lines were in temporary abeyance. At the other extreme was a group who felt that vows were vows; they would not look at or date any Australian girl. The vast majority of the young men (and the skippers) fell somewhere in between.

I suppose that I also fell somewhere in the middle group of the young submariners enjoying two free weeks in Australia. I was very much aware of the fact that I was married to a wonderful woman who had done everything that any wife could do to make me happy.

But the war mentality and psychology were abroad in full force. Every other week or so we would hear of another U.S. submarine that had been lost. Would we be next? Was this blissful two-week period to be the last we would ever enjoy? These thoughts inevitably altered our viewpoint.

Kathie Aberdeen was a major additional temptation. I could rationalize her to myself by saying that she was obviously a very nice, cultured, well-brought-up girl with impeccable manners who was an

The USS *Jack* is launched on October 16, 1942, at the Electric Boat
Company, New London, Connecticut. *Courtesy of Terence J. McCabe*

The bow of the *Jack,* showing some of her armaments. *Courtesy of Terence J. McCabe*

The *Jack* at rest at the submarine base, Pearl Harbor. *Official U.S. Navy photograph*

Above: The lookouts on the periscope shears. *Official U.S. Navy photograph*

Right: Loading a Mark XIV torpedo. *Official U.S. Navy photograph*

Above: The Christmas Tree and the hydraulic control manifold in the control room, the key spot from which almost all of the diving machinery was operated. *Official U.S. Navy photograph*

Left: Chow-down in the crew's mess. *U.S. Naval Institute Photographic Library*

Another Japanese *maru* heads for the bottom. *Official U.S. Navy photograph*

What a depth charge looks like from the surface. *Official U.S. Navy photograph*

Jim Calvert (*right*) receives a Silver Star from Admiral Charles A. Lockwood, Jr.

Kent Lukingbeal on watch. *Courtesy of Terence J. McCabe*

Gunner Frank Lynes holding forth. *Courtesy of Terence J. McCabe*

At a ship's party in San Francisco in 1945. The men in back row are (*left to right*) Gene Lewis, Al Fuhrman, Danny Deaver, and Jim Calvert. In the front row (*far right*) is Calvert's wife, Nancy. *Courtesy of Terence J. McCabe*

The crew of the *Jack* in Perth, Australia, after the third patrol. *Courtesy of Terence J. McCabe*

Class of prospective submarine commanding officers in New London in the summer of 1942. In the first row (*second from right*) is Tommy Dykers and in the second row (*far left*) is John "Beetle" Roach. *Courtesy of Submarine Force Library and Museum, New London, Connecticut*

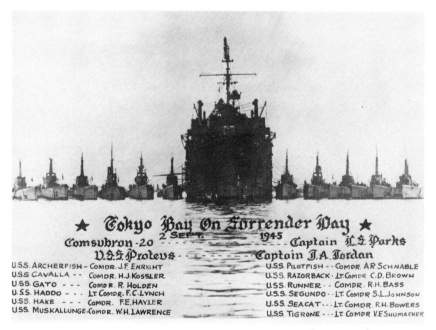

★ Tokyo Bay On Surrender Day ★
2 SEPT. 1945
Comsubron-20   Captain H.S. Parks
U.S.S. Proteus   Captain J.A. Jordan

U.S.S. ARCHERFISH - COMDR. J.F. ENRIGHT	U.S.S. PILOTFISH - - COMDR. A.R. SCHNABLE
U.S.S. CAVALLA - - COMDR. H.J. KOSSLER	U.S.S. RAZORBACK - LT. COMDR. C.D. BROWN
U.S.S. GATO - - - COMDR. R. HOLDEN	U.S.S. RUNNER - - COMDR. R.H. BASS
U.S.S. HADDO - - - LT. COMDR. F.C. LYNCH	U.S.S. SEGUNDO - - LT. COMDR. S.L. JOHNSON
U.S.S. HAKE - - - COMDR. F.E. HAYLER	U.S.S. SEACAT - - - LT. COMDR. R.H. BOWERS
U.S.S. MUSKALLUNGE-COMDR. W.H. LAWRENCE	U.S.S. TIGRONE - - - LT. COMDR. V.E. SHUMACHER

From the surrender ceremonies in Tokyo Bay. *U.S. Naval Historical Center photograph* extraordinarily good conversationalist. Who could object to my enjoying her company? After all, I kept saying to myself, it was the family I was there to see—Kathie just happened to be an added attraction. Didn't I spend a lot of time talking to Dr. Aberdeen? And to Mrs. Aberdeen?

This, of course, was unadulterated hogwash. When Kathie walked into a room, everyone noticed her. She had a sort of refined oomph. Every time I saw her, I gulped, swallowed, and did my best to keep my composure and to act as though I hardly knew she was there. But I did; believe me, I did. Still, I did not ask her for a date. I didn't think that was quite right.

Kathie was enrolled in a local college and was doing quite well in all of her courses except chemistry. That seemed to be an area in which she was having more than a little difficulty. Thanks to my premed experience at Oberlin, I had an excellent background in chemistry. In fact, chemistry was the only course in which I had stood number one in my class at Annapolis. It was inevitable that I would try to help her. I suppose that my frequent invitations to dinner at the Aberdeens' had something to do with the fact that I tutored Kathie with her chemistry after dinner.

We would sit at the dining room table after things were cleared (I even helped with the dishes). At first these sessions were strictly business. I was able to give Kathie some pointers that made the mysteries of chemical valence and bonds a little more reachable for her. She appreciated it, and I enjoyed it.

One evening about halfway through my two-week rest period, as we sat side by side at the dining room table working out of one chemistry textbook (partly to make reading easier and partly because I just wanted to), we started edging closer and closer together. Finally, as I pointed at something in the book, Kathie's hand came softly on top of mine.

"Haven't we had enough of this for tonight?" she asked. "Let's take a walk."

We did, and we held hands all through the walk.

That was the end of the no-date policy. Almost every day, after Kathie was through with her driving duties and her classes, we would do something together. We went on picnics, we went swimming, and we went for long walks. Kathie was an extremely fine golfer and had won some championships at the Cottesloe Country Club nearby. However, I did not play golf and wasn't about to duff around playing with a champion golfer. So we played tennis at the club, where we never had trouble getting a court. Here she proved that a good athlete is a good athlete in any sport. She could beat me at tennis—though not without a little struggle.

On these dates we talked . . . and talked. Kathie knew that I was married, and indeed I told her a good bit about Nancy. Still, we knew without saying so that beyond our enjoyment of each other's company there was also a strong physical attraction. Kathie had an inner warmth and friendliness that just seemed to radiate when we were together. It was good chemistry—of a different kind from that which we'd been studying.

Nevertheless, it was only at the end of my two-week rest period that I kissed her. We were standing on her porch in the late evening shadows, and I knew that I would not see her again before we went on patrol. I was finding it very hard to say goodbye and . . .

It was a very tender moment, filled with emotional statements on both sides.

All of this was interrupted by the gentle toot of the horn from a friend's car waiting at the curb to take me back to the Majestic.

As we drove off, he said, "It looks as though you and Kathie are getting to be good friends."

As I slumped down into the seat of the car, I said, "Yeah, I guess so."

I felt both happy and guilty at the same time.

At the end of the rest period, we sent almost a third of our crew back to new construction. Freddy Laing, proud of his part in the *Jack*'s great patrol, had gone on to get command of his own submarine. Alec Nading went back to a new submarine and was replaced with another young reserve officer. I was now the third-ranking officer in the *Jack*.

While waiting for an active submarine assignment, members of the relief crews in Fremantle had a barracks in which to live while working on submarines in from patrol. Most of the relief crew men, however, found more congenial quarters off base. With such a heavy proportion of females in the population of Perth and Fremantle, it was not hard to make arrangements out in town that were more home-like and friendly than a barracks, to say the least.

I suppose this was all to the good, but the men also became accustomed to this soft and pleasant life ashore, complete with good food, laundry service, and other kindnesses. Some had become so devoted to the good life in Perth or Fremantle that their enthusiasm for the rigors of a war patrol had waned almost to the vanishing point. Getting out of the relief crew in Midway was one thing; leaving it in Perth was another.

From my point of view, this was dangerous. We had lost nearly twenty-five experienced, war-hardened sailors, and we were going to have to replace them with these green and soft men. We would have to work them, train them, and bring them up to a state where they could at least begin to replace the veterans who had gone back to the States to man new-construction submarines. Were they up to doing this? Did they really want to do it? Were we up to the task of getting them trained?

To make matters worse, the Rottnest Island sea area, notoriously rough at all times of the year, had winds even stronger than usual this early April, with winter setting in. Our new shipmates were not only homesick: they were seasick, some of them so violently that training was out of the question. They had to be put ashore and replaced with others who, hopefully, could establish a better relationship with the ocean.

Beetle Roach's words about hard work came back to me again and again. I was determined that we were not going to get ourselves killed just because we hadn't worked hard enough. I said to myself through gritted teeth that we were going to get these new guys in shape if we had to half kill them in the process. One night we nearly did.

One of the new men was a young seaman named Newton, who had a serious weight problem and even more serious problems with the clear-the-bridge drills. The good life ashore had really gotten to him, and he just had trouble moving fast enough to enable us to make the required thirty- to thirty-five-second time limit on our emergency dives. (In wartime all dives are emergency dives.)

Early on we began getting complaints from the other seamen and firemen who made up the lookout gang.

"Newton always holds us up—he's like cold molasses getting down that ladder. We're never gonna make thirty-five seconds with him on the team."

"You know the rules," I responded. "If he's slow, ride his shoulders down. Just put your feet on him with your full weight and he'll speed up."

About two nights later, it was so rough that even the experienced crew members were having trouble holding on. It was really too rough to be working, but we had only a limited time before we had to leave on patrol, and our best diving times were still in the forty-second range. It was two in the morning, and we were still at it.

Kent Lukingbeal was the officer of the deck and his loud "Clear the bridge!" rang through the conning tower where I was standing. Newton was first off the bridge and down the ladder into the conning tower. The ladder had steel rungs about fourteen inches apart. In his determination to speed up, his foot and leg slipped between the rungs of the ladder.

Down came the crushing weight of the other two lookouts on his shoulders, with shouts of "For Chrissake, Newton, hurry up!"

The next thing I heard was a sickening cr-r-rack, almost like a rifle shot. It was Newton's leg, and it was serious. Both bones had broken and come out through the flesh—a serious compound fracture. We were halfway into the dive, so all we could do was carry him, moaning and bleeding, over to the after end of the conning tower and finish the dive. When we were leveled off at periscope depth, I went in and told Miles Refo and Dykers what had happened. There was nothing to do but return to port and get Newton to the hospital.

His seagoing days were over, at least for a considerable time.

We had practice attacks, both night surface and daytime periscope. It was clear that, whatever our problems with clear-the-bridge drills, our attack party was still up to snuff.

However, we made one hardware change. To shave off some of the relay time and inaccuracy that resulted when final bearings were passed down from the bridge to the TDC by intercom, we installed an old compass repeater by the TDC and hooked it in to the bridge pelorus with a buzzer. When Dykers was ready to shoot, he had Bennett sight on the proper target and then press the buzzer. We were sure this was improving our accuracy substantially. The accuracy of that last bearing is all-important.

Finally the day came to depart on patrol. It was April 6, a crisp fall day, when we steamed out of the Swan River, past the Rottnest Light, and on our way up the west coast of Australia, bound for the Japanese Empire again. As Rottnest Light faded over the horizon astern, I felt almost homesick—but my thoughts, I am somewhat ashamed to say, were all of Kathie. Would I ever see her again? I was by no means sure. The odds were less than comforting.

To make matters worse, I kept worrying about all the young officers Kathie would meet while I was away. She was a driver, and what better way to meet new men? I was a great respecter of our young submarine officers, but some of them were not exactly the guy you would pick to go out with your sister. They were slick talkers . . . oh, such slick talkers. But I had no right worrying about such things and did my best to put them out of my mind.

I was having enough guilt pangs as it was.

On our way up the west coast of Australia, we proceeded with another submarine, also headed for its patrol area. We exchanged both day and night practice approaches with him, and we made dives close aboard each other to familiarize the lookouts with the appearance of a real periscope cutting the water. This made good use of our transit time.

We were, however, to have an intermediate stop before reaching Japanese waters. In an effort to send the Fremantle submarines into their patrol areas with the maximum amount of fuel on board, the Navy had established a bare-bones fueling station at Exmouth Gulf, a large, protected bay at the extreme northwestern corner of the continent. The Navy did not have much there except a large fuel barge and the bleakest kind of living accommodations ashore for the men who ran the fueling station.

As we steamed down into Exmouth Gulf to get to the fueling station, we were struck by the stark emptiness of the Australian outback. There was no sign of any kind of human or animal life and very little vegetation.

"Looks like Kalgoorlie," laughed one of its veterans.

As we pulled up to the fuel barge, we were met by a reserve lieutenant whose contribution to the war effort was commanding this fuel station. He was glad to see some new faces and did everything he could to make us welcome and comfortable. He did not have much to offer besides fuel, however.

We took on nearly 10,000 gallons—about 8 percent of our total capacity of 123,000 gallons—so it was worth the stop. We left Exmouth filled to the brim with fuel, fresh water, and lube oil.

The *Jack* was ready to go at the Japanese again.

Although we were assigned to an area in the South China Sea, Dykers had decided to forgo the excitement of the Lombok and Makassar Straits and go through the archipelago near Timor, the island on which Captain Bligh fetched up after being put adrift by the mutineers of HMS *Bounty*. Although we had to dive for planes three times as we approached the Ombai Strait during the daytime, we had no difficulty getting through that night. As far as I know, we were not sighted.

En route to our area, we made contact on a Japanese convoy about eleven in the evening on April 12. It consisted of two main ships, possibly troop transports, and four very active escorts. The heavies were running abreast of each other, with two escorts out ahead on either bow and two astern on each quarter. We had about a half moon with numerous rain squalls all around. Light conditions fluctuated between total blackness and too much moonlight. The easterly trade was unusually strong, and we had much rougher seas than are typical in this part of the world. We were breasting them well, but they slowed our speed considerably.

As soon as we had the contact, I could feel the tension and excitement building up in the boat. Here we go again—this is *Jack the Pack!*

Dykers tried to work in between the two escorts on our side. Then, as we were beginning to get into position, we saw yellow tracers coming in our direction from the stern escort. Clearly we had been sighted. We pulled out, expecting the escort to follow us. He did not—apparently his orders were to stay with the convoy no matter what.

"These bastards must have radar. There's no way he could have seen us," muttered Dykers from the bridge. I could hear the low tones of Bennett singing—a different hymn this time. He must have learned some new ones in Perth.

Another effort to close into firing position had a similar result. No tracers on this approach, but the escort turned around and gave us a zero angle on the bow, heading right for us. Again we pulled out, and again he broke off and rejoined his convoy.

This convoy was making thirteen and a half knots, far above the average speed for marus. It had to be a very valuable outfit with such high-powered ships. We were on a line west of New Guinea and had reason to believe this westbound convoy might be returning to base to bring either more troops or more equipment for the effort against General MacArthur's operations there. We knew it was important, and we were doing our level best to get at them.

The convoy's high speed made it difficult for us to gain a new position. In the rough sea, we had a speed differential of less than four knots rather than the ten or eleven we had been used to. Instead of being able to duck in and out as before, we had a long, slow trek coming in, with too much time for the escorts to pick us up. There

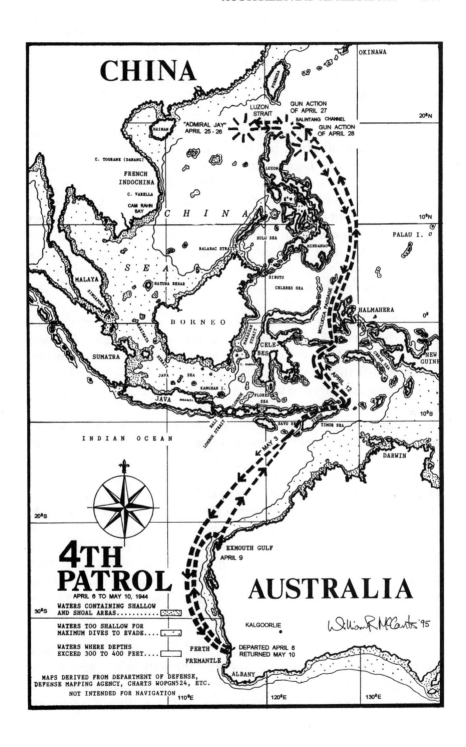

4TH
PATROL
APRIL 6 TO MAY 10, 1944

was no point in worrying about the bow wave—we had to make all the speed we could just to keep up and work around.

Dykers wasn't giving up, however. We spent the next three hours trying to pull into a good position. The on-again, off-again moon and the frequent rain squalls added to the difficulty of the task. Twice more we drew tracer fire from the escorts, making it apparent that they knew what we were trying to do. It was clear that they had radar, all right, but it was also clear that they were not going to desert their high-speed convoy just to play tag with a pesky submarine. I believe they thought the combination of their high speed and the rough seas would enable them to leave us behind.

Finally, about three in the morning, Dykers decided to try a very long shot. We simply could not get in any closer. We fired four torpedoes at forty-nine hundred yards, almost two and a half miles. Despite the fact that we had a good track on these guys and had set in the firing bearings accurately with our new system, all four missed.

Although I knew the odds were heavily against us with such a long torpedo run, I felt terrible about the miss. I had let the team down. I realized that we could have had a near-perfect solution and still missed at that long range. Nevertheless, it was a bitter blow to me—we were not used to losing. And it was not what I had expected after our great successes on the third patrol.

I began to reflect. Had we had all our luck on that third patrol? Were all the night attacks from here on going to be as difficult as this one? Where was the Dykers luck?

With the sea picking up, it was becoming harder and harder to keep up with the convoy, let alone work in around the escorts. The bridge was getting a shot of green water every once in a while, making it much harder for them to use their binoculars.

About five in the morning, we had a possible chance at one of the trailing heavies, but the torpedo run was so long that Dykers decided not to risk it. We were approaching a narrow pass, the Buton Strait. It was getting light, and we had absolutely no chance to run ahead and dive on their track.

Dykers broke off the attack.

And so, after a long night of hard work, we had nothing to show for it but four wasted torpedoes. About the only bright spot in the whole matter was that the men sleeping in the forward torpedo room now had more space. Four of their big sleeping companions were gone forever.

As Dykers said in the wardroom after he secured the battle stations: Round one went to the Japs.

After clearing the Molucca Passage, where we went west of Halmahera and east of the northern tip of Celebes, we worked our way up the east coast of the Philippines toward the Luzon Strait. Dykers planned to use the Balintang Channel to go north of Luzon and enter the South China Sea.

We ran on the surface as much as possible during the day but were forced down frequently by patrol planes. Our new lookouts were breaking in nicely and were doing a good job of spotting planes far enough away that we could get down before being seen. We were not bombed once during the entire nine hundred-mile-long passage up the east coast of the Philippines.

On April 25, shortly after completing our transit of the Balintang Channel, one of our new lookouts spotted a periscope on our starboard beam, in firing position. Following doctrine the OOD, Kent Lukingbeal, turned away and went to flank speed. It was about 5:30 in the morning, so it made reveille on a lot of us. No torpedo tracks were seen, but about fifteen minutes later, with everyone still talking about the periscope, one of the lookouts sighted a plane coming in fairly close. We went down immediately, hoping that perhaps he had somehow missed seeing us.

Click . . . *BANG!* As we passed one hundred fifty feet, we received this calling card from Tōjō. There was no doubt we had been seen. This was very bad news since we were just getting into position for a possible intercept given us by the code breakers.

The Japanese, desperate to reinforce their troops on New Guinea against MacArthur's operations, had organized a large convoy at Shanghai to lift new men and equipment to the New Guinea area. We were not told how many ships were in the convoy, only that it was large and that the convoy commodore was an admiral, connoting the convoy's importance. After our early-morning bombing, we knew that we had been detected and were sure the convoy would be rerouted around us. Nevertheless, we stood west, submerged, attempting to get away from the location of the bombing and hoping possibly to intercept the convoy's most logical new route. At our slow submerged speed, we did not have hope of moving very far.

To our amazement, not long after noontime the same day, we sighted the smoke and masts of many ships. They were to the east of us, passing southbound just about over where we had been bombed. None of us could understand this. There were only two possible explanations: either the Japanese communication system had failed, and the convoy commodore had not gotten the word on the bombing, or, more likely, the *Jack* had been confused with the Japanese submarine we had spotted in that exact position, and the Japanese command had decided the plane had bombed one of their own submarines.

Coming down from Shanghai, the Japanese admiral could have taken his convoy either west or east of Taiwan on the way down to Manila, where he was scheduled to stop either for material or for more troops. Judging from where we had intercepted him, he had gone east of Taiwan. When we made contact with him, he had some three hundred miles to go to Manila; he was probably planning to arrive there in the evening of the next day.

As we worked closer to the convoy, we could see that there were seven or eight heavy ships, some of them passenger freighters or troop transports. There were more escorts than we could count— certainly six or so. One patrol plane, obviously assigned solely to this convoy, flew low to the water, back and forth across the bows of the convoy, then from time to time in a complete circle around the whole group. This was the most heavily escorted outfit we had ever encountered, confirming our code-break information on its importance. It looked as though we were getting one more chance to help out with the New Guinea operations.

One way or the other, we had to get in on these guys. But there was no way we were going to catch up with them except on the surface. We waited, submerged, until all was clear, and then about three in the afternoon, we surfaced to close the range. Within half an hour, the escort plane made an extra-large circle around the convoy and we had no choice except to dive. As soon as the plane went back to his forward station, we were up again and pursuing at best speed. Twice more we were forced down by this character, but after dark he apparently returned to base.

We had made radar contact with the convoy at twenty-eight thousand yards—we were about fourteen miles astern of them. The thin moon was setting early, and by eight o'clock we were beginning to work ahead of them, staying out about seven miles on their flank, where we knew they could not see us or, we were reasonably sure, detect us on their radar. The reasons for our confidence were straightforward: first, we were fairly sure their radar was not as good as ours; second, a surfaced submarine presents a very small radar target, a fraction of the size of the large transports we were tracking.

During our time in Fremantle, the *Griffin* had equipped our radar with a Plan Position Indicator (PPI). The PPI took the echoes received by the radar and displayed them on a circular screen about eight inches in diameter, with the *Jack* in the middle of the screen. From this we could see the disposition of the convoy as though we were looking down on it from above.

From the PPI we could see that the heavy ships were disposed in two columns, with four ships in the west (starboard) column and three in the east column away from us. The convoy was, of course, headed south toward Manila.

As I looked at the escort disposition on the PPI, my stomach really tightened for the first time on this patrol. There was an escort about three thousand yards astern of each column. Two more escorts covered each flank about three thousand yards out, and one additional escort was on each bow about the same distance out. Eight escorts for seven heavies! None of us had ever seen anything like this.

In addition to all this, the whole outfit was constant helming about thirty degrees to each side of their base course. *Constant helming* means that each ship puts the rudder over only a very little so that it swings gradually until it is about thirty degrees to one side of its base course; then the ship reverses the rudder and swings gradually until it is the same amount to the other side; then it repeats the whole procedure over and over. The submarine tracking the target is thus given a continually changing picture that prevents the TDC from getting a firm course solution, as it can during a regular zig plan. It makes a dead-accurate TDC solution impossible.

One or two other submarines had reported seeing Japanese ships constant helming, but this was our first experience. I had to admire the way the Japanese admiral had gotten all fifteen ships in his armada to swing on just about the same frequency so that the whole formation stayed relatively constant in relation to its prescribed order.

"Swing and sway with Admiral Jay," cracked Gunner Lynes as he studied the impressive movements of the convoy on the PPI.

"Who the hell is Admiral Jay?" asked Kent Lukingbeal from the plot.

"I dunno, it's just my name for him. He's a Jap, ain't he?"

So here we had fifteen ships—seven heavies and eight escorts—along with a daytime plane escort; and all of this was opposed by just one submarine. Here we really *did* need a wolf pack to allow one submarine to attack from one side, distracting all escorts to that location and leaving the other side open to unopposed attack. We were alone, however, and *Jack* the Pack was going to do its best to take on the job single-handed.

The sea was almost dead calm, and we were able to make twenty knots, an eight-knot speed differential over their twelve knots through the water. Their constantly swinging helms slowed their speed of advance considerably below twelve knots, however, and in that way worked to our advantage.

We began driving ahead of the convoy so that we could swing in on their starboard bow, hopefully astern of that starboard-bow escort. The moon was down, and we knew the *Jack* was difficult, if not impossible, to see. As we started in, Dykers slowed down to minimize the bow wake and lessen our chances of being sighted. The gentle strains of "Nearer, My God, to Thee" began drifting down from the bridge. It was like old times.

But as we tried to slip astern of the starboard bow escort, with the range still too long for shooting, he turned around and headed right for us. No shooting, but there was no mistaking his intentions. Dykers turned away and started pulling out from the convoy. The escort kept chasing us.

Clearly this escort had radar. He picked us up when we were dead astern of him at a range where he could not possibly have seen us.

Suppose this guy has a big gun on board and is just trying to get within sure range, I thought. Once he opened fire, we would almost surely have to dive, and then we'd lose all chance of getting into attack position on these guys. There was also the chance that he would hit us, in which case we wouldn't be worrying about the attack. Shadows again, I thought to myself, and I tried to focus on the problem at hand.

"He's turned back and is rejoining the convoy," reported Dykers from the bridge. Here was another Japanese convoy commodore showing his unwillingness to abandon a valuable convoy in order to attack a submarine.

Almost immediately the convoy increased its constant helm plan to 50 degrees either side of its base course. This gave the ships a total swing of 100 degrees, too much even for Admiral Jay's well-organized outfit, and they began to get out of phase. While this may have been disturbing to the Japanese Admiral's sense of orderliness and good seamanship, it made it a lot more difficult for us. The relative position of the heavies and the escorts changed continually, and we did not know what we could count on.

Twice more we tried to get in from the western (starboard) side, and twice more the escort turned toward us with a bone in his teeth.

Not giving up, Dykers went all the way around the stern of the convoy and tried coming up its eastern (port) side. The night was slipping away; we were running out of time. Dykers and Refo discussed trying to drive on ahead to submerge on their track for a daytime periscope shot. With eight escorts and a plane added in the daytime, however, Dykers reasoned that his best chance was still for a night attack.

Twice more we tried coming in from the port side, once up ahead and once from their port quarter (halfway astern). Both times we were chased out by escorts.

As we looked at the formation on the radar and from the bridge, there were times when the convoy presented a solid, uninterrupted line of targets stretching a very long distance from one end to the other. About the same time, we all got the idea that a long-range shot was the only answer. Much as I disliked long-range shots, it seemed the only way. It seemed impossible to get by the escorts and into decent firing range, yet we simply could not let this convoy get by without even taking a shot at them.

Dykers came down to the conning tower, and we worked out a scheme whereby Kent, on the plot, would estimate the mean course of the constant-helming convoy for the period that the torpedoes would be running. Then I would set that course in the TDC. We would attempt to have the gyros set as near zero as possible to maximize the accuracy of the shot. We would use the Mark VIII Angle Solver (the banjo) to help us predict the firing bearing needed to get zero gyros from the TDC. That would help us put the *Jack* on the right course before firing—which would be necessary with this scheme.

This was a new and complicated way to shoot, and to work it out in the midst of a battle was really tough. Only a skipper who was a master of torpedo shooting could have done it. Miles and Kent were a big help also because they caught on quickly and knew exactly what we had to do.

The length of the torpedo run (over three miles) made it impossible to use the normal, high-speed setting on the torpedoes. We had to set them on low power, which meant they would run at about thirty knots rather than the usual forty-five. It was a somewhat desperate scheme, but it seemed the only way to shoot this heavily guarded and important convoy.

Dykers planned to shoot ten torpedoes this way, six from the bow and four from the stern. This large volume of fire was intended to cover at least some of the problems that would arise from the extraordinarily long torpedo runs.

All of this was carefully planned and executed for the six bow tube shots. It was too dark for Bennett to buzz in his bearings in the usual way, so Charley Caw gave me the bearing of the center of the target group from radar.

When I had the best bearing that Caw could give me, I started shooting.

"Fire one! . . . Fire two! . . . Fire three! . . . Fire four! . . . Fire five! . . . Fire six!"

I had never fired torpedoes from anything like this range before and never with so little confidence of getting hits. We arranged for two stopwatches, with two different men running them, to be certain that we got the time of the explosions (if any) accurately recorded. The torpedoes were going to take over six minutes to get there; it was going to be a long wait.

Without delay we swung around for the stern tube shots. The process of getting exactly zero gyros on the stern tubes took longer than Dykers wanted.

"What the hell's the holdup down there, Miles?"

The exec was supervising this complicated firing system, and I was glad he had to answer the bridge instead of me.

"It's taking longer to set up these zero gyros than we thought it would," Miles replied.

Getting the submarine on exactly the right course before shooting was not easy with the whole picture changing continually due to the now-confused constant helming of the convoy. For the sake of extreme accuracy, we had given up the flexibility of the TDC system, and we were having a tough time adapting to the change.

"The hell with it. Let's wait for these bow shots to hit before we shoot the stern tubes," from the bridge.

"I wish I were as sure as he is that there'll be some hits," I muttered to no one in particular.

"Aw, come on, Jim—we got these guys cold," said Kent with a smile from the plot.

It was turning out to be the longest six minutes of my life. Then, from Dykers on the bridge, "Two big-hit flashes out there—no doubt about it."

Seconds later, *WHAM!* . . . *WHAM!* . . . *WHAM!* . . . *WHAM!*

Four perfectly timed hits. We had known the range exactly from radar and had been able to predict the time of the explosions precisely.

Then, *Boom! Boom! Boom!* and many, many more. Depth charges all over the place. It seemed that each escort was dropping them as fast as he could. The escorts had apparently concluded they were being attacked by a submerged submarine from inside their screen since, they were certain, no surfaced submarine could have gotten past their radars. The one thing they had not considered was the possibility of a surfaced submarine shooting successfully from far outside their screen.

I had never heard such a depth charge barrage—it was like rolling thunder—but we were on the surface, and as we had learned, that makes all the difference.

Dykers pulled out and started a reload in the forward room so that we could go with a full torpedo salvo if we got another chance. During the reload Charley Caw studied the radar PPI carefully and gave out a low whistle.

"One of those seven heavies is missing—only six now."

We were all aware of the low opinion our bosses had of radar as a confirmation of sinking. There had been too many cases of ships reported sunk because of a missing pip on radar, only to have the code breakers learn that all the ships in that convoy had reached port safely. Still, Caw's report was encouraging to us.

With the reload completed, we took more than an hour to work into position again; but at about three in the morning, we were as ready as we could be. We were well outside the screen, with a good bead on the heavies.

Using the same awkward but accurate method, we got off six more bow shots without incident. As we swung around for the stern shots, we were all aware of the difficulties involved and did a little better this time. Kent gave us the approximate, then the exact, course we needed to come to. Caw gave us the center bearing again. Four more torpedoes went out of the stern tubes, as planned. Ten shots in this salvo! First time we had ever done that.

Again we had the long wait, with two men on the stopwatches.

Finally, after what seemed six hours rather than six minutes, a cry came from the bridge.

"Holy suh-*moly!* No doubt about those! Four big-hit flashes out there."

I could hardly believe it, but seconds later (the light of the flashes traveled faster than the sound) we heard *WHAM!* . . . *WHAM!* . . . *WHAM!* . . . *WHAM!*

Then, a little later still, the stern tube shots hit: *WHAM!* . . . *WHAM!*

Four hits out of six for the bow tubes, and two out of four for the stern! The stopwatch times had been within a second or two of the predicted values. Hard to believe, but equally hard to refute.

The depth charge barrage, which had calmed down and then stopped during the past hour of maneuvering, started again at an even more frantic pace. I don't think the escorts had a clue as to the source of the attacks, for they were roaming all over the place, dropping depth charges as they went. We never learned whether the Japanese Admiral thought he was being attacked by a wolf pack, but I don't see how he could have reached any other conclusion.

"Three ships burning now . . . big fires," from Dykers.

Kent slapped me on the back and said, "See, you just have to get the plot and the banjo in the act, and we can't miss. I think that TDC is outmoded."

I didn't care who got the credit; I was just grateful we had gotten in on this convoy, which was almost unbelievably heavily protected.

"One of the burning ships must be an ammunition ship. Looks like the Fourth of July. Pyrotechnics, explosions, rockets—everything!" said Dykers. He sounded pretty happy despite his misgivings about the long ranges and low-speed torpedoes.

About half an hour later, Caw reported that only three of the original seven heavies were showing on radar. Again, despite our lack of confidence in radar evidence, this was pretty encouraging. We were only a few miles away, and our radar had been working perfectly. These ships had been detected easily at nearly fifteen miles when we first intercepted them. If we couldn't find them now, they had to be gone.

About an hour after our ten-torpedo salvo, one of the heavies broke out of the convoy formation and started right for us. Was he a warship, too large to be a regular ASW escort? We didn't know but pulled off his track to see if he would follow us. He did not. We pulled off just enough to give us a nice shot. He was tracking at fourteen knots—much faster than the convoy speed, which may have been why he decided to chance it alone.

We had only four torpedoes left on board, and they were Mark XVIIIs, the new, wakeless electric torpedoes. The absence of wakes made them especially hard to counter.[1]

Despite their wakeless feature (not a big factor at night anyway), the electrics had us more than a little worried. Many other submarines had had trouble with them, and their low (thirty-three-knot) speed made them more difficult to shoot. The submarine was almost forced to get a track angle (angle of impact) forward of the beam to keep the torpedo runs from becoming unacceptably long. To put it another way, the Mark XVIIIs were too slow to catch the target—they had to be shot with the target coming toward them.

Dykers took all of this into consideration and worked into a beautiful position, with a torpedo run of only twenty-three hundred yards—practically point-blank range compared to what we had been doing earlier. With this fellow so close, Bennett could see him easily, and he buzzed in the bearings with no problem.

"Fire seven! . . . Fire eight! . . . Fire nine! . . . Fire ten!"

The first three electrics jumped out as expected, but the fourth one would not go.

"Torpedoes running straight and normal. They're very quiet but sound OK," from sonar.

"Try again on ten, Jim," said Dykers.

"Fire ten!" Still nothing.

About this time, from the bridge, "Hit flash—a big one!"

Then, almost simultaneously, *WHAM! . . . WHAM!* Two hits, exactly at the proper time.

We began to pull away while continuing to track the target. Unexpectedly, he did not stop but whirled around and headed back for the escorts. So much for going it alone, he must have thought.

---

[1] Allied intelligence had known almost from the beginning of the war that the U-boats were using electric torpedoes with devastating effect. By extraordinary good fortune—for the Allies—some of these German electrics had run up on the beach unexploded. They were recovered, and at least one of them went to Newport with orders that it be copied as quickly as possible. With Newport desperately behind on its schedule for manufacturing the conventional steam torpedoes, the task was given to Westinghouse Electric. Westinghouse made a good start, and the submariners were told they would have electrics sometime in 1942.

But as was so often the case with Bureau of Ordnance projects, this one went off track, and even in 1944 the electrics were still not entirely debugged. The *Jack* had left Fremantle with twenty steam torpedoes (Mark XIVs) and four electrics, the latter carried in the after room.

Then, Ker-*WHOOM!* An explosion from the target. Could have been a boiler. Would he stop now?

He did not stop, but Dykers spun the *Jack* around and got into pretty good position to get that last fish off as a killer shot. We had to hurry—it was beginning to get light.

"How's your setup, Jim?" from the bridge.

"Pretty good. We're gonna get him," I replied.

"Shoot when you're ready."

"Fire ten!" I ordered, with my fingers crossed. Still it would not leave the tube. Our last torpedo was a loser. Dykers began to pull out.

We had been at battle stations continually for nearly twenty-four hours, and we were all exhausted. We had left only one torpedo that would not leave the tube. The three heavies and the eight escorts were going over the horizon to the south. Our last target had been able to rejoin the convoy and apparently was having no trouble keeping up.

The fact that he had been able to absorb those two hits and the subsequent internal explosion without sinking showed us why our bosses were reluctant to accept sinking reports unless they were absolutely sure and confirmed. We *were* absolutely sure, however, that we had sunk four of the seven heavies.

They were nowhere to be found by a red-hot radar in a calm sea.

It did not seem worth it to chase the convoy any longer. Our punch was reduced to one electric torpedo of doubtful usefulness.

In any case, Dykers felt that the battle was over, and we submerged to get some rest. He needed it as badly as the rest of us. We all needed some food, also. I had had one sandwich, eaten hurriedly at the TDC, in that twenty-four hours. Neither Miles nor Kent nor Dykers had done much better. We had an early-morning brunch, as did the rest of the ship's company.

During the day the torpedomen in the after room pulled out the faulty torpedo and found that it was too long from its tail to the stop bolt. The stop bolt should have held the torpedo in place in the tube and lifted when the firing key was pressed. But with this error in dimension (a manufacturing error), the torpedo was jammed so hard in the tube after the door was shut that the bolt could not lift when the tube was fired.

This defect should have been picked up by the torpedo shop at Fremantle since checking the tail-to-stop-bolt dimension was part of their job. Clearly they hadn't done it.

So the mystery was solved, but it didn't make us feel any better. If that last fish had gone out, it might have made the difference between survival and sinking for our last target.

After a great meal from Domingo, I slept all day and wakened, feeling better, to realize that Miles had taken my eight-to-twelve watch so that I could sleep. Pretty nice of him—he had been up as long and was as tired as I was.

About dark we surfaced and set our course for the Balintang Channel north of Luzon, the start of the way home. We submerged at first light on April 27 and continued eastward at our slow, battery speed, about three knots. About 10:30 in the morning, I sighted a small, trawler-type patrol boat with the rising sun painted on his side. He was lying to and apparently just watching the Balintang Channel. He was definitely not transiting.

Ever since commissioning, we had worked on our battle surface procedure, and this seemed like a good opportunity to put our team to work. The *Jack* was equipped with a three-inch, fifty-caliber gun, mounted on the deck about fifteen feet forward of the bridge. On a platform just forward of the bridge, we had a twenty-millimeter Oerliken machine gun, and on the after bridge we had two fifty-caliber machine guns. The big-gun shells were three inches in diameter, the 20-millimeter shells about one inch, and the fifty-caliber shells about one-half inch. All told, we could put up a pretty good volume of fire, but it was the three-inch gun that we had to depend on to do any serious damage.

To aim a conventional naval gun of that time, there were two wheels, one located on each side, that were turned manually. The trainer turned it right and left, the pointer controlled it up and down. The firing key was in the hands of the pointer, and he pressed it when the roll of the ship caused the crosshairs of the sighting telescope to meet the horizon. The pointer also set the range to the target on a dial near his position; this automatically elevated the gun to the proper angle for the range. Normally a spotting officer would set the initial range and then spot the range up and down, based on the splashes he had seen from the rounds fired.

I reasoned that the availability of radar made it possible for one man to do both jobs, to be pointer and spotting officer all in one. Caw agreed with me that the splashes of the misses would be big enough to be seen on radar, allowing him to give me absolutely accurate ranges and spots over the phones. This was clearly better than my having to estimate them. It also allowed us to minimize the number of people on deck in a battle surface. If I did the pointer's job with phones on to receive ranges and spots, it would mean one less man on deck and easier communications.

We had drilled with this procedure over and over, and in practice it had worked beautifully. Due to the serious shortage of three-inch, 50-caliber ammunition, however, we had never done any live firing; we didn't know how our scheme would work in an actual engagement. We didn't even know for sure if the three-inch-shell splashes would show up on radar. So far as we knew, no other submarine was using this scheme, but Dykers went along with it.

"Stand by for battle surface" came the command over the ship's loudspeaker system. Everyone was tensed up—no one more than I.

"We want to get that first shot off in a hurry—before he wakes up and can man his guns," said Dykers to me quietly as he prepared to sound the surface alarm.

We surfaced about a mile away. The sea was almost dead calm, the sun blazing bright in a blue sky. The water was Caribbean blue.

I followed up the hatch right behind Dykers with my headphones in hand. I hotfooted it out to the still-dripping gun and took my seat. Gunner Lynes was in overall charge of the deck operations, which included getting the ammunition to the guns and making sure everyone was in place. He ordered the breach opened and the first round loaded.

I checked out with Caw on the phones. All OK there.

"All ready on deck, Mr. Calvert," from Lynes.

"Range eighteen hundred yards," from Caw on the phones.

I set the range on my dial, and on the slight roll of the ship, fired the first round. It was short.

"You need to come up sixty yards, sir," from Caw over the phones.

I put in the spot and fired again. It was a hit—our system was working!

Through the aiming telescope, I could see men jumping over the side of the ship. They were apparently not going to fight.

Our system was organized so that as soon as the next round was loaded, Lynes was to give me the OK.

"Round won't seat," came from Lynes.

I saw him using a special tool to extract the round, but it separated, leaving the projectile in the gun and spilling powder all over the deck. Lynes promptly inserted a clearing charge, which we fired. The projectile plopped harmlessly in the water a few yards out.

The next shell went in properly, and when fired it fell about one hundred yards on the other side of the target. Caw gave me the spot, and the next shell was a hit. No more men were jumping over the side, and I could not see any more on board.

It was soon easy to see that the trawler was finished. He was on fire from stem to stern, and sinking. We had fired about thirty rounds and gotten about twenty hits.

We did our best to pick up the survivors, but they were not anxious to be saved by us. Finally, two of them came on board. Following procedures we stripped them both completely to ensure they had nothing concealed. After stripping, one of the two jumped overboard and would not return. Almost immediately another indicated he would like to come on board. We took him—the rest remained steadfast in their refusal.

About an hour after we had our first battle surface, we submerged again and spent the rest of the daylight hours down. At dark we surfaced and, at high speed, completed our passage into the Philippine Sea, where we turned southward toward home. It was a good feeling.

Again following prescribed procedures, we put one of our prisoners in the forward torpedo room, the other in the after room.

All in all, our first battle surface had not been too bad. We had sunk the target, we had had no injuries or casualties, and despite two jams, both caused by oversize ammunition, we had had a pretty good rate and accuracy of fire with the three-inch.

We had read of other submarines getting valuable information from prisoners picked up after a sinking. We did not. Perhaps we lacked anyone with real language skills—we probably needed Billy Coleman back. Kent Lukingbeal, however, did his best over quite a few days. It was a nearly dry well. He learned that the name of the vessel was *Dun Sai*, that it had carried eight men, that it had a radio on board, and that they *thought* the job of the boat was to watch the Balintang Channel and report traffic. They stubbornly repeated that the man who knew all these things was the captain and that he had drowned. Not the first time this ploy had been used.

Since their real names were difficult for us, we called the one in the forward room Freddy and the one in the after room Adam. They seemed to like these names and answered to them freely. But what they *really* liked was the food. At first they couldn't believe it, and then they couldn't get enough of it. They had been living on a diet of rice and salted fish for so long that we were worried that our relatively rich diet would give them trouble. It never did—not one bit. They began noticeably to gain weight.

They were anxious to work, and the men in charge of the torpedo rooms set them to polishing the brass, of which there was plenty. Before long, when you entered the torpedo rooms, you were blinded by the wall of brightly polished brass and bronze around the torpedo tubes. When that was done, they started on every other piece of shinable metal in the rooms. Our torpedo rooms, with only one lonely electric fish to store, soon became relatively palatial living spaces.

Early the next morning, April 28, on the eastern coast of Luzon, we sighted another trawler-type vessel, similar to the *Dun Sai* except that it was larger and had two guns of pretty good size in addition to its machine guns. Dykers decided we needed another workout to perfect our battle surface procedure. Since we were already on the surface, this engagement could be a little more leisurely. We manned all our stations and had plenty of clearing charges in the event of more stuck projectiles.

We closed him at high speed, and at thirty-seven hundred yards (a long range for the three-inch gun) we opened fire. The first shot was a hit! The second and third were also hits. This seemed to take the fight out of him, and we could see a lot of his crew taking to the water. Soon he was ablaze all over. We came close aboard, but there was no point in boarding to look for intelligence material; he was too far gone. For reasons he never explained to us, Dykers did not take any prisoners from this ship. He may have thought that two were enough and more might band together to make trouble. In any case, Freddy and Adam were to have no competition, either for food or for metal shining.

We made the passage on the surface—down the east coast of the Philippines, through the Molucca Passage, and into the Banda Sea—without incident except for occasional dives for patrol planes.

Through these long, relatively quiet days, I thought of Australia and, of course, of Kathie. It began to look as though we were going to get there safely, and I could not wait to see her. But I could not think of her without feeling guilty. What business did I have feeling so tenderly and fondly for someone not my wife? Obviously, none. But I did not seem to be able to stop it.

I thought of our long walks and talks, of our tennis games, of the evenings spent over chemistry at the dining table, and I felt a real choke of homesickness. I was afraid I was getting myself into

a bad situation, and I resolved to do something about it. But not yet
. . . not quite yet.

About 3:30 in the morning on May 8, a couple of days out of Fremantle, we made radar contact on a small vessel to the east of us.
Since this part of the Indian Ocean was a sort of no-man's-land,
except for U.S. submarines transiting between Fremantle and the
Lombok-Timor barrier, we couldn't figure this contact out; we had
no word of any transiting U.S. submarine. Bennett got him up-
moon from us, and at about six thousand yards, he said he looked
like a small submarine. He tracked on course about south, speed
seven knots.

We ran up ahead about twelve miles and sent an urgent message to Perth asking for identification. Perth promptly replied that
it was the Dutch submarine K-15.

We had both British and Dutch submarines based in Fremantle. They patrolled mainly in the Java Sea because of their relatively
small size and their shorter cruising radius. We recommended that
their transit information be made available to the American submarines operating out of Fremantle. This might well prevent some-
body from shooting a friend and ally.[2]

On May 10 we sighted the welcome rays of Rottnest Light, then
made contact with our escort vessel, and then entered port.

Our welcome this time was considerably different from the one
we had received after our third patrol: no Admiral to greet us, and
a considerably cooler reception from our Squadron commander.
No invitation to The Bend of the Road.

Nor did our Japanese friends, Freddy and Adam, get a cordial
reception. They were taken off the ship by three U.S. marines who
did not treat them with the amused kindness our sailors had displayed. The marines' language toward the prisoners was rough and
unmistakably unfriendly. I remember one of them following Freddy
up the forward torpedo room hatch as he got ready to leave us. The
marine was not happy with Freddy's lack of alacrity, and he jabbed
him hard in the butt with his bayonet. Freddy left the ship with a
large bloody spot in the seat of his pants.

I didn't see Dykers until we had been in a day or two, and when
I did he was not happy. Admiral Christie, in a long interview, had

---

[2]After arriving in Fremantle, we learned that we *had* been informed and had apparently missed the message. Our fault.

given him several pieces of less-than-good news. First of all, the radar evidence was just not enough. Convincing as it had seemed to us on the spot, it wasn't acceptable to the admiral and his staff. There had been too many enthusiastic reports of ships sunk with the only evidence being radar. Christie would give us credit only for four large ships damaged. No combat awards for that.

"You have to bring back the skipper's pants these days, Tommy," Christie had told him.

In addition, it was clear the staff had thought Dykers made a mistake in attempting night attacks on such a heavily guarded convoy. They believed, from the comfort of their offices in Perth, that Dykers should have spent the night running ahead and then submerged for a daylight periscope attack.

There apparently was also an undercurrent of feeling that Dykers really didn't relish the prospect of a periscope attack on this convoy, with its inevitable heavy depth charging. Perhaps he had become too enamored of the night surface attack.

Naturally, all these opinions and innuendoes were accompanied by statements such as "Of course, the man on the spot has to make the decision."

While Dykers could not ask Christie directly about code-break evidence, he got the impression that they had not given the admiral anything on our attacks on the big convoy.[3]

During his interview with Christie, Dykers was also told that he had been selected for captain. Normally good news, this meant that he had made his last patrol. He would not go back to new construction for a new submarine, being too senior for that now. He was told he would be going to a carrier Admiral's staff as the submarine liaison officer. This was an OK assignment, but not the best he could have gotten.

My great skipper's face was drawn and tired as he told me all

---

[3] After the war, in 1946, we learned that our big convoy had been commanded by Rear Admiral Kajioka, a distinguished veteran of several early-war actions. (So it was Admiral Kay, not Admiral Jay.) The postwar accounting, which is discussed more fully in the Afterword, revealed that on the night of April 25–26 we had sunk at least two of the ships in Kajioka's convoy, including the very valuable *Yoshida Maru I*, a big troop transport carrying an army regiment of three thousand men. All the troops, including the regimental commander, were lost.

Stopping off at Manila, Kajioka picked up even more escorts for the remainder of his mission. But due to more sinkings by another American submarine farther down the line, none of Admiral Kajioka's heavy ships reached New Guinea in time to help the Japanese effort there.

Dykers and the rest of us learned none of this until 1946.

of this. I could not help feeling bitter. This was not the finale this man deserved. I knew that if the Admiral and his staff had been with us that evening, they would have been as certain as we that we had sunk four of those seven heavies. There was no other logical conclusion.

Dykers had always been conservative in his sinkings claims, and it was a bitter blow to be treated this way for his last patrol.

There was no word on who the new skipper would be.

We had two weeks at the Majestic ahead of us, so naturally I went to see Kathie as soon as I could. I was not quite prepared for what happened. I walked into her living room, and there she was, looking so radiant and so beautiful that I could scarcely believe it. We just walked slowly into each other's arms and said not a word. After a long time, I looked at her and saw tears streaming down her cheeks. Mine were wet too.

"I've been so worried . . . I was afraid I would never see you again," she whispered.

About that time Dr. Aberdeen walked in the room, and we both, rather hastily brushing back our tears, said hello and tried to act as though it were just another afternoon. Dr. Aberdeen took no notice and asked me how the patrol had gone. There was little I could tell him except that we had shot all our torpedoes save one that was faulty.

Naturally he asked me about the beer, and I was happy to tell him that I had once again succeeded in trading for six cases and had already made arrangements for them to be delivered to the Tennis Club. This put things in a little lighter vein, and after dinner the evening concluded without any more emotional trauma.

But I had plenty of trauma when the mail arrived the next day. There were seven or eight wonderful letters from Nancy that made me feel homesick for the States and terribly guilty about Kathie. Is it possible for a man to be sincerely in love with two women? There was no question where my duty was, no question about what was morally right; but that old wartime psychology was working overtime. After arrival we had learned of the loss of two more American submarines, one of them carrying a classmate and good friend. Just how much more time was I going to have to spend with Kathie—or Nancy—or anyone, for that matter?

Like Scarlett O'Hara I decided to worry about it tomorrow. I phoned Kathie and arranged a date for the late afternoon when her classes were over.

During that stay Kathie and I even went to church together, a sign in those days that people were really serious about each other. What I was doing was getting myself into a mess, and I knew it. There was no way this story was going to play out happily.

I resolved each day to do something about it . . . and then did nothing.

9

The New Skipper

Early in our two-week rest period, Commander Arthur Elmer Krapf, USN, was named as the new skipper of the *Jack*. He was a graduate of Annapolis, class of 1934—seven years younger than Dykers. He had a postgraduate degree in electronics engineering and was widely recognized as an expert in this area, particularly as it related to combat electronics. Art Krapf (pronounced "Kraff" to rhyme with "staff") was a trim-looking man, about five feet nine or ten, with a rather smart mustache and very black hair. He had a warm and friendly face with a wide, engaging smile. He smoked cigars—several a day. His uniforms were always crisp and immaculate.

He had had no wartime submarine experience except one patrol as a PCO (prospective commanding officer)—similar to the way that Freddy Laing had ridden with us on our third patrol. Krapf had, however, submerged himself in patrol reports for some time and was certainly familiar with what had been going on in submarines since the start of the war. He had practically memorized the reports of the *Jack*'s first four patrols and had even learned the names of officers and men he had never met. He had an unusually sharp and orderly mind, but he lacked the patrician air and command presence of his famous predecessor.

In the Navy, people are always cautious about the new skipper. So much depends on him. In a sense he *is* the ship. Its safety, its accomplishments, its reputation—all depend on him, and the ship quickly takes on the imprint of his personality. I suppose this was especially true in wartime submarines; they were small, they usually operated entirely independently, and their missions were dangerous. On larger warships the captain was isolated from the wardroom; in submarines he was part of it and indeed was accessible to and visible to all of the ship's company every day. He lived in a fishbowl.

Dykers had left an almost indelible imprint on the *Jack*. He had placed the ship in commission and had been with her since she had been just a few rings of steel on the building ways at Electric Boat. In addition, he had possessed such a strong personality, such an in-depth knowledge of submarines, such an intense interest in his peo-ple that the ship had *become* the USS *Dykers*. How could anyone else take the place of this unusual man?

The Navy, however, accustoms one to change. After all, Miles Refo and I were the only original officers still on board, and less than a dozen of the original crew remained. Dykers could not have remained forever; a change was inevitable. We were determined to do all we could to make our new skipper feel at home and welcome.

Gunner Lynes put it well when he said to the crew one morning at quarters, "Hey, he's our man now. We're gonna sink or swim with him—let's swim."

We had another important new face in the wardroom before Krapf's first patrol. He was Frank Deaver, a reserve officer, quickly nicknamed Danny. He was a red-haired, cheerful man from Arkan-sas, where his family was in the lumber business. He had a won-derful smile and fit in quickly. He was, however, a little less modest about being a reserve officer in submarines—this hitherto sacro-sanct monopoly of Annapolis blue—than the others. He genuinely felt that reserve officers were the mainstay of the war effort (he was not altogether wrong in that), and he occasionally groused about "those regulars who have been well paid all these years just for sit-ting on their butts and keeping the guns clean."

The first time I heard this, I cautioned Danny that it was OK with us junior officers but to soft-pedal that line when the exec (Miles) was around.

Because we had a new skipper, we did not have quite as large a turnover in crew as we had had the last time. However, a detach-ment that was particularly hard for us to swallow was our singing quartermaster, Bennett. We protested, but to no avail, and our key night vision man was off to new construction. We sent fifteen other men to new construction and received, as before, soft, green relief crewmen to replace them. The happy, temporary homes of Perth and Fremantle were still being devastated.

Jack O'Brien needed a rest and was transferred to be the division engineering officer, a job for which he was ideally suited.

Our training period in the Rottnest Island area was even more strenuous because we had a new skipper to break in. He and Miles got along well; that made it easier, but there was still a lot for Krapf to learn. Our training officer for the patrol was our division commander, Freddy Warder, and there was no one better for the job. He had always been a little reluctant to give Dykers too much help and advice because he didn't think it was really needed, but he gave Art Krapf an awful lot, and this was good for everyone. We had a good attack party, but with someone like Warder working it over from top to bottom, we were all going to learn things we needed to know. No one ever learns absolutely everything there is to know about shooting torpedoes.

We made many practice approaches, both night surface and day periscope. Krapf seemed more at ease with the night surface than with the periscope—however, we were used to watching one of the masters of the game at that position. I doubt if there were many people in the submarine force, of any age, who were Dykers's equal on the periscope.

Our diving training went better this time because we did not have as many new lookouts to break in. We had no more broken legs, and we reached our thirty- to thirty-five-second requirement a little more easily.

On June 4 we were ready to go. We departed Fremantle about midday. Once again we traveled up the west coast of Australia with another U.S. submarine en route to her patrol area. For the education of the lookouts, we made the same mutual exchange of night and day approaches and the same show-and-tell drill with the periscopes at various ranges. Because we had lost in Obie a top watch stander, Kent Lukingbeal and I had to go through another forced-draft drill to get Earl Archer ready for this responsibility. He was a quick learner.

In four days' time we were back at Exmouth Gulf for our last-minute fuel and water top-off. We stayed only over the lunch hour and at 3:00 P.M. were on our way to the Lombok Strait, filled to the brim with all that we needed for our war against the Empire.

The powers that be at Perth had decided we would take a different route to the South China Sea this time. They had more or less given Dykers his choice, but this time Krapf was being *told* which way to go. After leaving Lombok we were to turn west into

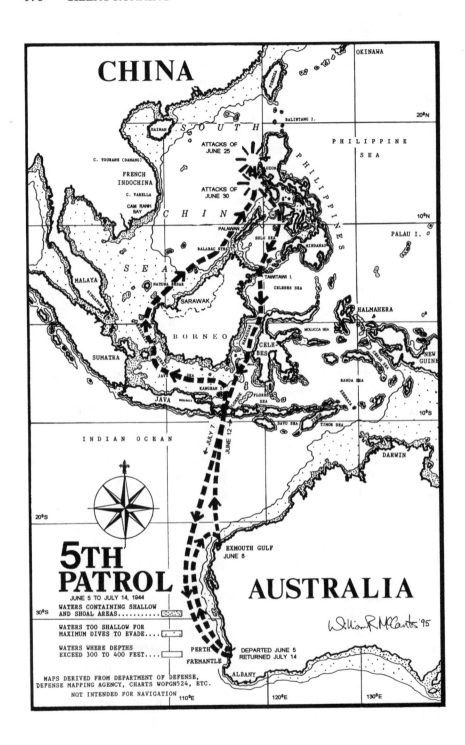

the shallow Java Sea; then northwest into the Karimata Strait, between Borneo and Sumatra; then north past Singapore and into the southern reaches of the South China Sea.

We went through the Lombok Strait on the surface at night at high speed. We saw no patrol boats nor did we detect any on radar. The next morning we had a long conversation about this in the wardroom after breakfast.

Kent started it off. "The Japanese must know that this pass is a key one for the Fremantle submarines going up to the Dutch East Indies. But here they are leaving it unguarded. What gives?"

"The only answer is that they are just so short of resources that they can't spare the ships needed to do it," from Miles.

"Well, the Japs are engaged in two life-and-death struggles, in New Guinea and in the Marianas. Think of what the loss of Guam and Saipan would mean to them. We could base our new long-range bombers there. They could reach the Japanese mainland easily from that distance," said the skipper.

"You mean they're just willing to take their chances with the Fremantle submarines that get through?" I asked. "That doesn't make any sense to me—they need that oil we're sinking to run their ships and to train their aviators at home. As far as I know, every drop of oil they use has to come from down here."

"Isn't it possible that the big operations in the Marianas are looked on as temporary emergencies? When they're over, one way or the other, the Japanese will get back to defending places like Lombok. I think that for right now they've decided to risk letting the submarines through this barrier," concluded Krapf.

"Well, let's make them regret it," grinned the irrepressible Lukingbeal.

Once past Lombok we knew we had to be careful on our route across the Java Sea and into the Karimata Strait. It was almost all shallow water, much of it ninety feet or less. The many patrol planes in the area called for emergency dives to be made quickly but correctly; there was not much room for error. Our practice of diving with such steep angles made it more difficult. In ninety feet of water, a mistake can land you on the bottom with some real damage.

Once through the Karimata Strait, we were told to keep an eye out for tanker traffic coming from the refinery ports of Sarawak, the separate nation that occupies the northwestern coast of Borneo. The tankers full of crude oil and refined products from southeast

Asia were the lifeblood of Japan's war machine—whatever decisions were being made about defending the Lombok Strait—and we had been told over and over that anything we could do to interrupt that flow would be a major contribution to the war effort. Tankers were still top priority.

About noon on June 19, we were patrolling submerged, in as close against the coast of Sarawak as we could comfortably get with due respect for the very shallow water there. About noon the periscope watch sighted smoke down to the southeast, between us and the shoreline. The convoy consisted of about seven ships, all small, with some escorts that were hard for us to identify—they were about the size of PT boats.

This miniature convoy was headed northeast, hugging the coastline and staying well inside the ten-fathom (60-foot) line. The only way we could get at them was on the surface, and we were not yet willing to try this in broad daylight only four miles off the coast.

We pulled out from the coast, surfaced, and started tracking the ships by high periscope and radar to see what they might do. They were headed for a known minefield off the Sarawak coast. We had no desire to get mixed up with that kind of thing, either surfaced or submerged.

It was soon obvious that they were so comfortable with their track in shallow water and through a minefield that they were not even zigzagging. We had hoped they might have a destination that would force them to come away from the coastline. But they stayed close in and soon were positioned so that they could remain in shallow or mined water all the way to the Balabac Strait, around the north end of Borneo and leading into the Sulu Sea. That was beyond our authorized area—we had to let them go.

I don't think we missed much with this group of midgets.

Within less than a week, we were in our assigned area off Manila. There, also about noon, on June 24, while on submerged periscope patrol, we sighted faint and distant smoke to the east. We closed the smoke at about four knots and soon decided it was a large convoy, a dozen ships or so, heading north up the western coast of Luzon and hugging the coastline. Some of the ships appeared to be of good size. An escort plane was flying lazy loops above the convoy. It soon became clear we were not going to be able to close this convoy submerged, so we surfaced and began a long end-around, keeping track of them by high periscope. Several times in the afternoon we had to dive for patrol planes, but each time we came back up as soon as possible and continued our pursuit.

By midnight we had worked up to a point about six miles on the port bow of this group. By this time we had had plenty of time to solve their zig plan and speed. We also had a fair, though not perfect, picture of their disposition. We had the heavies spotted, all right—twelve of them in two columns of six. The escorts were smaller than those of Admiral Jay's convoy and did not show up on the PPI nearly as well. However, radar did show escorts at least on both bows of the convoy. Although there was some moonlight left (the moon would soon go down), we could not see the escorts at this distance. We had all kept checking with the cooks to be sure Bennett's replacement on the bridge was getting plenty of carrots.

"He's stuffed with them," was the reply.

"I'm still having a tough time spotting these escorts on the PPI," reported Caw as we pulled in closer. "But I think they have one on each bow and one on each quarter—that's all I can see."

It was clear that this convoy was not as strongly defended or as aggressively run as Admiral Jay's big armada. Nevertheless, escorts are escorts, and they all can shoot guns and drop depth charges.

About two in the morning, we started in from the port bow but soon found that an unlucky zig had put us in a poor firing position; Miles recommended we pull out. The new skipper did just that—wisely, I thought.

It was a cloudy night, but the visibility was reasonably good, and the bridge had had a fairly good look at the heavies. We all missed Bennett's singing and owl-like night vision, but we weren't sure how the new skipper would have liked the hymn recitals at critical times. The singing could be unnerving and, all things considered, it may have been just as well.

It was another full hour before we worked our way in, again from the port side. This time we got a lucky zig and were able to sneak in about a thousand yards astern of the port-bow escort. He looked like a wooden sub chaser, and he apparently did not have radar.

As we were working into position, with the inevitable tension this brings, I found myself subconsciously listening to the tone of Krapf's orders and comments. He was new at this game, and if he was going to swallow his cud, this would be the time. But Krapf sounded as cool as a cucumber, as though he had been making night surface attacks all his life.

Just before we reached our firing position, Krapf reported with some excitement, "These are tankers! At least some of them."

"Pick out the biggest one and buzz the bearing down to the TDC," said the skipper. "Jim, we'll fire three bow tubes at the first ship, then three at the second. We'll buzz you a new bearing to start each salvo. Regular spread."

I got the buzzer.

"Fire one! . . . Fire two! . . . Fire three!" They all lurched out as planned.

Then the next buzzer.

"Fire four! . . . Fire five! . . . Fire six!"

The torpedo runs were short, and in less than a minute we heard WHAM! . . . WHAM! Very satisfying.

Then, from the bridge, "Wow! Look at that! A column of yellow flame shot up from the tanker, and it's lighting the whole sea! We can see the other target now. He's a maru, and he's been hit, too! Now the tanker's on fire from stem to stern!"

"That tanker is gone—I just saw him go under," from the bridge.

Then, a few seconds later, from the skipper, "The maru's on fire now—not like the tanker, but there's a big fire out there."

As we were spinning around for a stern shot, we heard depth charges being dropped in many different areas. However many escorts there actually were, they were dropping all the charges they could get into the water.

"Mr. Calvert, one of those escorts is heading right for us. Better track him!" snapped Caw, who didn't very often get excited. I tracked him, and he was heading our way at sixteen knots—and less than two miles away. We couldn't see him as there was a lot of smoke in that direction. Krapf turned away and put on flank speed.

"What's the range doing?" from the bridge.

"Holding steady," I replied.

"Maneuvering, pour on the coal!" snapped Krapf.

After what seemed like an eternity, the range began to open until finally it was about two and a half miles. Then Krapf began to pull off the track slowly to see if the guy could see us or still track us on his radar. Apparently he could do neither, for he slowed way down and started dropping depth charges about as fast as his men could handle them. It looked as though he had had us on his radar, then lost us as the range opened, and then concluded that we had submerged. Thus the frantic depth charging.

We were only fifty miles from the Manila-area air bases, and with all this night action and with day coming on shortly, Krapf decided we had had enough. As we were pulling away and were at some distance, Kent Lukingbeal, who had the deck, saw the burning maru flame up into a much bigger fire that suddenly enveloped the entire ship. Then the flame and smoke suddenly disappeared. At the same time, the radar pip disappeared. This was better evidence than just the disappearance of a radar pip and, we felt, established the sinking of the second ship beyond any reasonable doubt. Considering the way our bosses had roughed us up about our damage assessment after our attacks on Admiral Jay's outfit, we were all a little sensitive on this subject.

The morning of that same day, June 25, in the middle of my eight-to-twelve watch, sonar reported pinging to the north. Looking in that direction with the periscope, I saw two frigate-sized ASW ships heading our way. The sky was overcast, but visibility was excellent. They were regular Japanese Navy ships, painted gray and flying the rising sun. Both had signal flags flying from halyards on each side of their bridges. Clearly they were out looking for the culprit who had caused last night's sinkings.

The moment I saw them, I began to tense up. I don't know what was wrong with me, and I am not proud of what happened next. Maybe I was worn out from being up all night with the attacks, but I just froze.

Were we going to take these guys on? We'd try to shoot both, probably get only one, and then get worked over all day by the other one plus everyone in the area that he could call in.

I should have set the battle stations without delay, but instead I called the captain.

"I don't recommend we tangle with these guys. They probably have a lot of buddies nearby they can call in," I said as Krapf came to the conning tower.

Krapf took a long look at them through the periscope and then, clearly influenced by what I had said, went deep and rigged for silent running.

On the way down, I asked myself what Dykers would have done. I knew the answer—and it made me sick. I realized that if I had set the battle stations on sighting the vessels and then called Krapf with a gung-ho attitude, the results might well have been different.

This was my fifth straight patrol. Was I getting worn out? I didn't have a particularly vivid imagination, but it was vivid enough to realize that on some of our earlier depth charge attacks, a couple of those charges could have come a little closer, and then the *Jack* would have joined our growing list of lost submarines. Was I getting afraid of depth charging to that extent? Did I want us to finish the war making nothing but night surface attacks?

I remembered a discussion several months earlier between Dykers and Commander Warder about an officer from another submarine who was being considered for disqualification because he openly and disturbingly (to the crew) showed signs of terror during a depth charge attack.

"When you begin to get that afraid," said Warder, "there is just one thing to do—get out of submarines." The officer was disqualified and sent to shore duty.

Was I going to end up being the subject of a discussion like that? I had always been proud of being cool during attacks. But was it only because I was so busy with the TDC? When the decision was all mine and I wasn't busy with anything else, as had just been the case, was I going to show the white feather every time?

Later I told Miles the whole story. Wisely, he didn't say much. "Jim, you did what you thought was right at the time. I recommend you forget about it and get some sleep. You're not the captain, you know. It was his decision, and he made it. Probably right, all things considered."

Still, I didn't like it, and I am not proud of it to this day.

About three days later, on my evening watch, just as it was beginning to get really dark, one of the lookouts shouted, "Patrol boat on the port bow—and he's not very far away!"

I put my binoculars up and saw him, big as life. I asked the radar watch what the hell was going on. The immediate reply was, "We have him, bearing 340, range about eight thousand yards."

It's hard to understand why the radar did not have him much earlier. It was a quiet evening, and I guess the boys in the conning tower were relaxing over a cup of coffee—laughing and scratching, as they liked to say—and not watching the screen closely. Without doubt, they were awake now, and then some.

I quickly reflected that this was the way more than one German U-boat had met its death—relaxing in the evening on the surface and while its guard was down getting caught by one of our ASW ships. How many of our American submarines had gone the same way? We would never know. All I was sure of was that we had come close to joining the list.

In any case I called the captain, put our stern to this guy, and went to four-engine speed. Almost simultaneously the radar picked up another patrol boat nearly dead ahead as we ran away from the first. He was only three miles away. Our radar watch had *really* been asleep. Nothing to do now but change course to run between the two, inevitably showing a larger silhouette to the first guy. Krapf arrived on the bridge.

In a minute or two the first patrol craft turned a bright searchlight directly on us. He swept around with it but each time came directly back to us. Krapf set the battle stations.

While they were being set, our friend with the searchlight opened fire with what looked like about a four-inch gun. He was not using flashless powder, and each shot was a large, yellow-orange disk.

The patrol boat's fire was not too accurate, but the splashes were close enough to let us hear the explosions as they hit the water. They were also close enough to cause some real concern in the conning tower.

No matter how inaccurate the fire may be, there is something distinctly disconcerting about being shot at with a large-caliber gun at night. You see the large, orange flash, looking as though it is aimed directly at you; then, a few seconds later, you hear the loud *thump* of the gunfire arriving; then, a few seconds after that, the much nearer *whomp* of the shell hitting the water and exploding, sending a tower of water into the air. All in all, it is not a show that many people enjoy. Knowing that carelessness on my watch had gotten us into this mess did not make me feel any better.

Our pursuer was making a little less than seventeen knots, so in the relatively smooth sea, we slowly opened the range. When it got to about five miles, the shooting stopped. All told, our friend fired about fifteen shots; none of them came really close. Shortly after he ceased firing, he turned off his searchlight. The second patrol craft never did fire, nor did he use a searchlight. As we pulled out to seaward, he slowly converged the course of the first boat and joined him in pursuit. Neither one ever dropped a depth charge.

By 11:30 that night, we had lost contact with them, both by sight and by radar. I don't think they were connected with a convoy. They were just making a routine patrol in the coastal waters near

Manila. At any rate, they had given us a hell of a scare and had a good sea story to tell their barracks mates.

After this Krapf and Refo had a brief council and decided to pull away from the coast and patrol farther to seaward, west of Manila. Being this far away from the coast, we could patrol on the surface and with the high periscope have a much better chance of making a daytime contact.

On June 29, after a few dives for patrol planes, our high periscope sighted smoke down to the south-southwest, very distant. We never would have seen this contact had we been patrolling at periscope depth. We started closing them on the surface but had to dive twice for patrol planes, which slowed us down considerably.

I couldn't help reflecting that earlier in the war—even in early 1943, the time of our first patrol—no American submarine would have dreamed of chasing a convoy on the surface this close to an active base like Manila. But over time we had all learned that if we had really sharp lookouts and could dive in thirty seconds, we usually could get away with it.

We could see only the tips of the convoy's masts through the high periscope, but from that evidence and radar, we concluded that there were about nine or ten heavies. We were too far away to see their surface escorts, but we could see a plane that circled them overhead all day long. The convoy was on course due east, headed right for Manila.

The sun was setting, and as is always the case in the tropics, darkness came quickly. With the darkness the wind picked up from the northwest and was soon brisk. We felt some rain—heavy at times, as the weather forecasters like to say.

The pitch-black night was broken by occasional lightning flashes. The northwest wind was making the sea fairly rough. This slowed us down and made it a long haul to get around the convoy. It was after midnight before we were even beginning to get into firing position. The moon, which had been in and out of the rain clouds, set just after midnight. With the driving rain, steady now, it was literally impossible for the bridge watch and lookouts to see anything.

From the radar we had determined there were nine heavies, in three lines of bearing (abreast of each other in those lines). They were using a conventional zigzag plan averaging about thirty degrees to each side of their base course. There was an escort on each bow of the convoy and one out about three thousand yards on each wing.

We planned to work in astern of the beam escort on our side. The convoy was due for a zig toward, which we got about when we expected it. The escort, though only a thousand yards away, could not be seen from the bridge due to the rain squall. If we couldn't see him, as tensed up and alert as we were, the chances were that he would not see us. We were in luck.

Krapf came down to the conning tower to get the picture from the radar. Neither he nor his quartermaster could see a thing from the bridge. We might as well have been a hundred miles away from the convoy for all they could see up there.

"We'll shoot six bow tubes at the second line of heavies, then turn and give the four stern tubes to the third line," said Krapf, returning to the bridge.

Obviously there would be no buzzes from the quartermaster, so the skipper told Miles to take charge in the conning tower and get the shots off using only radar.

At about two in the morning, in utter blackness, with the rain coming down in buckets, Caw gave me the final buzzer.

"Fire one! . . . Fire two! . . . Fire three! . . . Fire four! . . . Fire five! . . . Fire six!"

As soon as the sixth torpedo went, Miles swung the ship around smartly, and I got a new final bearing from Caw for the stern shots. Then, before I could start firing,

WHAM! . . . WHAM! . . . WHAM! . . . WHAM!

Four hits from the bow tubes!

I got a new bearing from Caw.

"Fire seven! . . . Fire eight! . . . Fire nine! . . . Fire ten!"

Then, right on the stopwatch time, WHAM! . . . WHAM!

Six hits out of ten fired, with no visual bearings! Pretty good in any league.

Krapf was pretty sure he saw at least one flash through the driving rain. The quartermaster thought he saw two.

As we pulled out and began our reloads, both forward and aft, one of the heavies opened up with his deck gun. Judging from the size of the big, orange flashes, Krapf thought it was probably a five-inch gun.

If he was shooting at us in this visibility, he must have radar. No way he could see us. Every once in a while, the rain would blot him out altogether, and then we could hear the gunfire but couldn't see the flashes. No trouble hearing the explosions when the shells hit the water near us, however.

The escort we had passed close astern of while getting in firing position was now only seven hundred yards away. According to Caw, who was the only one who could tell, he was heading in our general direction but not directly for us. After he saw a few rounds from the big gun, we saw him. In a break from the rain, he flashed a strong searchlight in the direction of the firing ship and began to pull away. He had no desire to become a victim of friendly fire!

Depth charges were being dropped by every escort, as far as we could tell, and the convoy was scattering in all directions. At the same time, the visibility began to improve, and we could see at least two potential targets.

After a lot of weaving and ducking, we got a fairly good setup on one of the remaining heavies. We fired the four torpedoes remaining in the forward room. It was a short run, but we heard only one *WHAM!*

The bridge saw the explosion and then a blue flash that ran the entire length of the target's waterline. Almost instantly the harrowing sound of a human scream was heard—it was loud enough to carry across a half mile of water. (We were downwind, which doubtless helped.) This was followed by a long Klaxon alarm sound—probably their collision or torpedo alarm warning. Krapf saw the ship start to go bow-up and slide under the water. Wherever that one torpedo hit, it had found a vulnerable spot.

Without delay we picked up another heavy and began to make a rapid setup on him. We had only the four electrics left, and they were all in the after room—always a more difficult shot. But within less than ten minutes, Krapf had worked us into a satisfactory position on this unfortunate ship. The visibility had improved so much that the bridge could give me buzzers on this ship.

"Fire seven! . . . Fire eight! . . . Fire nine! . . . Fire ten!"

The run was longer than I liked, and I still had my doubts about the Mark XVIIIs. Our wait lasted more than two minutes, during which I was distinctly uneasy.

Then, *WHAM!* . . . *WHAM!* . . . *WHAM!* Three hits out of four—maybe I'd been wrong about the Mark XVIIIs.

The bridge could see this guy clearly. Within two minutes after the explosions, he was gone.

A depth charge barrage rumbled from all directions, once again like rolling thunder. But we were on the surface, headed away from the coast with all torpedoes expended. There is no sound quite so sweet as the sound of depth charges being dropped while you are on the surface and getting away at flank speed in the darkness.

We submerged about dawn. Everyone needed something to eat and some rest. This had been a sixteen-hour battle with plenty of tension. Batting around in that pitch-black night in driving rain while we were the target of a five-inch gun was not a prescription for calming the nerves.

All day long on June 30, as we remained submerged, we heard the sound of continual depth charging from the scene of our attacks, like the sound of artillery fire from some distant battlefield.

It was music to my ears.

That night (June 30–July 1) we threaded our way through the picket fence of the small islands north of Palawan and made our way into the Sulu Sea, bound for Fremantle. About the middle of the day on July 1, we heard pinging and saw the smoke of a Manila-bound convoy. We just had to go deep and let these guys go overhead. This was the second time the *Jack* had had to let a big convoy go by because it was out of torpedoes.

Nobody was too upset about it, however. We knew our new skipper had won his spurs on his first patrol. The *Jack* was still on track despite the roughing up that Dykers had gotten from our bosses after his last patrol.

En route to Fremantle I began to think more and more about how our bosses had assessed that patrol. No sinkings, indeed! What had they thought all those explosions and pyrotechnics from one of our targets had been—a celebration of the emperor's birthday?

Most of all, I still resented their implication that Dykers had chosen to make the long shots at night rather than to run ahead for a daytime periscope attack because he had had enough depth charging to last him for a while. How could anyone have gotten in there and slugged more than Dykers had? I was really ticked.

Fortunately, I kept all these thoughts to myself. But the treatment that Dykers got on his fourth patrol rankled deeply—and it still does to this day.

Well, in any case, Dykers had turned over a damned well trained boat, and it certainly had performed for its new skipper.

After a relatively uneventful trip down through the Makassar Strait and into the Java Sea north of Lombok, Krapf decided to try a new method of getting through the famous Lombok Strait. On each previous passage, we had noticed a strong southerly set through Lombok. He decided to take advantage of the set and go through submerged in the daytime.

At dawn we submerged north of the strait and started our transit. The huge mountain that dominates the eastern shore of Bali made a fine navigational mark for us all through the morning hours, as we took our bearings through the periscope.

Our navigation showed that with our propulsion set for a speed of about two and a half knots, we were making more than five over the ground. We were being helped home, all right. By three in the afternoon, we were clear of Lombok, having seen only one native sailboat during the entire time.

The trip south through the Indian Ocean was pleasant, with unseasonably good weather—after all, the Australian winter was getting well under way.

On the morning of July 14, we saw the welcome loom of Rottnest Light, and we knew we were home again.

Our welcome was much warmer than the one for our last patrol. Admiral Christie was there to meet us, and although he did not pin a Navy Cross on Art Krapf's chest on arrival, it was clear that the assessment of our patrol was going to justify that kind of an award. Our new skipper had really started with a bang.

We had pretty conclusive evidence on the sinking of four heavies and a certainty that at least three more had been damaged. This wasn't equal to the spectacular total of our third patrol, but it was away up there in the general picture.

Another invitation to The Bend of the Road was given, and at that luncheon Krapf was told he was being recommended for a Navy Cross, this time to go through regular channels.

The arrangements for our two-week refit by the relief crew were accomplished without a hitch. The crew was off to its various rest areas, and we were off to the Majestic. Once again I had been successful in the beer-for-liquor swap, and I made arrangements for the six cases to be delivered to the Tennis Club.

I was anxious to see Kathie, of course, but somehow I was reluctant to go. All through the patrol I had been wrestling with myself about the seriousness of what I was getting into. So many of my shipmates, and also good friends from other submarines, seemed to have developed much easier friendships with Australian girls—perhaps of more modest backgrounds. Yet these friendships were also more lighthearted. My shipmates could either take them or leave them, not feeling the least bit guilty about the friendships and not worrying about them when out on patrol. They were just a kind of comic relief, good fun for two weeks and then forgotten.

What was wrong with me? Why had I, a happily married man with a wife at home, let myself get into such a serious situation with this lovely girl from a wonderful family?

Maybe I was all wrong, I thought. Maybe Kathie had met someone while I was out on this patrol, someone who had made her forget all about Jim Calvert. Then I would be very sad for a time, but the problem would be solved. I half wished this would be the case—and half wished it would not.

When I went to see Kathie at her home, after dinner on our first night in, I realized that this was all empty speculation. Our meeting was as warm as ever. She looked so radiant and so happy to see me that all my somber intentions and worries went out the window. We were back where we had been six weeks ago.

The next night was a singing night at the Majestic. Kathie and I joined in for an hour or so, then went to another room where we could talk. Kathie said, "Why don't we sing that song about Honey that I like so much?"

> Honey, honey, bless your heart,
> You're the honey that I love so well.
> I done been true, my gal, to you,
> You're the honey that I love so well.

This old, old college song seemed to have special meaning for us both, and we sang it looking at each other and holding hands.

"I do love you so well; you know, don't you?"

"Yes, I do know, Jim; and I love you just as much in return."

After this exchange I felt guilty again, more guilty than I had ever felt about my friendship with Kathie. We had never used such words before, and now that they had been said, they were awfully hard to unsay. But I put all this aside, at least for the moment. I was being Scarlett O'Hara again.

After a long pause without any words, we changed the subject and talked about the submarine news. When the *Jack* returned from its latest patrol, I learned that, short as it was, this period had seen the loss of four more of our submarines. All of them had held friends, two of them classmates. Kathie had known several of them.

In another way this was not a change of subject because the frame of mind generated by such news had much to do with our outlook and our care for each other. Significantly, I never talked to any of my *Jack* shipmates about these losses. But I had to talk to someone about them, and Kathie inevitably was that person. The more we talked, the more closely we clung to what we had with each other.

I suppose it was a sign of softness on my part, but I wanted to share my anguish, sorrow, and worry with her—and she seemed to want to share it with me.

From the earliest days at Electric Boat, the *Jack* and *Harder* wardrooms had been good friends. The *Harder* wardroom was an unusually talented one. Her skipper, Sam Dealey, later to be a Congressional Medal of Honor winner, was a warm and friendly man who seemed to take a special interest in his junior officers. His exec, John (called Jason) Maurer, was a particularly talented man with considerable war patrol experience. The third officer was Frank Lynch, the five-striper (regimental commander) in the class of 1938 and a man who was looked on by many as a future chief of Naval Operations. The fourth officer was Sam Logan, Annapolis class of 1942 and, as previously mentioned, a Submarine School classmate of mine. He had stood number one in his academy class and also number one in our Submarine School class. He was *Harder*'s TDC operator, and so we had much in common to talk about.

Sam was a brilliant young man, and many of the ideas I used in my own TDC work were originally gotten from Sam—both in New London during our building period and later in the Pacific.

All of these men were friends, and the *Jack* and *Harder* had a friendly competition going during all of 1943 and 1944. We were squadron mates, and we both were cursed with the awful HOR engines.

Harder was tough competition. She early on made a top place for herself in submarine annals. On patrol after patrol, she turned in extraordinary performances, sinking four or five ships on each one. During 1944 *Harder* developed a tremendous reputation as a destroyer killer. On Dealey's fifth war patrol, assigned the area around the Japanese fleet anchorage at Tawitawi Island, he sank five destroyers in almost recklessly aggressive attacks.

On this patrol *Harder* sighted a large Japanese task force, including three battleships and four cruisers with screening destroyers. An escort aircraft spotted *Harder*'s periscope and vectored one of the screening destroyers toward her at thirty-five knots. Dealey waited at periscope depth until the range was very short, then fired three torpedoes on a down-the-throat shot before starting down to go deep. There were two hits, and the destroyer exploded with violent force just as it was over *Harder,* then only at eighty feet. The blast shook *Harder* violently, but the Japanese destroyer was gone.

This was, doubtless, one of the great patrols of the war. Not only did Dealey wipe out these badly needed destroyers, but he also transmitted reports on the movements of the Japanese fleet that were of great value to Admiral Spruance in his planning for the Battle of the Philippine Sea. In addition, *Harder*'s actions around the Tawitawi anchorage entrance were so vigorous that they convinced Admiral Toyoda, the senior Japanese officer there, that the anchorage was surrounded by submarines. As a result, he had Admiral Ozawa's Mobile Fleet leave a day early on its way to the Battle of the Philippine Sea. Many believed that this upset the Japanese timing and contributed to their defeat in that battle.

Rarely had a single war patrol received such unrestrained praise and enthusiasm as *Harder*'s fifth. All of the American submarines were, quite naturally, in competition with each other and somewhat reluctant to make wild praises of others. This was an exception, however. Every submariner in the Navy tipped his cap to the *Harder* for this one.

Naturally the stories grew about such a determined and aggressive skipper. There were even wild (and untrue) tales about Dealey intentionally flaunting his periscope near destroyers to get them to make a run at him so he could make the now-famous down-the-throat shot.

Of course, fame carries its price. When Admiral Christie decided, in 1944, that he wanted some firsthand war patrol experience, he arranged to meet *Harder* in Darwin (in extreme northern Australia, less than six hundred miles southeast of Timor) and extend its fifth war patrol for about three weeks to take him into the war zone. This move was not overwhelmingly popular with the *Harder* crew. After the wild ride they had already had on that patrol with Sam Dealey, and having shot all their torpedoes, they were looking forward to the peace and quiet of Fremantle, not to a fresh load of torpedoes and a three-week extension of their already exhausting patrol.

The patrol with Christie was such a success, however, that when it was over, Sam Dealey didn't get just an invitation to The Bend of the Road for lunch; he was invited to stay there for his entire two-week rest period. To my knowledge he was the only skipper ever to be so honored.

But none of this unmatchable success harmed the relationship between the two wardrooms. After our fifth patrols, we stayed at the Majestic together, shared meals and bull sessions, and sat in front of the fire singing. Some of my best memories of the Majestic are tied to the *Harder* officers and our good times together there, many of them shared with Kathie, who knew all the *Harder* wardroom well.

In many of these bull sessions with the *Harder* folks during that July of 1944, the subject was whether Dealey would make the sixth patrol or whether, instead, the boat would be turned over to her exec, Frank Lynch. Frank wisely stayed clear of all these discussions. They were mainly between Sam Logan and me and the other junior officers. We were just gossiping, so to speak, as junior officers love to do. In most cases they have been given no inside information, so they don't have any secrets to keep and feel free to speculate.

Speculation ceased, however, when we finally got the official information. Even for the most successful skippers, the policy was usually five patrols and then back to new construction. Admiral Christie, however, gave the famous skipper his choice, and Dealey said he wanted to make one more patrol. Jason Maurer had already been detached to command his own submarine, and Frank Lynch was to be left in for *Harder*'s sixth patrol with the understanding that he would take command on its return. My friend Sam Logan became the exec and, I think, was moved from the TDC, where he had been since building days at Electric Boat.

If true, this was an important and perhaps fateful move. If there were to be any more down-the-throat shots—and the chances of more of them with this ultra-aggressive skipper were great—they were going to place a heavy burden on the new TDC operator. Not many of them could handle the tremendous pressure of a destroyer hurtling down on them, only a few hundred yards away, without making a mistake in the last few seconds. In effect, the skipper was betting the life of his ship and all in it on those torpedoes hitting their target. One slight slip on the TDC, or any kind of misunderstanding between skipper and TDC operator, could mean death for all on the submarine. I am by no means sure I could have done it. Sam had proved that he could.

As the *Jack* prepared to go out on one of its training days for its sixth patrol, we all went down to the dock to wave *Harder* off as it departed on *its* sixth. All of the *Harder* officers were either on the bridge or on deck, each wearing an Australian Army hat with the brim pinned up on the left side in the matchless Australian fashion. From Dealey on down to the youngest ensign, they looked tanned, handsome, and unbeatable.

The last few days with Kathie were very special. Rightly or wrongly, I had given up all guilt feelings for the present, and we just went right ahead and had a good time. We went dancing, we went to church, we played tennis, we sang at the Majestic, and we talked enough to fill a thousand books. We even tackled a few chemistry lessons, in which, I was pleased to note, Kathie was doing much better. Her professor had even asked her if she was getting some special tutoring. She didn't tell me her response.

And so I prepared to go on my sixth patrol, with nothing resolved except that Kathie and I cared deeply for each other and that there was no chance it could ever work out happily for either one of us. So why didn't we just drop the whole thing?

Because both of us believed that, whether we liked to think about it or not, we might be enjoying each other's company for the last time, and we were not going to miss it—no matter what.

10

A Gallant Retreat

Since our next patrol, the sixth, was to be Krapf's second, our bosses no longer took any pity on us, and we suffered a heavy hit, with some twenty-five veterans being sent back to new construction. Naturally they did not want our recently acquired men; as a result we kept losing well-trained and experienced sailors.

Fortunately, Jack O'Brien felt rested enough to rejoin (I'm not sure he really liked remaining in port while all his old buddies went to sea), but to balance this, Earl Archer felt, and looked, worn out. He took Obie's place as division engineer. So the wardroom remained perilously low on wartime experience.

To show how we had been stripped down by these high-command raids on our personnel, Miles Refo and I were the only two officers remaining from the commissioning wardroom. We had only four chief petty officers remaining from the commissioning crew, but they were dandies. Miles and I agreed that our bosses would get them away from us only over our dead bodies. First, there was Gunner Lynes, Chief of the Boat and a priceless leader and morale builder.

Probably second in importance was Terence J. McCabe, the head of all the engine room gang. McCabe was not only technically superb, he was a great leader and a fine example of the very best in our World War II submarine crew members. In my opinion the enginemen had the toughest job on board. They had to stand their watches in a terribly noisy environment (earplugs were necessary); they had to accommodate the engines' continual need for care and attention; and when a breakdown occurred (though much less frequently now with the GM Wintons), they had to make the repairs, sometimes in weather so rough that they could barely stand up.

These men needed good on-the-job, ever-present leadership, and Terence McCabe provided it.

Bob Craig, the third of our plank-owners, as commissioning men were called, was a leading electrician and another exceptionally fine man. As I have said, he and his running mate, Sandy Sanderlin, our fourth remaining commissioner, were the battle station controller operators, in charge of all the main propulsion, whether on the surface or submerged.

Miles frequently went to the chiefs for opinions on how things were going and for ideas on how we might improve them. Gunner Lynes had made an important suggestion before the fifth patrol, Krapf's first.

"Mr. Calvert's always talking to the bridge during a night attack, and down here in the control room, I can hear most of it and have a pretty good idea of what's going on.[1] But the rest of the ship doesn't have a clue. Isn't there some way we could rig that circuit so it would go into the ship's announcing system and everyone could hear?"

Miles and the skipper approved the idea if we could work it out electrically so that it did not in any way interfere with the present communication setup between bridge and TDC. Bob Craig and his men were able to do this, and consequently, during all the attacks of Krapf's first patrol, my communications with the bridge had gone throughout the ship by loudspeaker.

By and large this was a success, but there were one or two dissenters. One of them came to Miles with this comment:

"Hearin' that talk between Mr. Calvert and the bridge is scarin' the livin' shit outta me. I was happier when I didn't know what was goin' on but could only imagine it. Do we hafta have it?"

The overwhelming sentiment, however, was to continue the shipwide announcements during attacks. Men are generally more afraid of what they don't know than of what they do know. And, after all, with four main engines roaring away, quiet in the rest of the boat was not a factor. (The announcing system volume in the engine rooms was already set high enough so that the men could hear anything said over that system with the engines running.)

Once again Commander Warder was our training officer, and as always he did a superb job. He was able to set up a Royal Aus-

---

[1] Gunner Lynes's battle station was in the control room, on the hydraulic manifold, the center of diving control.

tralian Navy cruiser as our main target, and he arranged for two Royal Australian Navy ships and two U.S. Navy ships to act as screens. We were able to make both night surface and daytime periscope approaches on this group; it was a really good workout, despite the miserably rough conditions in the Rottnest Island areas.

Perhaps I was getting old and grouchy, but it seemed to me that the new men from the relief crew were softer and greener than ever before. However, tightening our belts and taking a deep breath, we went to work on them. With most of them seasick, as usual, we hammered in the importance of lookout and of getting under in thirty-five seconds or less. Slowly but surely they began to round into shape. But when it was over, I asked myself, How many more times can Miles and I do this? It is getting to be an awfully old story, and it seems harder each time to bring these guys up to the necessary level.

More than once during this training period, I broke out Beetle Roach's words about training and used them to reinvigorate myself. I sincerely wanted to live through this war.

Miles was a tower of strength during this whole time. If he was ever tired or discouraged, he never let anyone know it. I was beginning to understand the importance of a true professional naval officer amongst all the beginners and amateurs.

On August 6, the day after we saw the *Harder* depart on patrol with the Australian Army hats, and just about three weeks after our return from our fifth patrol, the *Jack* once again set out to do battle with the Japanese. It was clear that the bosses were driving the horses pretty hard, but I could see the reasons for it. The war was going well; we really had the Japanese on the run, and this was no time to ease up on them. They had lost the New Guinea campaign and were losing the Marianas. Their backs were beginning to be put to the wall. Any oil or refinery products that we could deny them now would really be a significant contribution to the overall war effort.

Also, the occupation of the Philippines was the next big target for the Allies. We knew that the sinking of any ships loaded with troops, supplies, and ammunition for the defense of the Philippines would be a special help right now.

As had become standard practice, we made the transit to Exmouth Gulf in company with another U.S. submarine bound for its patrol area. We exchanged practice approaches, both night and day, and once again tried to educate our lookouts on what a real periscope looks like up close and out far. We refueled at Exmouth on August 9.

Our orders on this patrol were different, however. Instead of proceeding directly from Exmouth Gulf to our patrol area, we traveled up the northwest coast of Australia to the port of Darwin, located in the Beagle Gulf almost at the northern extremity of Australia's Northern Territory.

Darwin had two claims to fame. First, it was named after the famous English natural scientist, the father of the theory of evolution. The name of the gulf came, of course, from the Royal Navy warship in which he made his famous voyage, HMS *Beagle*.

Darwin achieved further fame in the beginning of the war. In the early spring of 1942 the Japanese started two major thrusts down into the Dutch East Indies. The western group came down through the South China Sea and captured Borneo and Sumatra. The eastern group came down to Celebes, Ceram, and Timor. Admiral Nagumo's carrier force, fresh from its strike on Pearl Harbor, was in general support of both groups.

The only resistance against these powerful forces was a patchwork command called ABDA (American-British-Dutch-Australian). ABDA had difficulties from the beginning, due mainly to the sharply divided goals of its partners. The Americans wanted to do everything possible to strike back from Pearl Harbor and revitalize their Asiatic Fleet; the British wanted mainly to preserve their important possession at Singapore; the Dutch wanted to save their priceless oil and refinery resources throughout the East Indies; and the Australians wanted to prevent the invasion of their country.

The ABDA command and what was left of the U.S. Asiatic Fleet were headquartered in Surabaya, on Java. The only real base of support for the Asiatic Fleet was Darwin. It also supplied some support to the ABDA forces in general.

After the occupation of Timor, Admiral Nagumo's planes dealt quickly with Darwin, damaging it severely and forcing its abandonment as a support base for any forces—U.S. or ABDA. Not long after this, ABDA fell apart as a meaningful military organization. The U.S. forces withdrew, some of them to Fremantle, and Darwin was left to lick its wounds in relative peace.

When we arrived in Darwin in August of 1944, any threat to the area from the Japanese was essentially gone, but the scars of battle were evident everywhere. There were four or five sunken merchant ships with their rusting bows or sterns still protruding from the waters of Port Darwin. Doubtless there were many others totally sunk by Admiral Nagumo's raids. There were still damaged warehouses and other structures ashore. Darwin was not only a true frontier town but a war-torn one at that.

By 10:00 A.M. on August 15, we were tied up to the dock in Darwin and refueling. After some repairs and tune-up on our SJ radar, we were under way about ten that night, heading for the pass east of Timor and further battle with the Japanese.

We worked our way through the chain of islands east of Timor and then through the Banda Sea into the Molucca Passage. Through all of this period we had mirror-calm seas and cloudless weather. Being so close to these Japanese-controlled islands we had to submerge during the day and do our transiting at night.

During these nights, while threading our way through the islands, the phosphorescence of the sea was scary. Our bow wave seemed to put out so much light that it looked like a huge, blue neon sign. And the tiny sea creatures putting out this light were so disturbed by our passage that they persisted in illuminating the sea all through our long wake. I couldn't believe that we were not being observed by some watcher on the islands we were passing so close aboard. If they saw us, however, they either were not friendly to the Japanese or were too slow in getting their messages through to do us any harm.

In due time we entered the Celebes Sea, right in the heart of the East Indies. It was to be our main area of action. We had a number of quiet days here, with only an occasional dive for a patrol plane. Now that we were clear of the islands, we did all of our patrolling in the new mode—on the surface using the high periscope. The Celebes Sea, east of Borneo and south of the Philippines, is roughly circular in shape and is over three hundred miles in diameter—much too large to cover effectively with submerged patrolling. Here also we had smooth seas and cloudless skies, and being just a few miles north of the equator, it was *hot*.

This daytime surface patrolling increased the pressure on the lookouts considerably, but we all knew it was necessary for the greatly increased scope of vision it gave us.

Increased scope of vision or no, we had a long, dull period when we arrived in the Celebes Sea. Day followed day, night followed night with no contacts. Our earlier patrols had been so full of important contacts that this was a relatively new experience for us.

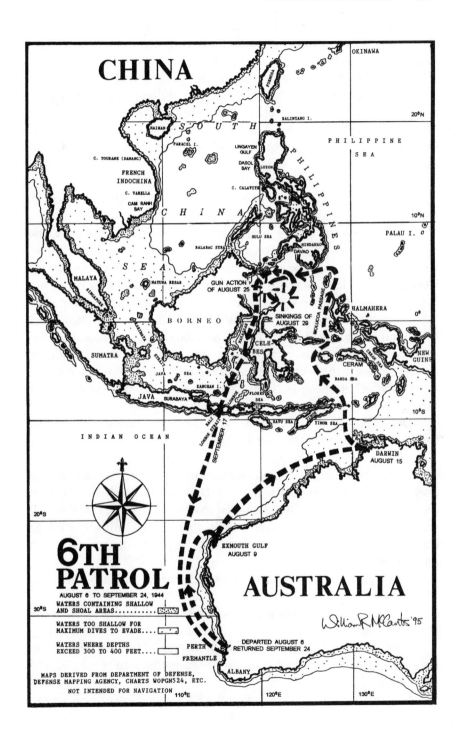

Nevertheless, we fell into that dull routine that is the peculiar property of ships long at sea: events fall into a rhythm, and time passes in an event-free blur.

The most exciting events of the day were seeing what was for dinner and enjoying the evening bridge game in the wardroom. Since I had the eight to twelves, I usually missed out on the bridge game. But once in a while when I got down from watch at midnight, the game was still going on, though without its fourth, who had gone up to relieve me.

"Come on Jim—just one rubber. That's all. We promise."

Protesting that I was too tired to play, I would sit down, the cards would be dealt, and there would go part of my precious sleep. Occasionally when the bridge game really got going hot and heavy, the next thing I'd know, Domingo would be coming in to set up for breakfast. The night would be gone with no sleep, and after breakfast it would be time for my morning eight to twelve on that burning-hot bridge. Oh well, we were young and strong.

Occasionally something would happen that was at least good for a laugh. Danny Deaver, as the new boy on the block, had the midwatches, so he was my relief after my eight to twelves. Since we always relieved the watch fifteen minutes early, it was the custom to call the relief about half before the hour so that he would have time to get dressed and get a cup of coffee.

One evening, at exactly 11:30 P.M., I called down to the control room, "Please call Mr. Deaver for the watch."

The response came quickly and reassuringly, "Aye aye, sir."

I stretched a bit and yawned comfortably, thinking of hopping into that nice soft bunk. I was tired. Danny had been very prompt on previous reliefs, so when he failed to appear at 11:45 I was mildly surprised but didn't think too much about it. At midnight I was getting a bit perturbed but didn't want to let the control room watch know how I felt.

At 12:15 I called down to the watch below, "Please check on Mr. Deaver."

In a moment the answer came back. "He's up, sir; not in his bunk, and there's no one in the wardroom. Must be in the head."

I thought this was logical, though it seemed he was being a bit long. At about 12:30 I called down, "Please check in the head and see if he is OK."

In a few minutes, "He's not in the head, sir. Don't know where he is."

"Well, look more carefully for him—he's got to be on board," I said somewhat grumpily.

In about five minutes, "We found him, sir. He was asleep in the pantry refrigerator." All this with a chuckle and much laughter in the background.

The wardroom pantry was adjacent to but closed off from the wardroom itself. Domingo always left some lemonade or iced tea in the little pantry refrigerator (it was about three feet high) for the night watch. Danny had knelt down to get into the refrigerator, put his head down on his arm, which was resting on the top shelf, and fallen sound asleep. He might have dozed there all night had someone not found him hidden away in that cozy nook.

He might also have gotten a bit chilly.

We had a new steering device on this patrol. Realizing the importance of constant helming, we had been using this method of zigzag for some time. We had been doing it all by hand, swinging slowly back and forth about thirty degrees to either side of the base course. Now, however, we had an electrically driven cam that gave the helmsman a constantly changing course with very little effort on his part. All he had to do was follow the ordered course on his compass repeater. Thus, the cam would slowly and automatically change the course of the submarine. It would go sometimes ten degrees away from the base course, sometimes thirty, and sometimes forty—but always constantly changing. With the cam the submarine was never on a steady course, not even for a moment. The device repeated the cycle only about once an hour, infrequently enough to prevent a submerged enemy submarine from ever determining the pattern.

On August 25 we were in the Celebes Sea, not far from the northern branch of Celebes island itself. About noon the quartermaster of the watch, on the bridge as an extra lookout, sighted a periscope close to our stern, about fifteen hundred yards away. It was a smooth sea, and the periscope was showing quite a feather. The sighting was confirmed by Danny Deaver, the OOD, who had just relieved me. Following doctrine, Danny put him exactly astern, put on flank speed, and watched like a hawk for torpedo tracks. None.

We were all certain that this Japanese submarine had been making an approach on us but had been frustrated by our constant-helm cam and had ended up astern of us. This incident dramatically drove home something we had all known but hadn't paid enough attention to—patrolling on the surface in enemy waters in the day-time greatly increased the risk of submarine attack. We had placed such heavy emphasis on the necessity of spotting patrol planes early in this situation that we had not focused on our greatly increased vulnerability to submarine attack.

Needless to say, we were believers now. We changed our procedures so that the three lookouts would continue to look for patrol planes, while the quartermaster of the watch and the OOD would look only for periscopes. It goes without saying that we continued to use the new constant-helm cam—we were all convinced that it had saved our lives.

About 3:45 that same afternoon, the assistant OOD on the high periscope watch sighted just the tops of a ship to the south. We closed him on the surface until we could get a good TDC track. It showed that he was coming our way, and we could close him successfully submerged. So down we went. As we got closer, we could see that he was a small coastal freighter, unescorted and too small for a torpedo attack. He had a fairly good-sized gun forward and some obvious machine gun emplacements. After a period of careful thought, Krapf decided to battle surface.

We surfaced about two and a half miles away and took great care in setting our range. Our first shot was a miss, but so close that Caw could not get a spot on the radar screen—splash and target merged into one pip. It took us three more shots before we got a hit, but when we did it brought down one of his two masts and the radio antenna strung between them.

As we got closer, he opened fire with his forward gun. We realized that our safety depended on getting some hits on him in a hurry. A couple of near splashes drove this point home forcefully.

In my hurry to get up with the battle surface crew, I had forgotten my earplugs, an important safeguard when you are sitting about ten inches from the gun barrel. This was no time, however, to be sending down for forgotten items. We kept firing as fast as we were able. We were getting hit after hit—both masts were down and a fire had started on his deck.

Our Japanese friend was not finished, however. I had noticed his two machine guns on our side blazing away but had not paid too much attention as we were too far away for them to be very effective. All of a sudden, I heard a yelp of pain and saw one of the ammunition handlers holding his arm. It was Mayo, one of Domingo's assistants in the wardroom. Big and strong, he was a first-rate ammunition handler.

His arm was bleeding, and it was clear that he had been hit by the machine-gun fire. He was the first *Jack* sailor to be wounded in the war. He said it was just a grazing shot and wanted to stay up and continue the fight, but we sent him down below for bandaging and better examination by our pharmacist's mate, Chief Bill Tucker. It was indeed just a scratch—harder on his shirt than it was on him—but a few inches to the left, and it could have been serious.

By now the entire forward deck of the freighter was covered with flames, and the firing from his large gun had stopped. The flames were putting out such huge billows of black smoke that I believe he had been carrying more than just his own supply of fuel. When the larger gun stopped firing, we came somewhat closer to our target and could see that the crew was abandoning ship. They had put a small boat in the water and were diving overboard to get to it. All machine-gun fire had stopped. The battle was over.

I had been so seized with what we were doing, and so anxious to get as many hits as possible before the freighter could do us any harm, that I had forgotten all about my earplugs and the pain in my right ear. Now I felt it, and in spades.

"You've got blood running out of your right ear, Mr. Calvert. Looks like you might have a broken eardrum," from Gunner Lynes with obvious concern. I put my hand up to my ear. Sure enough, blood.

As our target was gurgling its last gasp before going to Davy Jones's locker, we saw that all, or most, of the crew had gotten into the small boat and were pulling away from us as fast as they could go in the smooth sea of that day. We submerged.

When the diving officer put pressure in the boat to test the seal, it was as though a red-hot poker was being put into my right ear. I went to see Chief Tucker without delay. We had no doctor on board, but Tucker was a mighty good substitute.

He looked at the eardrum and said, "You have a small tear in there, all right, but I think it will heal pretty quickly. The main problem will be the pressure in the boat. In the meantime here is something to help with the pain."

About three days later—almost all of which was spent on the surface, to the great relief of my ear—the high periscope watch sighted distant smoke to the north. All we could tell was that the bearing of the smoke kept changing to the east, so we started off to the north-east to get into position either for a periscope attack or, failing that, a night surface attack later.

Before long we had to submerge for a patrol plane, and as a result of being down, we lost sight of the smoke. We surfaced as soon as we could, but he was not in sight, and we had no radar contact. It was now getting dark. We had no recourse except to head for his most logical position, and hope.

Had we lost this guy, the only worthwhile target we had found yet on this patrol? There was gloom on the bridge and in the conning tower as we continued the search, without results. But the gloom turned to joy when, about 8:00 P.M., at the start of my watch, Charley Caw called out from the radar, "Got him! There he is, dead ahead at 25,500 yards!"

We had made contact at about thirteen miles in just about the location we had projected. I called the skipper and set the battle stations.

We got a good TDC and plot track on him and found he was zigzagging around a base course taking him to the east. As we got closer, Caw said that the formation consisted of one large ship, one good-sized escort on his starboard bow, and a smaller escort on his port bow that he could see "only from time to time."

There was a half moon, due to set about midnight. While waiting for that, we continued to work ahead of the heavy to get into position for an attack. All of a sudden, the formation changed course to the north. We didn't think we had spooked them since we had not been closer than eight miles or so, but there was a possibility they had radar detection equipment and had picked up our SJ radiations. Had he decided to head for the base at Davao in the Philippines?

We continued our tracking, and in about an hour the formation reversed course in a wide, slow circle to head roughly south toward Celebes island. The moon had set by now.

"Looks like they've decided to run for shelter in Celebes," said Krapf on the intercom. "How far before they can reach a port there?"

After a quick check, Miles said they had nearly sixty miles to go. It would be well past sunrise before they could get in.

"Good, we'll have time. Let's go after them," from the bridge.

The large target, apparently a supply ship of some kind, and his large escort were both in sight from the bridge now. If Bennett had been with us, I think he could have seen the small escort also; but Bennett wasn't there. The bridge seemed uneasily silent without him. His singing during attacks had been our trademark.

We were attempting to work in behind the port escort and had gotten to about three thousand yards when the whole formation zigged right toward us.

"Do you think they've sighted us? Have they changed speed?" came somewhat alarmed questions from Krapf. Both Kent, on the plot, and I checked as quickly as we could.

"It looks like a routine zig to us. No change in formation, and no change in speed," I reported.

"Nothing to do but show him our full broadside and pull out," from Krapf. We showed the escort our full-beam view at about twenty-eight hundred yards and kept the speed down to minimize the wake. I'll admit I held my breath and expected the next report from the bridge to be of gunfire from the near escort. Had the phosphorescence here been like that in the islands, there would have been no doubt about it.

It was, however, pitch dark with almost no phosphorescence, and we were not sighted. We pulled out to a safe distance without mishap. In about six minutes, the whole formation dutifully zigged to the right and gave us a fairly good shot. The zig was forty degrees, which put them a little farther away than we wanted. But this was no time to be choosy.

"We'll shoot four at the big fellow and two at the big escort. All from the bow tubes, Miles," from Krapf.

The buzzer giving me the bearing on the heavy sounded.

"Fire one! . . . Fire two! . . . Fire three! . . . Fire four!"

The buzzer sounded again for the big escort.

"Fire five! . . . Fire six!"

Sonar reported all six fish to be running hot, straight, and normal. Krapf swung around with full rudder and put our stern on the near escort. In the conning tower, we were glued to the stopwatch to see how we had done. The first four seemed right on as we shot them, but the two to the escort were rather hastily set in and showed more of a change from the generated bearing than I had expected. Not a good sign, usually.

"Mr. Calvert, I think that escort was changing course as we fired the last two," from Caw on the radar.

WHAM! . . . WHAM! Two hits, right on time for the big cargo ship—but apparently no hits on the escort.

"Wow! That flame must have gone up a hundred feet in the air—big yellow flame!" from Krapf.

While opening the range as fast as we could, we tracked all the ships in the formation. The big fellow was dead in the water, but both escorts were streaking away from us—they were going in exactly the wrong direction! They must have assumed the attack had come from the opposite side. Apparently they thought we were still on the surface because they were not dropping depth charges.

Faced with this situation, Krapf did a very aggressive thing— he turned around and started after the escorts. When he made this decision, we were about three miles away from the stopped, burning freighter. The escorts were roughly the same distance on the other side of the fire, and pulling away—the larger escort at about seventeen knots. We put on flank speed to attempt to close the range on the fleeing watchdogs. Were they running away, or did they still think they were chasing us?

As we shot past the burning cargo ship, we saw it beginning a regular Fourth of July show with rockets, shooting stars, and major internal explosions. The ship was literally exploding as it sat there in the water. It must have been a heavily loaded ammunition ship. Nothing else could have explained such a series of spectacular pyrotechnics.

"That's a load of ammunition that won't get used against us— or against anyone! Good going, Jim," exclaimed Miles as he laughed and slapped me on the back.

Refo was not a very demonstrative guy, and this was a truly exceptional outburst for him. It made me feel pretty good.

Suddenly the big escort slowed to about eleven knots, a big decrease. What gives? Then, almost immediately, he turned around and headed nearly for us.

"Who the hell is chasing who?" grunted Krapf from the bridge, somewhat ungrammatically but very pithily. He swung the *Jack* around and put our stern on our new target.

It was soon clear that the big escort was not chasing anyone— at least not anyone on the surface. He kept on at eleven knots and started pinging. Apparently he was convinced we had submerged— or perhaps had been submerged all the time.

As he kept plodding along at the same speed, now about five miles away from his still fiercely burning former charge, we began to work into position for a shot at him. The natural thing would have been to pull out for a stern shot, but his course put him too far away for that, so Krapf swung around for a bow shot.

With the torpedo run just a little over two thousand yards, we shot four bow tubes with the fish set at ten feet on a good track.

WHAM! . . . WHAM!

Two for four—not bad with all the excitement that had been going on.

Then, about three seconds after the last of our hits, came the loudest explosion I heard in the war. Even though we were on the surface, it shook the *Jack* from stem to stern like a dog shaking a rabbit.

"Good Lord! The whole stern of the target has disappeared!" came from the skipper. Krapf was not much for profanity.

I tried to explain briefly to the crew over the announcing system what had happened, and to assure them that we were not damaged. Undoubtedly some of them thought our last hour had come.

"I can see searchlights back aft on the target, looking at the stern—or where it used to be," came from Krapf.

Unbelievably the target was still afloat. He was dead in the water but not sinking. The bridge could see, and the radar confirmed, that he was smaller but still floating firmly. Krapf decided on a killer shot.

We moved in to about a thousand yards and let it go at the stopped target—a can't miss situation.

"Torpedo is running erratic!" came from sonar.

This was hard to believe; it had been so long since we had had any torpedo failure for which we did not have at least a partial explanation. But clearly it was true—there was no explosion.

Krapf was now the one shaking the rabbit, however, and he was not about to give up. We pulled out and shot two more from the stern tubes. It was easy because the target was dead in the water.

WHAM! . . . WHAM!

Both had hit, and he sank almost immediately, in plain view of everyone on the bridge. He sank, literally, in less than fifteen seconds.

We reasoned that the ship must have been a minelayer. There was no other explanation for the tremendous explosion shortly after his second hit. We knew also that the Japanese frequently used minelayers to escort larger ships.

We then headed back to the vicinity of the burning ammunition ship. As we closed it, it suddenly disappeared both from sight of the bridge and on radar. Both of the two main ships had been dispatched. We never learned where the smaller escort went—probably back to the safety of a Celebes port, as fast as he could travel.

We secured the battle stations about five in the morning and submerged to give everyone a rest. This had been another all-afternoon and all-night session, for a total of some fifteen hours with no food and no rest. I was tired out and hungry. This time, however, after some breakfast and a short nap, I took my regular eight-to-twelve watch. I knew that Miles was as tired, or more tired, than I was. However, we stayed submerged for the day, expecting the bloodhounds to be out after us during the day.

Perhaps as a sign of how far the Japanese ASW forces had been drawn down, no one showed up. No patrol plane, no ASW craft—nothing. We were all surprised but weren't complaining.

We had now shot thirteen torpedoes, and had eleven left—plenty for lots of excitement if we could find some targets. But targets were scarce in the Celebes Sea in August and September of 1944.

Day after day went by with no contacts, not even a patrol plane. The sea seemed empty to us. We did all of our patrolling on the surface. Using the high periscope during the day and the radar at night, we were giving the area good coverage. There just wasn't anything there.

The *Jack* had never had a patrol terminated by the time limit in the operation order. On the first, third, fourth, and fifth patrols we had fired all of our useful torpedoes. Our second patrol had been terminated early by engine failure. But here we were, with eleven good torpedoes, patiently waiting for the end of our assigned time while we scoured an empty sea.

During this long period of empty search, I began to notice a change in our skipper. Always a bit tense, he had nevertheless conducted his attacks with coolness and determination. But something was eating at him, and I could not tell what. I talked to Miles about it, and he said he had noticed it too but didn't think it was anything important.

I did. Night after night, I would come down from the eight to twelve and find Krapf alone in the wardroom, smoking his ever-present cigar and just staring into space. He was not reading, not listening to Tokyo Rose, just sitting. He almost never participated in the evening bridge game, and while it was going on he kept to his room.

One night after coming off watch at midnight, I sat down with him in the wardroom and ate one of the snacks that Domingo always left for us.

"Jim, I don't know what I would have done on this patrol without you and Miles."

This was a very courteous and nice—but highly unusual—statement for a wartime skipper to make to one of his officers.

"We've just done our job, sir. We're all a team."

"Yes, but I think you two are doing more than your share. You're taking part of my load."

That ended the conversation for that night, but I noticed again and again that no matter what time of the night I was up, our skipper was always there, usually alone, in the wardroom, smoking his cigar.

Finally the day came when we were due to head for the barn, torpedoes left or not. We threaded our way down through the Molucca Passage and through the phosphorescent seas of the islands near Timor. We dove only once, for an early-evening patrol plane, and even then neither the lookout nor the OOD were absolutely sure it *was* a plane.

"Could have been a frigate bird," said Kent, referring to the large tropical bird that was famous for being mistaken for a plane due to its habit of soaring for long periods of time without moving its large, black wings.

When we were clear of the islands and were transiting along the northwest coast of Australia, the skipper said he wanted to see Miles and me in his room. We came in and sat down on the bunk while he took the only chair in the room. Aside from the bunk, which was full-length and looked comfortable, the room consisted only of a space about four feet by four feet, with a fold-down desk and a fold-up wash basin. Both could not be used at the same time.

Krapf shut the door carefully and told us there were a couple of things he wanted to tell us. He made it clear they would be for our ears only and were not to be talked about with anyone else on board before we arrived in Fremantle.

"The first thing I want to say is that I am recommending you, Miles, for command of a submarine now. You're ready for it in every respect. This means that you will be detached at the end of this patrol.

"Secondly, I'm going to recommend that you relieve Miles as executive officer, Jim. You're pretty young for it, but you've had the experience, and I believe you can handle it now.

"Last of all, I have given it very careful thought and intend to ask to be relieved of command after we return to Fremantle. Although I don't believe I have given any outward signs of it, I am just worn out. I can't take the responsibility for all these lives unless I feel that I am in tip-top condition—and I'm not.

"Frankly, Miles, I just don't think I could do it again without you, and I'm not going to hold you back just so that you can bolster me up on patrol. I believe there are other things I can do to help the war effort, and I am going to do my best to do them."

Long pause. This was a lot of news to absorb from one speech.

"Well, you certainly haven't given any sign of it," said Miles, not altogether truthfully. We had both noticed his strained and withdrawn condition. Whether any of the other people on board had noticed it, I will never know.

"I'm grateful to have the chance to be the exec here. I'll give it my best, sir," was all I could muster.

"I've served with a number of skippers by now, and I've never known a finer or more dedicated man than you, sir," added Miles.

"Thanks, Miles."

We got up, shook hands with our skipper, and walked out, both of us feeling deep admiration for the manly way in which Krapf had handled a terribly difficult matter.

Our transit down the western coast of Australia was uneventful and, considering the winter weather, reasonably smooth. On September 24, just forty-nine days after we had departed on patrol, we saw the loom of Rottnest Light. It had been the *Jack's* longest patrol.

Our reception at Fremantle was warm, but not unusually so. We had done well with the only worthwhile contacts we had, but there had been many other much more productive patrols during the same period.

Meanwhile, the whole atmosphere of Fremantle was dominated by one devastating piece of news: The *Harder* had been lost while we were on patrol.

I can still remember where I was standing and how I felt when I heard this news. It came as the worst shock of the war. Not only had I lost good friends and men that I admired, but our finest, our most aggressive, our most battleworthy submarine had fallen to the Japanese. I could not believe it.

Slowly, bit by bit, I got most of the story. Dealey had been put in command of a three-ship wolf pack—*Harder, Haddo,* and *Hake,* all Squadron Twelve boats, all based in Fremantle. Chester Nimitz, Jr., was in command of *Haddo,* and *Hake* had a new skipper, Frank Haylor. *Harder* had left Fremantle on August 5, the day we had seen them with the Australian Army hats.

After a series of very successful attacks in the vicinity of Manila, Chester Nimitz in the *Haddo* was out of torpedoes; he told the others he would go to the advance base at Biak island, New Guinea, to pick up more torpedoes. This would take him quite a while since Biak was more than a thousand miles away.

In the meantime, *Harder* and *Hake* rendezvoused off Dasol Bay, a small place in the thumb of land that goes up on the west coast of Luzon to form Lingayen Gulf.

On the morning of August 24, a destroyer-minesweeper exited Dasol Bay, and both submarines closed to attack. Haylor did not like the looks of the converted destroyer and went deep to evade. Not long afterward Haylor heard a string of fifteen violent depth charges. Sounds as though the *Harder* is catching it, thought Haylor.

Everyone in the *Hake* thought it somewhat strange that they had heard no warhead explosions. Had the *Harder* shot and missed? Not likely, they thought. They heard nothing else, and on surfacing about dusk, they attempted to raise the *Harder* on the radio. Nothing.

For two long weeks, Haylor tried to raise the *Harder* by radio, without success. On September 10 Nimitz returned to the area with his reload. Haylor hoped that Chester might have gotten news of the *Harder* while at the advanced base. He had no news. After talking it over with Haylor by megaphone, Nimitz reached the inevitable but unthinkable conclusion. He sent a message directly to Admiral Christie:

"I must have to think he is gone."[2]

---

[2] Much later I learned from Chester Nimitz that the destroyer-minesweeper that had killed the *Harder* was probably the former USS *Stewart* (DD 224), an American four-stacked destroyer captured by the Japanese at Surabaya at the beginning of the war. She was heavily damaged by the attack on Surabaya, and she had to be largely rebuilt. Her topside was altered to take on Japanese lines so as to avoid attack by her own forces. She was recovered, in Japan, by the United States at the end of the war and returned to the U.S., where she was eventually scrapped.

Irony had been added to tragedy.

*   *   *

I don't think that the loss of any submarine during World War II hit the entire submarine force as strongly as this one. Had Sam Dealey, the destroyer killer, fallen to a mere minesweeper? Fierce arguments ensued over whether or not Dealey should have been permitted to make this sixth patrol. Many thought he had been too tired and worn out. Others thought he had become relaxed and even contemptuous of Japanese ASW measures. Clearly Admiral Christie, the man who bore the responsibility for making the decision, had felt that he was up to one more patrol.

Whatever the truth of the matter, the U.S. had lost one of its finest men of war, and I had lost some very dear and close friends. Squadron Twelve would never be the same without *Harder*, and the Majestic would never be the same without her officers.

Two days later another bombshell was dropped. The *Jack* was to go back to San Francisco for overhaul, making a war patrol on the way in the South China Sea. At the same time, it was announced that Commander Krapf would be relieved by Lieutenant Commander Albert S. Fuhrman as commanding officer. It was also announced that I would be the new exec.

So this was to be our last refit period in Australia. This was going to be the last time I would ever see Kathie.

As I unpacked my things at the Majestic, I knew I would never see it again after these two weeks or so. I knew that I had had some of the best times of my life there. I knew that I had grown up there far more than such a short time would normally permit. And I also knew that the coming parting from Kathie would be hard—hard, indeed.

As usual I arranged for the cases of beer to be delivered to the Tennis Club—but I knew it, too, was for the last time. There were too many lasts, and I was letting it get me down.

At lunch I sat with Kent Lukingbeal, and this wonderful guy, this endless source of good humor, clapped me on the back and said, "Why so gloomy, James? We're here to rest and have a good time. And don't forget—we'll be on our way home when we leave. Bit of a delay en route, but we're heading in the right direction. California, here we come!"

"Yeah, I know, but I'm having a little trouble reconciling myself to the fact we won't ever be back here again."

"Jim, I think I know what's eating you, but it will pass. You've spent a lot of time telling me what a wonderful girl Nancy is. Kathie will fade into the background after a time. Get things in perspective—wise up."

It was good advice, but like a lot of good advice, awfully hard to take.

That afternoon, alone in my room, I sat down and thought for ω long time. I had nothing to read, no radio to listen to—I just sat and thought . . . and prayed.

Did I really care so much about Australia, about Kathie, that I wanted to rip up my whole young life and come here after the war to live? Was I enough in love with Kathie that I wanted to marry her, with all the trauma that would bring to Nancy and her family, as well as to my own parents? Did Kathie really care that much about me?

My answer to all these questions was a resounding no. Not only no but *hell* no. I told myself that I had a childish weakness about attractive places into which I had been thrown by fate. I thought back to my feelings about the paradise of Maui. All my yearning for that kind of a life soon passed and was forgotten. Was Australia just another Maui?

Not quite, I realized. Maui had been two weeks of paradise, with no emotional attachment except an enchantment with the beauty of the place. Australia had been my home for the better part of a year. Kathie's family had become almost like my own family. And Kathie had become a confidante, a friend, a playmate. But not a lover.

That last barrier of faith and trust had not been broken.

That evening I was due to go to Kathie's home for dinner again—probably another last. I had made up my mind before going that I was going to have a long talk with her and set straight some of the things that I had been thinking about that afternoon.

I walked up the familiar porch and into the Tiffany-shaded living room with grim resolve. Then I saw her, standing there looking more beautiful than I had ever seen her before, and all my resolve melted. How could I hurt this lovely girl with all the things I had intended to say? As I had so often decided before, it would have to wait for later. Scarlett again.

After dinner I sat down and talked with Dr. Aberdeen. As usual he wanted to talk about the war.

"Don't we have them pretty much on the run?" he asked.

"Well, it's a lot harder to find targets. We had only one really good opportunity on this last patrol. Fortunately, we took it," I said, probably telling more than I should have.

"What will you do when the war is over, Jim?"

Was there more to this question than appeared on the surface? Was this just a friendly question, or was it the concern of a worried father who had been talking with his daughter?

"You know I'm married." I had often discussed Nancy not only with Kathie but also with her parents. "I'll be going back home and will pursue my career in the Navy."

"Of course you will," Dr. Aberdeen replied, in a tone that didn't entirely set my mind at ease.

The subject was changed to the economic condition of Australia, and no more delicate questions were asked.

Naturally I saw a good bit of Kathie in the evenings, and although we studiously avoided the subject of my departure, the awareness of it ran through everything we did or said.

One evening, late in my two-week stay, a house party was given by a friend of Kathie's who lived in Perth. Kathie and I arrived a bit late, and the party was well under way when we got there. The house was larger and more pretentious than any I had visited before in Australia. There was drinking, then dancing, then some singing. Since no one was paying much attention to us, I suggested we go to a quieter place to talk.

"Come on, I know a place," she said.

We walked to the back part of the house, where there was a sort of combination den and library. In it was a large sofa with some colorful pillows stacked on it. There were heavy draperies at the windows and a small, shaded lamp in the corner.

We sat down side by side on the sofa to talk.

I suppose what followed could have been predicted. We cared for each other, very tenderly, but simmering underneath that tenderness was a strong passion, not far below the surface.

Before long Kathie looked directly at me and said, "Jim, you're the only one who knows what to do from here on—and I trust you . . . completely. But I don't think this is right for either one of us."

That did it. Suddenly I knew just how right Kathie was.

Her family had taken me in without reservation and made me one of their own—and she trusted me . . . completely.

I had a vivid picture of myself talking with Dr. Aberdeen in the Tiffany-shaded living room, explaining just how it came about that his lovely daughter was in trouble.

Finally, I had a very clear image of myself explaining to Nancy, waiting faithfully and patiently at home, what had happened in Australia and wondering if she could ever trust me again.

"Kathie, as much as I love you and ache for you, you are right—this *can't* be for us . . . it *can't* be. It's as important for me as it is for you. It matters a great deal, both for now and for later."

"I understand that . . . and I agree," she whispered softly.

We got up from the sofa, straightened it, and walked hand in hand back to the living room to rejoin the group.

They were still singing.

I have always been glad, even thankful, those words were spoken and the harder course taken that night. For I am wise enough now to know that, had we yielded to the passion driving us, no matter what might have happened, the relationship between Kathie and me would have been forever changed and been made less sparkling, less precious, and less joyful. And my marriage with Nancy would have been gravely and seriously marred, no matter how much I might have tried to put the memories of that evening behind me.

Kathie phoned me the next day and told me that her parents wanted to see me one last time before I left Australia. Could I come over that evening?

I felt a sinking sensation. Was some parental scolding about to take place? Had I betrayed their trust? Had Kathie had some frank and serious discussions with her parents?

I appeared at the appointed time with some apprehension, not only about what might be in store for me from the senior Aberdeens but also about how Kathie might feel about what had happened the night before.

When I walked in, however, nothing seemed changed. Dr. Aberdeen offered me a beer (he always kept a few bottles from my cache aside for special occasions), and we talked about how the training was going and how it would be only three or four days before the *Jack* left Australia for good.

"We're going to miss you, Jim. You have become a good friend to all of us—almost like part of the family."

I thought briefly about how that statement would have sounded had last evening gone differently.

Over Dr. Aberdeen's shoulder, I saw Kathie standing in the library door and beckoning me with a wink.

"Excuse me for a minute, Doctor," I said and went into the library with Kathie. I did not know what to expect. This could be a very difficult scene. After all, last night had not been just a routine date—and maybe her reaction to it was different from mine.

We walked away from the door. Then Kathie put her arms around me and put her head on my shoulder. As I held her, I could feel her trembling. I was afraid she was crying, but as I looked at her, I could see that she was not.

"Wasn't last night *wonderful?*" she said softly, smiling again as she looked at me in that direct way of hers.

It was clear that she realized that the decision made the night before had been as important to her as it had been to me. I was sure that I didn't understand everything that was going through her mind, but I was grateful that we had nothing, absolutely nothing, to regret.

We walked together back into the living room and sat down to talk to Dr. Aberdeen. The crisis was over. Scarlett's tomorrow had finally come.

I saw Kathie twice more before we left on our seventh patrol. They were the same half-joyous, half-sad times that we had always had before. Nothing was changed, except that there was a finality about this goodbye that had never been there before.

And I knew that no matter what happened in the future, I would never, not ever, forget Kathie.

11

Farewell, Forgiveness,
and Tragedy

Our new skipper, Al Fuhrman, was in the Annapolis class of 1937, a full ten years junior to Tommy Dykers and three junior to Art Krapf. In the five months from May to October of 1944, our skippers had dropped ten years in seniority. The flood of new-construction submarines was causing ever younger men to be given command. Fuhrman was only thirty years old.

Al Fuhrman may have been young, but he was also, by far, the most war-experienced of our three skippers. He had completed nine war patrols, half again as many as Dykers and Krapf combined. The *Jack*, however, was his first command. He was a shorter-than-average man with wavy black hair and a sort of tough-guy look that was partially but not altogether misleading. He had a reputation in the submarine force as being a bit of a wild man ashore, but no one doubted that he was all business once he crossed that gangway to get on board his submarine.

This might be a good time to set the record straight as far as alcohol on board World War II submarines is concerned. It was strictly against Navy regulations, and since Dykers was a strictly regulation guy, the *Jack* started out with crystal-clear rules on this subject. That was our tradition.

We knew all about the submarines that broke out beer for everyone after a successful attack, and we had heard plenty about the skippers who had a few bottles of scotch carefully stashed away in their rooms for "medicinal use" during war patrols.

The *Jack* just wasn't in for this kind of thing. So far as I know, the only alcohol we ever had on board was made by one of the Filipino stewards (not Domingo), who fermented some fresh pineapple to produce an alcoholic drink to be used "to celebrate when

211

we had a sinking." This was sniffed out (literally) early in its production and thrown over the side, to the accompaniment of great lamentation and wailing by its brewer.

All of this is not to say that there wasn't plenty of drinking ashore during rest periods. There were a few times it got competely out of control, but on the whole, it was reasonable given the circumstances.

One morning, during this time ashore, I had an experience that left a lifelong impression. As the new exec, I had to take some papers over to Lucknow for Fuhrman. It was maybe nine in the morning when, after ringing the doorbell with no success, I stepped into the living room, which was open. Through an interior door I could see into the dining room. Sitting at the table and leaning over it was a terribly disheveled and hungover man, whom I recognized as the skipper of one of the new submarines just reporting in. He was dressed only in his underwear and needed a shave badly.

He didn't see me in the living room, as he was entirely preoccupied. On the table was an open bottle of scotch and a tumbler full of what looked like straight whisky. A towel was draped around his neck. He had grasped each end of it and, in his right hand, also the tumbler of scotch. To get this up to his mouth without spilling it, he was pulling on the left end of the towel. His attempts were not succeeding. He was trembling so violently that, even with support from the towel, half the whisky was being spilled before the tumbler reached his mouth.

And this was a man to whom we were entrusting the lives of some eighty men and a multimillion-dollar submarine badly needed in the front line? I was thankful that he had nothing to do with the *Jack*.

I left the papers and exited quickly and quietly, being careful not to disturb the labors of the towel-puller.

All the way back to the Majestic, and for many days later, I had this scene vividly in my mind. Was anything worth this kind of a mess? I didn't think so.

If that's what you needed to relax, I decided I would choose to stay tense.

Before we left on our seventh war patrol, we had three important personnel changes. We had lost our senior cook to new construction, and Commander Warder, seeing our distress, gave us a man who had been with him in the *Seawolf* for four patrols before being put ashore because of a serious leg injury. Commander Warder's friend was now ready to go to sea again and at the beginning of our training period, Chief Commissary Steward D. W. Watson reported on board the *Jack*. We knew that he came highly recommended, but we little suspected what a significant role Rebel Watson, as he was called by everyone, would play with us before the war ended.

A second change involved the wardroom staff. After losing Domingo to new construction, we needed a new senior steward. Again Commander Warder came to the rescue with an old Filipino friend, Chief Steward Fernandez. Bald as a billiard ball and almost always smiling, Fernandez was a truly superb cook. Many times, when he did not approve of the general mess offering, he would cook a special meal for the wardroom, and some of these creations were truly memorable. Domingo had been a mighty good steward, but if possible Fernandez was better. We continued to be pampered in the middle of a war.

The third change was equally welcome. Earl Archer came back on board, so we had both of our mustang (up-from-the-ranks) officers (Archer and Jack O'Brien) back with us again. All through the history of the *Jack*, they had been worth their weight in gold. I don't know how we could have gotten along without these two fine men.

One change we did not make was on the TDC. Since I was now the exec, the normal thing would have been to have one of the younger officers, probably the gunnery officer, take over this job at battle stations. Possibly thinking of *Harder*—or maybe just because he did not see a logical replacement on board—Fuhrman told me I would remain at the TDC.

"I expect you to act as the assistant approach officer, Jim. You can do that from the TDC as well as from anywhere—maybe better. I'll have Danny Deaver read the bearings and ranges from the periscope on submerged attacks."

Actually it proved to be an excellent arrangement, one that was, I believe, followed by other submarines that had a long-experienced TDC operator who had fleeted up to be the executive officer.

World War II submarines tended not to let their good TDC operators go.

All during the training period for our seventh patrol, the battle to regain the Philippines was under way. The landings at Leyte Gulf had already occurred before we left Australia for the last time on October 27. Excited as we were about these pivotal actions in the overall Pacific War, we knew that as far as the *Jack* was concerned, it was business as usual. We were going to the South China Sea again and being routed through Lombok and west to the Karimata Strait, near Singapore—undoubtedly to keep us clear of the many complex Allied surface naval operations taking place in and around the Philippines at that exact time.

We were assigned to a patrol area just off the coast of what was then French Indochina (later Vietnam). We would be some six or seven hundred miles west of the Philippines.

As we pulled away from Fremantle for the last time and Rottnest Light began to fall astern, I cried harder than I had since childhood. There was a finality about this departure that just wrung my heart. I would never, ever, be back there again. Fortunately, I was back on the cigarette deck where no one could see me when I really let down. Australia, and Kathie, had come to mean more to me than I had wanted to admit to anyone—even to myself.

I had to face the fact that I would never see Kathie again—never . . . never . . . never.

After the *Jack* fueled at Exmouth Gulf, as usual, Fuhrman decided to transit the Lombok Strait at night. The pass between Bali and Lombok island is narrow indeed, without much room to maneuver around a patrol vessel should one be met. We entered the strait at dark, with the nearly full moon due to rise within an hour. It was partially cloudy with only a light breeze.

With the huge moundlike mountain on Bali soaring more than three thousand feet high to the west, we rang up flank speed, which in the calm water gave us twenty knots. But our navigation soon showed that we had a five-knot southerly set, so we were making only fifteen knots over the ground. That familiar smell of jungle—rotting vegetation and other mysterious odors—wafted over the water from the nearby islands and permeated the air as we battled the current through the strait.

About a half hour after moonrise, we picked up what looked like a patrol boat almost dead ahead. We decided to go around him to the west to get him up-moon; the nearly full moon was in and out of the clouds but was out and shining most of the time.

Shortly after turning west, we picked up another patrol boat, dead ahead. Were we being boxed in?

Fuhrman decided we would have to evade to the east, even though that put *us* up-moon from the patrol boats, something we had learned the hard way not to do. We had, however, no choice if we were to get through the strait that night. We turned to a course just a little north of east with the intention of curling around to the north after we had passed the boat ahead of us. I had this, the second, patrol boat set up on the TDC while Kent had both of them on the plot.

Could the patrol boats see us? Did they have radar? We took some comfort in noting that the phosphorescence, while present, was not nearly so strong as what we had seen around Timor. We kept on the four-engine speed—Fuhrman believed the sooner we got through the narrow part of the strait, the better.

We had been working slowly east-northeast for some time when we picked up a third patrol boat, dead ahead. Again I wondered if this was, in truth, a boxing operation, and if they had us dead to rights. Was our last scheduled transit of Lombok to be really our last in every way? I was seeing shadows, all right.

At this point Fuhrman showed us that shadow-seeing was not part of his makeup. His words came down from the bridge, loud and firm, "I don't think these guys have any idea that we're here. Are either one of the other boats showing any sign of following us?"

Kent answered, "No, they're both plotting on about course north, at about six knots. Could be just their regular patrol pattern."

"OK, we'll go between the two up on our bow and see how that works," came from Fuhrman. This was going to bring us much closer to both of them than I would have liked—but I wasn't driving.

After about ten minutes of this, more word came from the skipper. "The guy up to the north is sweeping with a searchlight now but doesn't seem to be settling on us—he's gone right by twice without stopping." His voice was as calm as though he were commenting on the weather.

Did the patrol boat suspect something, or was he just following his instructions to sweep every now and then? As we passed between the two boats, the searchlight suddenly turned off. But there was no change in the course of any of the three boats.

Another twenty minutes went by with no new developments. All three boats were beginning to fade into the background.

We were through the strait.

Ten days later we had completed our passage through the Java Sea and the Karimata Strait and were off the coast of French Indochina, near Cape Padaran (later Cape Dinh). One of the China-based Allied

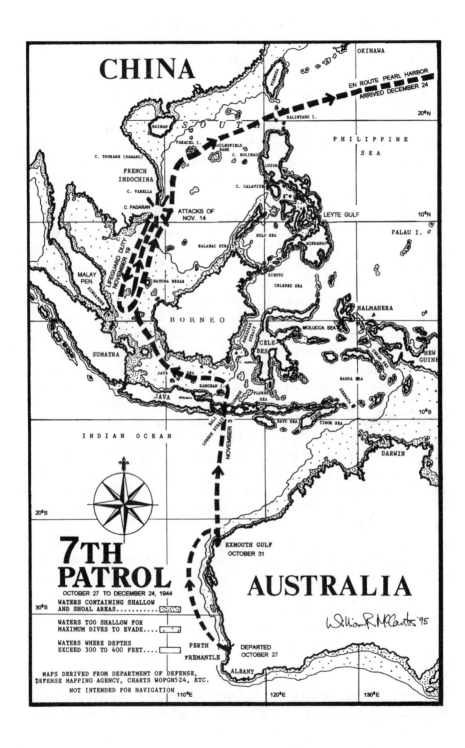

patrol planes had alerted us to a "large convoy off the Indochina coast consisting of many ships but course and speed unknown."

With this tantalizing but not altogether helpful information, Fuhrman decided to close the coast, despite the fact that we would be getting into water too shallow to afford much protection if we had to dive. We submerged at dawn, close enough in to be sure that the convoy could not pass between us and the coast without being seen.

We saw nothing all day, so at dark we surfaced and started up the coast to the north. With the information we had, one direction was as good as another. We couldn't even be sure that the convoy would be running along the coast; that was just the most probable of the several possibilities.

About ten in the evening on November 14, after several hours of fruitless searching, Lady Luck showed she was still a friend of the *Jack*.

"Sir, I'm pretty sure I have a group of ships on our port bow, close to the land," the radar operator reported to Kent Lukingbeal, who had the deck. I was called and came up to the conning tower to have a look. Were they really ships, or were we just seeing a promontory of the land? I called in the battle station radar operator, Charley Caw, to consult. After a long pause and much shifting around of the radar controls, he said, "I don't think it's land. These are ships, but I can't get the same one often enough to tell which way they're going."

With that I called the skipper and asked him to come to the conning tower.

Fuhrman wisely decided to stop. That would give us a chance to find out which way they were moving. No sooner were we stopped than we got a report from sonar.

"We have pinging up ahead coming from at least two or three different ships. They're pretty far away, but it's definitely pinging."

The old giveaway again. Where there is echo ranging, there is a convoy.

"Which way is the bearing drawing, sonar?" snapped Fuhrman.

Long delay. Then, "Definitely to the left, sir."

The convoy was headed south. Fuhrman immediately set the battle stations, put on four engines, and turned to parallel and track the convoy, all the time converging them slightly. The water depth was less than a hundred feet. We drew sixty-eight feet at periscope depth, so we could submerge here in an emergency. Yet we needed at least two hundred feet of water to maneuver and evade with any effectiveness. If we had to dive in this depth, we would be a sitting duck for any good ASW vessel.

There was a heavy overcast, and it was pitch dark. Not even cat-eyed Bennett could have seen anything. As we paralleled the convoy, however, Caw on the radar was able to pick out seven heavies and three escorts. All the escorts we could spot were on the seaward side. The heavies were three abreast in the front line and two abreast in the next two. The convoy was hugging the coast and was, as far as we could see, unprotected on the landward side. There was, of course, no way we could get in to attack him from that side. We were going to have to come in through the escorts.

About this time our new radar-detection equipment picked up a Japanese-frequency radar sweeping around. Soon it detected another. Clearly the escorts had radar—perhaps some of the heavies did also. Well, we would just have to deal with that.

At Cape Padaran the Indochina coast takes a definite turn to the west. We wanted to get in our attack before the convoy reached that point as we would then be chasing them rather than paralleling them. We had a good track on them. The convoy was zigging every four or five minutes, with no course changes more than forty degrees, most of them around thirty degrees. Speed was about ten and a half knots. This somewhat higher-than-average speed plus the radar-equipped escorts indicated that we probably had some valuable targets here.

Fuhrman planned to come in on their port bow and shoot the closest heavy of the front line. They were coming our way now, and we were shaping up for a good shot when the radar detection operator reported, "One of the radars has steadied on us—not sweeping any more. His signal is very loud."

Almost simultaneously from the bridge, "Searchlight from the close escort—sweeping in our general direction, but hasn't steadied on us."

At this point Fuhrman wisely decided to break off and retreat into the darkness. Would they follow us? They did not.

"I don't think they were ever sure they had anything," said Fuhrman. It was becoming clear to all of us that our new skipper was a cool customer.

By now, however, we had lost so much time that the convoy was rounding Cape Padaran. When we were ready to go in again, we were chasing after the ships, with the resulting longer torpedo runs.

Within less than an hour, Fuhrman was threading his way through the escorts in an effort to shoot the closest heavy in the third line. We passed close astern of the middle escort with no sign that we were detected. We then had the after escort almost dead ahead of us. With the middle escort now on our port beam and the after one still dead ahead, we were getting into a possible shooting position. Even though I had been through this a dozen times or more, my heart was in my throat, and pounding more than I wanted. I had learned not to like escorts with radar.

"Jim, we'll shoot four bow tubes at the close heavy. Regular depth setting and spread," from the bridge. It was all quickly arranged.

"Go ahead and shoot when you're ready, Jim. I can't see a thing from up here," said Fuhrman.

Without visual bearings from the bridge, we had to be extra careful to get the best possible bearings from radar.

"Fire one! . . . Fire two! . . . Fire three! . . . Fire four!" I snapped.

"Right full rudder, all ahead flank," came from the bridge, very calmly.

About a minute later, "Kee-*rist*, what an explosion!" came from the bridge, not so calmly.

Almost immediately in the conning tower, we heard one tremendous *WHOOM!* followed by a regular torpedo *WHAM!*, both at the correct time.

"There was a column of fire and smoke at least a thousand feet straight up—never saw anything like it," from Fuhrman. "It was almost blinding, even at this distance."

In about a minute, Caw reported from the radar, "Whatever happened, that pip is disappearing—there, he's *gone.*"

Fuhrman immediately started pursuing the convoy and working into position to get another of the trailing heavies.

"Gunfire from the close escort!" came from the bridge.

The tracers were speeding through the pitch-dark night like huge, arcing, yellow neon lights, Fuhrman told me later.

"Some of those shots from the escort are landing close, but no hits yet. I'm going to keep pressing in," from Fuhrman.

Was that gutsy, I wondered, or was it just irresponsible? Well, tracer fire won't sink us, but it sure can do a lot of damage to the bridge. I guess he knows what he's doing, I concluded—and he's up there in the midst of it all.

Then in the conning tower, we heard a heavy *thump, thump* that we had not heard before.

"Large-caliber gunfire from one of the big ships! Wow, he knows where we are, all right. Those shells are exploding when they hit the water, and some of them are *close*," reported Fuhrman, now less than calm.

I had a brief thought as to how this sounded to the men in the engine and torpedo rooms, where they couldn't do a damned thing about it except listen and pray.

"How long is the torpedo run now on the ship you're set up on, Jim?" asked the skipper.

"About thirty-three hundred yards."

"Too damn long, but we'd better shoot right now, Jim. Get four off as quick as you can—we gotta get the hell outta here."

I did not need any prompting. We were only a little more than two miles off the coast, in very shallow water, and being shot at by two different ships. I was motivated.

"Fire one! . . . Fire two! . . . Fire three! . . . Fire four!"

"Right full rudder, all ahead flank," came from Fuhrman, more than a little urgently.

We could still hear the *thump, thump* of the heavy ship's gun as we moved away, and it was now so frequent that those of us in the conning tower were sure there were now two heavies shooting at us.

However, we didn't bother to ask the bridge. We were too busy staring at the stopwatch measuring the torpedo run. We had a considerable wait because of the unusually long torpedo run. But right on time, *WHAM! . . . WHAM!*

Two hits in about as tough a spot as we had ever been in the *Jack*. Gunfire is very distracting, even when you're not on the bridge to see it.

As we pulled out to the east, the large-caliber gunfire stopped. Either we had hit the only ship with a large gun, or they had decided there were better things to use their energy on. The tracer fire continued however, then became sporadic, then stopped altogether. I think they didn't know where we had gone and chose not to go off on a wild-goose chase. The escorts did not want to desert the remaining five heavies and so continued to plow on with the convoy on its way southwestward. No depth charges were ever dropped, so

I assume the escorts believed we had stayed on the surface. Apparently the escort's radar was not nearly as effective as ours. And we were grateful, once again, that a submarine on the surface makes a surprisingly small radar target.

As we pulled farther and farther away, Caw said the pip on our target was disappearing. But I knew right away that we would never get credit for that sinking. Disappearing targets on radar were becoming less and less acceptable as evidence of a sinking.

Shortly after the gunfire ceased, Fuhrman came down to the conning tower to look at the navigational chart. He was interested in water depth and how close we were getting to the very shallow water south and west of Cape Padaran. Since I was the exec, I was also the navigator, but I had been a bit preoccupied for the past eight hours on the TDC. Fortunately, my chief quartermaster, Olsen, had been navigating all through the attacks, getting occasional ranges and bearings on prominent landmarks from the radar. He was able to show the skipper that the convoy was heading into water not only too shallow for us to submerge in but also known to be mined in places.

Fuhrman deliberated a bit and decided to break off. He deemed it too dangerous to pursue them into the really shallow water—too shallow for us to dive at all. I'll admit I breathed a good bit more easily.

These are the kinds of decisions that, although hard, can make the difference between getting home and not getting home.

On November 15 we dove at dawn, as we had so many times in this war. We got some rest while we made some progress up the coast of Indochina. That evening, on surfacing, we received orders from Admiral Christie. He was sending us to a position near Singapore to act as lifeguard for carrier strikes scheduled for that city. It was well over six hundred miles south to our assigned position, and we had only a little more than three days to get there. Time would have been no problem if we could have run on the surface all the way. But with the heavy patrol plane and other traffic in the whole area en route to Singapore, we knew we might have to spend a lot of the daylight hours submerged.

Now came a time when some of the old *Jack* daring was recalled for Fuhrman. We told him of our success in running surfaced in the daytime in many parts of the South China Sea, counting on the lookouts to get us down in time. I gathered that the skippers he had served with before coming to the *Jack* had not been of this persuasion.

After some thought he said, "OK, we'll do it. But you'd better give those lookouts a real sermon."

Over the next three days, we dove over and over again for planes but nevertheless made much better time than we would have submerged all day. No bombs—our lookouts did a sterling job. As we closed in on the Malay Peninsula on the third day, we had to stay down during all the daylight hours. It was like Times Square. But even with all the delays, we arrived at our assigned station slightly ahead of time, on November 19.

The concept for lifeguarding was to have the submarine at periscope depth at a precise location known to the carrier aviators before their strike. They had our call sign, and we had theirs—right down to the individual planes. When a strike was scheduled, we would move into position ahead of time and be sure all was in readiness with the rescue party.

We stayed at periscope depth during the strike despite being disturbingly close to the beach. All was in readiness to pick a crew up if they had to splash anywhere near us, but fortunately none of the planes had need of our services. After two days we were released to head back to the coast of Indochina, this time in the vicinity of Cape Varella, some 120 nautical miles north of Cape Padaran.

There we waited . . . and waited . . . and waited. We tried pulling out from the coast and using the high-periscope patrol on the surface. We tried getting in close to the coast so as to be sure not to miss any small traffic hugging the beach. We tried everything but saw nothing, absolutely nothing. We had sixteen good torpedoes left and no sign of a target.

At the end of our assigned patrol time, Admiral Christie bade us farewell and told us to change operational control to Commander Submarines Pacific (ComSubPac) and proceed to Pearl Harbor.

We arrived at Pearl on Christmas Eve, 1944.

We were awarded credit for sinking one medium (who could tell the size?) cargo ship and for damaging another. Judging from the size of the explosion we saw, this first ship must have been carrying ammunition or some sort of explosives. However, we were given credit merely for a "cargo ship." It wasn't much, but it came at a time when submarine after submarine was returning from patrol without anything at all on the scoreboard. The air was clearly going out of the Japanese balloon. Leyte, Guam, and Saipan had been secured, and plans were well under way for the recapture of the rest of the Philippines. We knew plans were being made to invade the mainland of Japan; this, we knew, would be a bloody, bloody undertaking.

The *Jack*, however, was heading home, home to San Francisco, where we would be overhauled at Bethlehem Steel's submarine repair facility at the Hunter's Point Yard.

We arrived at the yard with a work list six feet long. The *Jack* had made seven war patrols; had traveled enough miles to go twice around the world; had been bombed, depth charged, and shot at; had been driven through mountainous seas that poured green water into the engine rooms, all over the main generators; had been driven for long hours at speeds far beyond her design limits; and had several times been taken well below her design test depth. In short, she had been driven mighty hard and was in need of some tender loving care.

In addition, the war experiences of the past three years had shown the necessity for alterations to submarines of the *Jack*'s vintage; she was getting to be an old-timer by World War II standards and needed to improve her battle efficiency. All of this was going to take time.

We spent the next two days in long conferences with the yard people, explaining what we needed done and going with them on board the *Jack* so they could see exactly what we meant.

We moved off the ship onto a barge again, as we had at Mare Island. But we knew that this stay would be longer—perhaps as long as three months. Fittingly, the barge was a bit more comfortable than its predecessor. It was larger, newer, and better heated.

As we were moving onto the barge, the exec of the submarine crew that had just moved off told me he had a deal for me. A bit suspicious, I sat down and listened.

"Jim, I have these two slot machines, one nickel and one dime. We used them all through our overhaul, and believe me, they're gold mines. The yard workmen are always coming over to the barge to mooch coffee and sandwiches, and they can't resist the slots—they'll be going day and night."

"How much?" I asked.

"Three hundred bucks. You can take it out of the crew's welfare money, and it'll be paid back many times over."

Realizing this maneuver was more than a little illegal, I was willing to take the chance without bothering the skipper but wanted to talk to the chief of the boat about it. The welfare money was for the crew, and he could speak for them better than anyone else.

I found Gunner Lynes, explained the whole thing to him, and asked him what he thought.

"Hell, let's do it, Mr. Calvert. There's a lot more than three hundred bucks in the fund, and I don't see any immediate need for it. If we make as much money as some of the other submarines have, we can use the dough to put on a ship's party to end all ship's parties," Lynes said.

So we bought the slot machines. We were told they were set to pay out the maximum amount possible but that we would still make a hatful of money.

Well, they were used all right. From the instant they were set up in a big general room in the center of the barge, they never stopped. There was always a line of yard workmen waiting to play them. We told our crew not to play the slots, but even then not everyone could resist the lure of the whirling cherries, oranges, and jackpot bars. It was, however, mainly the yard workmen who played the slots, and since the ship was being worked on three shifts a day, seven days a week, we got plenty of their money. The slots practically never stopped except when Gunner Lynes, who was in charge of this operation, interrupted them to scoop out our profits.

A few days earlier, as we had passed under the Golden Gate Bridge, I realized that not only was the *Jack* coming home but so was Jim Calvert. We had left Australia for good, had crossed the equator and the international date line, and were returning to the land of our birth. We would never see Australia again. For the past two months at sea, I had thought long and hard about Nancy, Australia, and Kathie.

It would be just about a year since I had said goodbye to Nancy at Mare Island, and the amount of living that had gone on in that year exceeded any in my young life to date. I had been scared to death, exhilarated, angry, lonesome, gladdened, saddened, and burdened with responsibilities far beyond any I had even dreamed of a year ago. I was only a year older, but I had grown up a lot more than that.

I knew that I had had a close call in Australia. I had narrowly escaped an involvement that could well have changed my life forever. And in hindsight it would not have been good for Kathie or for me. More important, I had avoided a heartbreak for Nancy beyond any description.

I also knew now that my place was in America, in the Navy, and above all with Nancy. I was extremely fortunate to have her for my wife, and I vowed never again to do anything or become involved in anything that would risk losing her.

A few days after our arrival at Hunter's Point, I met Nancy at the San Francisco airport. The sight of her smiling and beautiful face, her warm embrace, and her obvious joy at seeing me alive and in one piece all combined to make our reunion more sweet and wonderful than I could have imagined.

The Navy once again provided Quonset huts for families whose ships were undergoing overhaul. Once again they were adequate if not very luxurious. But young lovers do not need luxury, and very soon our little hut was taking on all the attributes of a home. Above all, it was a place where love was, and, as the Bible says, that is far better than a grand and luxurious palace in which there is no love.

I realized that, sooner or later, in order to live with myself, I had to tell Nancy about Kathie.

I told her about it, very slowly, and I did not leave out much. When I was finished, I said, "Sweetheart, I have worried about this for most of the year. I have no excuses—it was just plain wrong. Can you forgive me for it?"

Long pause. She was holding my hand while she looked directly at me.

"Jim, I hope you won't worry about it any more. I hope you won't talk about it any more. Kathie sounds like a wonderful girl, and I think I understand. There is really nothing to forgive. I love you—and that covers everything."

I have loved her ever since for those words and for the sweet and generous thoughts behind them. They were better than I deserved. But the words and the thoughts were totally in character.

That was the way she was.

During the overhaul the conning tower was lengthened and its equipment rearranged to suit the night surface attacks that were becoming more and more the norm. Radar was installed in the number one (thicker) periscope, enabling dead accurate ranges to be taken during a periscope attack. What an advantage that would be!

There were many engineering improvements made and new armatures were installed in our four main generators—the old ones had had so many doses of saltwater in rough weather that they were beyond repair.

Our old three-inch gun was replaced by a five-inch, twenty-five-caliber gun, a huge improvement in striking power. A forty-millimeter machine gun was installed on the cigarette deck, and twin twenty-millimeter guns on the forward bridge platform. We retained our fifty-caliber machine guns to be mounted in stanchions on the deck. We were becoming a floating arsenal.

As late March and the end of the overhaul rolled around, it was time to count up the profit on the slot machines. I knew it was going to be a lot, but the final results astounded me—we had made slightly more than five thousand dollars from those machines in less than ninety days—and they had been set to pay out the maximum to the players. Ever since counting those profits I have been unwilling to play a slot machine. It is just a method of throwing your money away, without any mathematical chance whatsoever of winning over a period of time.

In addition to all this, I was able to sell the two machines to the next submarine occupying our barge for the same three hundred dollars. It was one of the best business deals I have ever made.

About this time we received a piece of wonderful news—the *Jack* was being awarded the Presidential Unit Citation for her first, third, and fifth patrols. The Presidential Unit Citation was awarded only to ships or other military units that had distinguished themselves far and above the crowd and were worthy of special recognition. It entitled every officer and man on the ship to wear the Presidential Unit Citation ribbon, a distinction that mighty few of the participants in the war could share.

We had a lot to celebrate.

So we planned to make the ship's party even bigger. Gunner Lynes did almost all of the work. He lined up a club in San Francisco that was willing to close and give us the entire place for the evening. He arranged to have an orchestra, food, an open bar—the works. Even a juggler and a man with card tricks. We had everything but a trapeze artist.

The party was a huge success. It was only three days before our scheduled departure, and most of the work on the ship was done. She was cleaned up and looking beautiful after all her refitting. We had no worries there, so we just relaxed and enjoyed the party.

Ship's parties are always better if the officers leave early, so at an appropriate time we all departed, leaving Gunner Lynes in charge to keep control and to pay the bill when it was over.

About four o'clock the next morning, the phone rang in our Quonset.

"Something must be wrong on the boat," I mumbled as I staggered sleepily out of bed to answer.

It was Danny Deaver, who had had the duty and had missed the party. He was on board the boat, where a phone was hooked up.

"Gunner Lynes has been in an automoble accident and been very seriously injured. The doctor I talked to isn't sure he's going to live."

"Oh no, oh no, oh no-o-o," I gasped. I just couldn't believe it. "Was there anyone with him? Another car involved?" I asked.

"I was told he was alone and hit a telephone pole—no one else involved," Danny replied.

"Where is he?" I asked.

Danny gave me the name of the hospital, and while I was getting dressed, I told Nancy what had happened. I left with no more delay.

It was five in the morning before I got there.

"Sorry, no visitors. Doctor's orders," snapped a prim-looking Navy nurse at the main reception desk. She was wearing a starched white uniform, and her manner was as stiff as her uniform.

"Look, I've got to see him. I'm the executive officer of his submarine, and he's my Chief of the Boat."

"I don't care what he's the chief of; you can't see him."

I insisted on seeing the senior medical officer of the watch and was told that he was sound asleep and couldn't be bothered.

"Well, he's going to be bothered this time. I'm going to his room," I said.

No one stopped me, and after a delay in finding it, I went in and woke him up. Fortunately he was an understanding man and gave me authority to go to the ward where Lynes was.

When I got into the ward, I asked the nurse in charge if I could see Chief Petty Officer Lynes. She looked at her list of patients, then looked up at me.

"You can't see him . . . and you don't want to see him," she said softly.

"Oh, yes, I do. Where's the duty doctor?"

She shrugged and nodded in the direction of a short, mustached man wearing a white coat and glasses.

"Doctor, I hope you can let me see Chief Lynes," I asked.

"No."

"Well, I have to." I explained my situation and how much he meant to me both personally and professionally.

"Then come here," the doctor said brusquely.

We walked over to the corner of the crowded ward, where a white curtain supported on pipe rails had been pulled around a bunk.

He abruptly pulled back the curtain, as though unveiling an exhibit. There was our shipmate, one of the best Navy men I ever knew. He was horribly bruised and bloody, trembling from head to foot, and gasping desperately for every breath.

"Isn't there something you can *do* for him," I asked in anguish.

"Nothing. He's had severe head and spinal trauma, and he'll die within the hour," was the reply.

"Why isn't someone here to at least *try*? You can't leave him alone like this."

"Look, lieutenant, we have a lot of men in this ward who need our attention because they have a chance to live. Most of them are battle casualties. Your man has no chance to live. If you can't keep your sailors from going out and killing themselves in automobiles, you can't expect us to stand around and wring our hands over them."

I know that doctor was probably exhausted from being up all night with one serious case after another, but I have never seen a medical man speak so heartlessly about a patient. I have never forgotten it, and I never will.

I waited, and within the hour I was told that my friend was gone. I now had the task of telling his parents.

We were leaving for Pearl in two days. Shortly after arrival there, we would go on war patrol—and we had lost our key enlisted man, the heart of the crew in more ways than one. Lynes had been a most unusual man. He was no angel but he combined mental ability, physical toughness, and leadership skill in a way that one does not find very often in any walk of life. More than a little of what the *Jack* had accomplished had been due to his influence on the crew.

To make our dilemma worse, we had no one on board who seemed at all right to take the job of Chief of the Boat. Fuhrman and I discussed the problem at length but came to no conclusion.

After making arrangements to have his body shipped to his parents in Virginia, we held a brief memorial service for Frank Lynes in the chapel in the Yard. I believe every officer and man who was not required to be on the ship was there.

The Navy chaplain opened the service with

> I know that my Redeemer liveth,
> and that he shall stand at the latter day upon the earth:
> and though this body be destroyed, yet shall I see God.

I reflected on these words and on the life of this so promising young man. Why should this have happened to him? So young, so full of life.

What a waste, what a waste, what a waste.

During the service I watched Chief Rebel Watson, and almost as though I had received a message, I decided that he could be the man. At first thought everything was against him: he was a cook— no submarine had ever made a cook Chief of the Boat—and he was new on board. Many of our other chiefs might be considered to have priority simply because of their length of service on the *Jack*.

But Watson had that magic ingredient called *leadership ability*, which is so hard to define and yet so immediately recognizable. As I sat there in that small chapel and thought about it, my conviction became stronger. This was the man.

When we got back to the ship, I talked with the skipper about it. I gave him all my reasons as well as the obvious objections.

"Does he want the job?" Fuhrman asked.

"I don't know."

"Why don't you ask him, and also get a private opinion from Chiefs McCabe and Craig—you seem to value their ideas."

I talked to them both on a confidential basis, and after a little pause to get used to the unusual idea of having a cook for Chief of the Boat, they both agreed it ought to work.

"Rebel is very special," said Bob Craig.

"He's a North Carolina cracker—he can't be all bad," added Terry McCabe.

The next person to ask was Watson himself. I asked him to come into the wardroom and sit down.

"We think you could take Lynes's place as Chief of the Boat. What do you think about it?"

After getting over his surprise, and reflecting a minute, Watson said, "I'd sure like to give it a try. I think I can do it."

I announced it to the crew at quarters the next morning.

"We're just twenty-four hours from sailing, and we have a lot to do," I told them. "I know you'll give Chief Watson your support and get the job done. We can't get the Gunner back, but we can show him we are doing our best to fill his place with a good man."

They gave Rebel that support to a man, and the next morning, April 1, we were passing under the Golden Gate Bridge, bound for Hawaii, with a ship well prepared for sea—and the feeling in my mind that we had made a difficult, but correct, decision.

12

Decisions at Guam

We arrived back in Pearl Harbor from the Navy Yard on April 9, 1945. Because of the many personnel changes, both officer and enlisted, made during the overhaul, the *Jack* was going to have a longer prepatrol training period than usual.

We were in the midst of it when, one afternoon after a busy two days at sea, I was sitting in the Pearl Harbor Submarine Base Officer's Club having a quiet beer with Kent Lukingbeal. Suddenly the club's announcing system broke in on our conversation.

"Our president, Franklin Delano Roosevelt, died this morning at Warm Springs, Georgia."

The voice went on with some details, but the impact of the announcement blotted out all the other words. Although in my childhood, my father used to have near-seizures of anger when we talked about Mr. Roosevelt, he had nevertheless been our commander in chief for almost as far back as I could remember, and certainly since long before I had gone to Annapolis. I was aware of the superb leadership Franklin Roosevelt had given our nation during the war, of his special interest in the Navy, and of the critically important friendship between him and Winston Churchill. What would we do without him?

I could well remember how one of my professors at Annapolis, a retired naval officer called back to teach navigation at the academy because of the war, had talked about Mr. Roosevelt.

Waving the stub of a pencil about two inches long, he had said, "This is how far we had to use our pencils down to save money before Mr. Roosevelt took over. We didn't even have enough to buy *fuel* to get under way. We just swung around the hook for month after month."

The old gentleman was wearing his blue service uniform with a captain's four gold stripes—now tarnished with age—on its sleeves; he said all of this through gritted teeth, with a deep tone of bitterness in his voice. I can still see his shock of white hair and angry face as he spoke and shook that pencil stub in our faces. I was learning that not everyone shared my father's views on Mr. Roosevelt. The Navy had a different perspective.

Kent interrupted my musing. "This means that Harry Truman is now the president of the United States—what does that mean to us?" he asked.

A terrible, sinking sensation hit me at this thought. Our trusted war leader was being replaced at a critical time by someone about whom we knew scarcely anything. I felt a deep sense of loss and emptiness but did not know how to express it.

"I don't know. I hope he likes the Navy," was my inadequate answer.

And so, an important page in the history of our nation was turned while we sat quietly sipping a beer at Pearl Harbor.

Both Jack O'Brien and Earl Archer had been detached at San Francisco and replaced with two absolutely green reserve officers. Kent, Danny Deaver, and I were the only war-experienced officers left. Almost all of our old enlisted crew from the Australia days was gone to new construction and replaced with men who had never been to war. We were just about starting out from scratch.

After a few days of training, it was clear that one of our new reserve officers was not up to making a war patrol. We couldn't find anywhere to fit him in comfortably. We tried him as the assistant plotting officer, but Kent, himself a reserve officer, said it just would not do. Fuhrman decided to send him to shore duty in the Pearl Harbor area. This didn't seem to be too much of a blow to our young man, but asking an officer to leave a ship because he doesn't measure up is never pleasant. I was glad when it was over.

After this troubling shift was over, our skipper was even more concerned about the lack of experience in our wardroom, and he arranged to have Lieutenant Bill Logan put on board in place of the young reserve officer just departed. Bill was a mustang officer, having worked up from enlisted ranks like Obie and Earl. He had made nine war patrols, the most of any officer on board—except for the skipper, who was starting out on his eleventh patrol. Logan was third in seniority.

Bill Logan was a tall, husky, sandy-haired officer with a quiet voice and relaxed manner. He could, however, be tough enough when the situation demanded it. He became the battle stations diving officer, which gave us all a sense of relief. Either Jack O'Brien or Earl Archer had held this position for the last six patrols, and although Danny Deaver was working into the job, we really wanted him back in the attack party. In short, we were all happy to have Bill Logan on board.

We seemed to have more trouble getting this new crew shaped up to go on patrol than any I could remember. The new men just didn't seem to have the desire that I had been used to. We worked and worked with them, diving over and over again to try to get them to realize that it took agility, skill, and determination to get a submarine under the water in thirty-five seconds or less. During this training a new thought began to invade my mind more and more: Was I really going to live through this war?

It was clear to most of us that the war with Japan was winding down. The Great Marianas Turkey Shoot of June 1944 had wiped out much of what was left of Japan's first-line carrier aviation. Admiral Lockwood had moved his headquarters from Pearl out to Guam to be closer to the scene of action. Bases for the bombing of mainland Japan were being built on Guam, Tinian, and Saipan with great speed.

These bases, however, were more than twelve hundred miles from Japan, and the land-based fighters, essential to protect the bombers, could not make this long haul. Thus Iwo Jima, located only five hundred miles or so from Japan, became a necessary part of the strategy. Not only would this tiny volcanic isle provide a base for the bombers' fighter cover, it would also serve as an emergency landing area for bombers in trouble en route home. Iwo Jima was assaulted and secured at great cost in American lives while we were being overhauled in San Francisco. The first landings on Okinawa took place the day the *Jack* departed San Francisco, in early April.

The grand strategy of the Allies was beginning to take shape, and the unmistakable drumroll of the Götterdämmerung for Japan was beginning to reverberate across the Pacific.

Having made seven war patrols when the outcome of the war was much more in doubt, was I now going to be lost when the end was almost in sight? Was I going to be killed just because we had a green crew and I had been too lazy to shape them up? Not if I could damned well help it, I said to myself over and over again.

We worked far into the night almost every day of the training period, and I'm sure that many of the new crew thought the exec was a real bastard about training.

I didn't let that worry me.

Finally, on April 26, our training was completed, and we were ready to depart on patrol. When I saw our assignment, I realized how much the war was changing for the submarines. We were assigned an area just south of the main island of Honshu, where I could see there would not be much traffic. Our real purpose there was to act as a rescue ship for the carrier planes making bombing attacks on the Japanese mainland. We had had a short taste of lifeguarding off Singapore on our seventh patrol and hadn't found it very challenging.

We were not altogether right about no challenge. Our lifeguard assignments kept getting closer and closer to the beach. One day we were so close, we could see individual buildings along the coast. We began to worry about whether or not we would survive surfacing this close to the beach to pick up a downed aviator. Part of this would depend on how quickly we could do it. So, on the days when no strikes were scheduled, we pulled well out from the coast and held lifeguard drills. In these we surfaced, got the entire rescue party on deck with all its equipment, simulated picking up an aviator from a rubber raft, and then submerged again as quickly as possible. The inevitable stopwatch was held against all of these drills, and our time, while slow at first, did begin to improve.

The month of May dragged by without a single contact worth a torpedo. When we were in close to the coast on a lifeguard assignment, we would see an occasional wooden coastal freighter, not big enough for a torpedo but too close to the beach to make a gun attack feasible. In short, we had no action except for the lifeguard assignments, and they came only about every fourth or fifth day.

Finally, on June 8, our lifeguard team went into real action. We were stationed about three miles off the beach and had seen carrier planes going in for the strike earlier in the day. We all thought it would be another day, like so many in the past, with no need for our services.

Suddenly in the radio room we heard, *"Jack! Jack! This is Colorado Nine. Have been hit and will splash near your position."*

The use of our real ship's name shocked all of us. In the war actual names of all warships were kept as secret as possible, and all radio calling was done by encrypted call signs. Each submarine had a code nickname, just for this lifeguard mission, and we expected only it to be used. However, a little thought made us realize that the pilot had probably looked at his call sign list quickly and thought "Jack" sounded like a radio call, not the actual name of a ship.

The radio room passed the word to the conning tower without delay, and the OOD began to look through the periscope for an incoming plane.

"There he is! Trailing a plume of smoke and heading this way!" said Danny Deaver at the scope.

"It's an F-6," added Danny, showing off his aircraft identification skills. The Grumman F-6 was the workhorse of the carrier fighter planes, and this one probably had been part of the fighter cover for the bombing strike.

"Prepare to surface. Radio, tell Colorado Nine we are surfacing," snapped Fuhrman.

Three raucous blasts followed, and in a few seconds we were on the bridge, just in time to see the fighter plane go into the water, not more than five hundred yards from us.

As we turned toward him, we could see the pilot pulling back his canopy and preparing to leave his plane. He was also inflating a small rubber raft, into which he hopped about the same time as the F-6 sank beneath the waves. We could see the steam coming up from around the engine cowling as the hot cylinders hit the cold seawater. It was a cloudy day with almost no wind, so the sea was calm.

In accordance with our procedure, we rigged out the bow planes so that our rescue party would have a platform right at the water's edge.

As we neared the pilot, he gave us a wave along with a big grin. In a minute or two, he was standing on our starboard bow plane, and his rubber raft was being taken on board, deflated, and struck below. The pilot had scarcely gotten wet.

Our people hoisted him up on deck. Then all hands hastened below through the forward torpedo room hatch, which had been opened in the calm water to make it easier to get everyone down below quickly. We heard it clang shut when the last man had gone down to the torpedo room. The control room reported it had a green light on the torpedo room hatch.

OO-gah, OO-gah. *Dive! Dive!*

By this time we had adopted the practice of backing up the

alarm with a 1MC announcement just to make certain that everyone knew what was going on.

We submerged without delay and resumed our lifeguard station, as all the carrier planes had not yet returned from the strike. I went below along with the skipper to greet our new shipmate. He was sitting in the wardroom having a bowl of soup. He looked relaxed and right at home.

"Well, I guess I'm destined to spend the war in submarines. This is my second rescue," were his first words.

Almost unbelievably, during a carrier strike against the Japanese base at Truk in the Carolines in early 1944, he had been shot down, had been rescued by an American submarine, and was on board her for five weeks before returning to Midway, from whence he was flown back to the States.

"I qualified as an assistant OOD during that patrol, and I'm ready to go to work again," he said cheerfully.

Our new shipmate was Tim Collins, a former schoolteacher from Texas who was making his contribution to the war effort as a carrier fighter pilot. After his rescue at Truk, he had undergone complete retraining and had joined a new air group. His air group was finally embarked in the new carrier *Ticonderoga*, and before long he was off the coast of Japan, ready for air strikes. On this, his very first mission, he had again been shot down and now rejoined the submarine Navy in the *Jack*. No wonder he felt submarines were his destiny.

Collins stood assistant OOD watches for the rest of the patrol, and, indeed, made friends all over the ship. We had picked up a good shipmate.

Five days later our assigned patrol period came to an end without a single torpedo or round of ammunition having been fired. For a submarine that used to pride itself on finishing every patrol with no torpedoes left, this was quite a comedown.

On June 18, fifty-three days after leaving Pearl Harbor, we tied up alongside the submarine tender at the new submarine base in Apra Harbor at Guam. In the less than ten months since Guam had been secured, the Navy Construction Battalions had accomplished wonders. They had, of course, built bomber bases for striking Japan and in addition had built the new harbor at Apra, complete with breakwaters, heavy piers, and huge mooring buoys capable of handling an aircraft carrier. Beyond this they had built a complete town for the logistic support of the activities in the Marianas as well as—if not as important to others, still of great interest to us—a handsome submarine rest camp on a beautiful beach not far from Apra Harbor.

Not only did the new rest camp have comfortable living quarters and a fine, white beach, it also had good athletic facilities. There were softball diamonds, horseshoe pits, two tennis courts, and a real competition swimming pool, blasted out of the coral, with sea water coming in and going out all the time. It was named Camp Dealey after the great *Harder* skipper.

Unlike the arrangements in Australia, the officers and men were all together in the same camp, and it worked very well indeed. There was an elaborate athletic competition during the whole two-week period; officers and men were both eligible for these teams—the best athletes got to play regardless of rank.

I was into everything. I swam on the swimming team and played on both the softball and volleyball teams. I tried out for the tennis team but didn't make the cut. A cup was given at the end of each two-week period, and the *Jack* won it for our stay. There was, however, a controversy. We had been short one good athlete and had recruited Lieutenant Jake Laboone, then temporarily in the relief crew, a husky, athletic man well over six feet tall, who just dominated the volleyball court. He also had several home runs in the softball competition.

The submarine team that finished second behind us claimed that if we had not had a ringer, namely Laboone, we would not have won the cup. They said that relief crew people were not eligible to compete. We turned this claim over to our resident lawyer, Kent Lukingbeal, and he prevailed easily. Kent was the real ringer—the competition never had a chance against this legal hawk. The cup went to the crew's mess of the *Jack*.[1]

After winning the cup, it seemed altogether appropriate to have a celebration. We planned a ship's party right inside the rest camp grounds, as walking outside it was prohibited. In the jungles there were still Japanese troops who had not surrendered.[2]

---

[1] Many years later Jake Laboone became one of the most well-known and well-loved chaplains in the Navy. We can claim no credit for that, but it was a pleasure and an honor to have had him on our team.

[2] Not long before our stay at Camp Dealey, seven men from one of the submarines resting at the camp had gone on a strictly forbidden souvenir-hunting expedition into the jungles near the camp. A group of Japanese soldiers who had not surrendered killed five of the crewmen. The other two, badly wounded, managed to crawl to safety and survive.

The ship's party was for all hands. After a softball game, horseshoe competitions, and much beer, we all sat down to enjoy some wonderful steaks prepared by our cooks. After the meal a quiet crap game started in one corner of the field. I saw it and did not want to spoil the fun, so I asked Rebel Watson to make sure that no one got really hurt—losing more than a few dollars or so.

I watched the crap game for a while and noticed that they were playing on a blanket but bouncing the dice against a board erected and braced at one end of the blanket. Watson was watching the game but not participating, as I had asked.

At a lull in the game, he called me over and said, "Mr. Calvert, let me show you why you should never shoot craps with sailors."

He interrupted the game, picked up the dice, proceeded to shake them vigorously, and then rolled a pair of aces on the blanket (not using the "bang board," as they called it). He then picked them up, shook them vigorously again, and rolled a pair of deuces. He went all the way up to a pair of sixes and back down again to the aces. While he missed a couple of times, his overall control was phenomenal. His skill in picking up the dice, adjusting them, shaking them convincingly, and then rolling out what he wanted was just about unbelievable to a neophyte like me.

"You gotta pick 'em up just right, glance at 'em quickly, and then shuffle 'em in your closed hand to the right position. It ain't easy, and you can't do it against a bang board, and it's impossible if they make you use a cup," went on Rebel.

"Mr. Calvert, not only is he showing you why you shouldn't shoot craps with sailors, he is also showing you why no sailors will ever shoot craps with Rebel Watson. He can even do it about half the time off a bang board," grinned one of our crew.

About halfway through our rest period, we received a message from the carrier *Ticonderoga*, which was anchored in Apra Harbor. The wardroom of the *Ticonderoga* was inviting the officers of the *Jack* over for a dinner of thanks for having rescued Tim Collins off the coast of Japan.

It was a gala evening with a large banner inscribed "Thanks to the *Jack* from all of Tim's Air Group" hung over the wardroom. There were many toasts and speeches by the Air Group commander, our skipper, and the captain of the *Ticonderoga*. On this evening I also learned that the strict prohibition of alcohol on board Navy ships was not so totally strict on wartime aircraft carriers. We had a great time, complete with a long talk after dinner with Tim's shipmates about carrier aviation—what they did day to day and how they lived. Tim joked that he knew more about submarines by now than he knew about carrier aviation. I really enjoyed the evening, and it left a lasting impression.

At the end of the rest period, I received a message asking me to come and see the Squadron Commander in his cabin in the tender. The new Commodore (as Squadron Commanders are called) was our old friend Frederick B. Warder, now a four-striped captain. What could be wrong? Was I in trouble because of the ringer controversy at the rest camp? Because I allowed gambling at the ship's party? Because of the drinking on board the *Ticonderoga?*

As I put on a clean shirt, I thought of everything either the *Jack* or I had done wrong in the past two weeks. I then hopped up to the Commodore's cabin without further delay.

"Have a seat, Jim. There's something I need to talk to you about."

"Yessir," I said anxiously as I sat down.

"You've made eight war patrols—that's enough for now. I'm sending you back to new construction. You'll be an exec."

I was glad I was sitting down. I had been absolutely sure that I would be on board the *Jack* until the war was over.

"Who'll be the new exec of the *Jack?*" I asked weakly.

"Bill Logan. I've talked to your skipper about it, and that is satisfactory with him—although he would rather keep you. But I am going to stick to my guns on this. I've watched you pretty closely over all the time you've been in the *Jack,* and I think it's time you had a rest."

I was stunned. All sorts of things ran through my mind. Joy at going home to see Nancy, relief from the seemingly endless routine of working up a new, green crew for each patrol, and sorrow at leaving my old ship and shipmates. But more than anything, I was convinced they could not get along without me. It wasn't very modest, but I didn't see how they could possibly do it.

I had done everything for so long. Who would train the new crew? Who would be the TDC operator? Who could navigate? Who could run the watch bill?

"This is going to leave them awfully thin," I said weakly.

"I know how you feel. I thought the *Seawolf* would sink when I left. But she did all right . . . for a long time."[3]

"What will I do now—go to the relief crew?" I asked with some trepidation. That was not a fate I looked forward to.

"Just for a few days. I'm arranging air transportation for you back to the States now. Your orders from the Bureau will be here soon. You can pack your trunk and send it home. Tell Nancy you will be on the way before too long."

Thus ended the first of three fateful interviews with Captain Warder during our stay in Guam.

Returning to the *Jack*, I sat down in my room and had a long think. I had been fascinated with what I had seen of carrier aviation from the lifeguard side and became even more intrigued after our visit to the *Ticonderoga*. I was convinced that the submarine war was winding down, and I wanted to be in on the invasion of the Japanese mainland, which we all knew would be coming within a year or so. I didn't see how the submarines could have a very big part in that.

Could I go back, get through Pensacola and all the other aviation training, and return to the Pacific in time for the action?

Without really knowing all that was involved, I decided to put in for flight training. As long as I was needed in the *Jack*, I wouldn't have dreamed of it. But the Commodore and the Bureau had made it clear the *Jack* was going to get along without me—so why not?

I talked to Fuhrman about it, and he said, "If you want it, go ahead and apply. It's a long road. You'll have to start with the physical exams right here. Not everyone passes them."

I reported in to the flight surgeons at the Naval Air Station on Guam for my physicals. There were endless eye exams, strength tests, and tests where you had to look down a long, lighted box and try to line up two sticks by pulling on strings attached to them. Depth perception, I guessed.

There was also an interview with a psychologist, who wanted to know just why was it, exactly, that I wanted to go into carrier aviation. Didn't I realize that I might end up flying land-based planes or even a helicopter? He made it clear that carrier aviation was not for ev-

---

[3] After a long series of successful patrols, the *Seawolf* had been accidentally sunk by Allied forces in September of 1944, the only U.S. submarine known to have been killed by friendly forces. It had been a bitter blow for Warder and all of us who knew and admired the famous old ship.

eryone—the Navy was not going to allow me to kill myself in an airplane if I didn't have the aptitude for carrier landings.

With the boundless confidence of youth, I brushed all of these points aside and said I was sure I would be a carrier fighter pilot.

About halfway through these examinations, I moved up to the tender and off the *Jack* for the last time. A few days later, on July 12, she left on patrol . . . without me.

I stood alone on one of the other submarines nested alongside the tender. The merciless tropical sun beat down on the submarines, making the day stifling hot. There was not a breath of air, and the water of the harbor was like a mirror. The *Jack* tossed off her mooring lines, leaving them behind as we always had when departing on patrol.

As I stood there and watched her pull away from the nest, I broke down and cried for the second time in the war. The first time, leaving Fremantle, I had half expected it. This time, watching the *Jack* leave, I had not expected it at all. I kept telling myself the *Jack* wasn't a living being, just a heavy steel tube with miles of wire and pipe inside, nestled around four big diesel engines.

But it was clearly more than that to me. Not only had it been my home and the center of all my work attention for three event-filled years, it also continued to be the home of some dear friends, both officers and crew. How were they going to survive without me? No one else knew where anything *was*. No one else understood the TDC. No one else understood the watch bill. No one else knew how to navigate. A whole series of childish thoughts went through my mind, but the *Jack* pulled, imperturbably, away from her nest and out into the stream without shedding a tear or uttering a cry.

My old home seemed totally indifferent to the parting.

The next morning, after recovering from the departure of the *Jack*, I packed my trunk (actually a cruise box made for me by the carpenter shop of the tender), sent it off, and wrote a long letter home explaining that I was either going to a new construction submarine or to Pensacola, depending on how the flight physical turned out. I realized that covered a lot of variables, but it was wartime and we were young. I just expected that Nancy would adjust to it. She always had.

Then I was off to the Air Station again to finish up my flight physical. The eyes were no problem, and one way or another I had gotten by the psychologist. In fact, I had gotten by everything, and

I was declared qualified. The next step was up to the Bureau of Naval Personnel and the Bureau of Aeronautics.

In the Navy everything is done by endorsements, and the package with my letter of application, covered by about one-half inch of medical papers, also had endorsements of approval by my skipper, Al Fuhrman, and by our new division commander. All was in readiness except for the required signature from Captain Warder, which, given my old friendship with him, was a foregone conclusion.

As I was sitting in the wardroom of the *Proteus* talking with one of my new friends, the squadron lawyer, a steward handed me a note asking me to go to Captain Warder's cabin. Probably congratulations on completing the flight physical so well, I thought.

"Have a seat, Jim. I need to talk to you," Warder said very seriously and somewhat grimly, I thought. This wasn't the start I had expected.

There wasn't much talk, however. He took my half-inch-thick folder of flight papers and, leaning over a large wastebasket, slowly tore them all to bits without a further word. The pieces fell into the basket slowly, like the first flakes of a large snowstorm.

"Jim, some day you will thank me for this," said Warder, looking directly at me.

I was aghast. How could my old friend, who had seen more of me during the war than any other officer, do this to me? How come no explanation?

Uncharacteristically, I kept quiet for a long time. I thought to myself that he was undoubtedly my friend. He knew me. He wanted the best for me. He knew far more about the Navy than I did. He probably knew more than I did about just how much aptitude I had for flying. I decided that no discussion was really necessary.

"Sir, if you think that it's best for me to stay in submarines, that is what I'll do," I said with more confidence than I really felt.

"You won't regret it," the Commodore replied with a smile.

I picked up my hat and excused myself. The visit was over— and so was my short career in naval aviation.

My flight back to Pearl Harbor was due to leave in two days. I had written home about the decision on flight training. All was in readiness for me to leave, when one of our squadron mates, the *Haddo*, returned from patrol. Her exec was very ill and had to be hospitalized.

The *Haddo* skipper was Frank Lynch, whom I had known well when he was in *Harder*. Had Dealey survived his sixth patrol, Frank would have been the new skipper of *Harder*. I had a long talk with Frank about old days and about how things were going with the *Haddo*.

The patrol he had just returned from had been in the Yellow Sea. Attacking a four-ship convoy with two escorts in a dense fog and in water too shallow for diving, the *Haddo* had sunk two of the heavies and then dodged one of the escorts as it charged by him, firing away. Undoubtedly the fog had enabled the *Haddo* to escape. Lynch had then dived in water only eighty feet deep and had sunk the escort with a special new acoustic torpedo called a Cutie. The other escort had had enough and had broken off to pick up survivors. It had been a brilliant patrol.

As I sat talking with Frank, I realized what a truly huge man he was—some six feet four and weighing about 230 pounds. He had been a great athlete at Annapolis and, more importantly, had been the regimental commander in his first-class (senior) year. In addition to all this, Frank had a brilliant mind with a great deal of creative ability. It was almost universally agreed in the Navy that Frank had a most promising future and was one member of his class who would certainly be an admiral—if not the Chief of Naval Operations. Such agreement among men who are in intense competition with each other is not common.

Frank and I talked over my flight training escapade, and he said, with no sign of hesitation, that Warder had done me a favor. That made me feel a lot better.

The next morning I got another note asking me to step into the Commodore's cabin. This was getting to be a routine, I thought.

As I entered the sunlit cabin, I could see from Warder's rather solemn face that this visit was not going to be fun and games.

"Jim, we're in a tough spot here. We have absolutely no one here—or at Pearl for that matter—who can take over as exec of the *Haddo*. The old exec won't be out of the hospital for some time. Frank Lynch would very much like to have you. Are you willing to do it?"

What could I say? I was flattered to be asked by such a famous skipper. But what about Nancy? What a blow to her. What a blow to my mother and father, who had been silently worrying out the war and had been overjoyed to know I was coming home for at least a time. But in thinking it over, I realized I really had no choice. I had to do it.

"I'd be honored to have the job," I answered.

"Good—I thought you would. You can report on board right now to work with the relief crew while the rest of the *Haddo* crew are at the rest camp. Frank Lynch will come in to talk to you several times, I'm sure. I'll take care of the change in your orders."

So ended my third talk with Captain Warder in less than three weeks. Back to new construction . . . no, back to flight training . . . no, still in submarines but going home very soon . . . no, going out on patrol again in a few days.

I had been told many times at the Academy that in the Navy you had to expect the unexpected, stay loose, and adjust to change without complaint.

I was beginning to see what they had been talking about.

The training period with the *Haddo* went well, although it was apparent that the *Jack* had not been the only submarine that got hit for new-construction people. The *Haddo* had almost one-third new people on board.

What also became apparent to me was that the *Haddo* attack party was sharp. Frank Lynch had introduced a lot of new ideas, mainly in plotting but also in the way the TDC was used. I had a lot to learn and was enjoying every bit of it.

As we departed Guam for patrol in early August, I still did not know our area assignment. Lynch had been more tight-lipped about this than my previous skippers.

After we had cleared the harbor and set course to the north, the skipper asked me to come in his cabin. He shut the door and showed me the operation order.

For my ninth war patrol, we were going back to Tokyo Bay. I had come full circle.

I knew there would be no lifeguarding there. This would be for real.

13

Deliverance
by the Bomb

"Mr. Calvert, I think you oughtta look at this right now."

I received this word after a vigorous shake of my shoulder by one of the new ensigns on board, who had been decoding messages. It was about midnight of August 6–7, and I was sound asleep.

I snapped on the light and read.

THIS MORNING A NEW U.S. WEAPON WAS DROPPED IN HIROSHIMA RESULTING IN ALMOST COMPLETE DESTRUCTION OF THE CITY. YOU WILL BE KEPT INFORMED.*

"Please show it to the captain now and to the rest of the officers. Don't worry about waking them—they'll want to see it," I told the young ensign.

Within a few minutes, all of the officers were gathered in the wardroom, talking about the message. Nobody really had a clue as to what the new weapon was, but the skipper said, "Only one weapon could have the power to wipe out most of a city at one shot—one using atomic energy. I've heard some vague rumors that the Germans have been working on such a weapon, and it only makes sense that the U.S. would have been doing it too."

Lieutenant Al Viebranz, always cheerful and wide awake, regardless of the time of day or night, said, "Good Lord, if we really do have a weapon of this kind, this war won't last long. The Japanese are tough, but not that tough."

"Al, it won't change just this war. It'll change all wars from now on," mused the skipper.

---

*This may not be the exact wording of the message, but it conveys the meaning and, to the best of my memory, the wording.

We continued to speculate on the new bomb, if that was what it was, and its implications for the Japanese and for the war. We went on for hours. Finally the stewards came in to set up the wardroom for breakfast.

Frank Lynch ended the conversation by commenting rather grimly, "Well, the Japanese wanted war, and they got it . . . in spades."

The stewards were putting down the white tablecloth and the silver for breakfast, so we had to leave the wardroom. As we broke up, I had the same feeling I had had after the Japanese attack on Pearl Harbor: The world will never be the same after this.

All of this happened as we were quietly charging batteries in the middle of Sagami-nada, about twenty miles south of Uraga Strait, the entrance to Tokyo Bay proper, which, as I have said, was too shallow for submerged submarine operations.

We had transited the thirteen hundred or so miles from Guam without any opposition. En route we had the thrilling experience of seeing a huge B-29 flight go overhead on the way from Guam or Saipan to the mainland of Japan. This was a sight to remember.

Their course was almost due north, the same as ours. They came by in seemingly endless numbers, flying in a narrow formation that reached from horizon to horizon. Amid crystal-clear skies the northbound planes would be disappearing from sight while the seemingly endless formation continued to appear from the south. The sun glinted on their shining aluminum bodies, while the roar of their engines seemed to come at us from every direction.

I had never seen such a manifestation of American power. As those planes roared overhead on their way to drop death and destruction on the Japanese people, I had a bit of a return of the feeling that had plagued me at the beginning of the war. What had these civilians, as individuals, done to deserve such a fate? What could they do in their own defense against such a mighty airborne armada as this? Each one of those B-29s carried enough destruction in its belly to destroy most of a city block.

The Japanese military had wanted the war, but now the Japanese people were the ones who would have to pay the price. I felt a real sense of bitterness toward the military leaders of Japan. They were beaten beyond any shadow of doubt, yet they remained in ultimate control of the Japanese government and were digging in to defend their homeland to the last man. We had seen enough of

Japanese determination on Pacific islands such as Peleliu, Iwo Jima, and Okinawa to realize that the assault on their homeland would be the bloody fight to end all bloody fights.

The military would get their emperor to tell citizens to fight to the last man, and we knew that the Japanese would do just that. In effect, the Japanese military were willing to sacrifice most of their countrymen to do . . . what? To save face?

The whole thing made me sick.

The *Haddo* was a different ship from the *Jack*—not better, not worse, just different. The histories of the two submarines were somewhat parallel. The *Haddo* had been commissioned about the same time as the *Jack* at Electric Boat and, of course, had been cursed with the same HOR engines. After their total failure, she had been re-engined with Winton 278-As, then sent to Fremantle, where she had made several successful patrols under Chester Nimitz, Jr. In late 1944 she had been sent back to California for overhaul. Then, like the *Jack*, she had been sent back to the Pacific war.

While the histories of the two ships were more or less the same, their characters were quite different. As is always the case, the character of the *Haddo* had been molded mainly by her skippers—particularly the last two.

The first, young, fiery, restless Chester Nimitz, Jr., had run a relatively loose, happy, and very effective ship. He took seriously the task of rising above the complexity of the submarine and was always keeping in mind its real purpose. Chester wasn't about to let things like Title A cards (the Navy's system for keeping track of important equipment) and deck logs get in the way of the main task. His goals were to forget the record keeping and emphasize the destruction of Japanese ships. He was unusually successful in both aims.

The second of these young shapers of the *Haddo* was its present skipper, Frank Lynch. As I have said, he was huge physically, and in addition he had a powerful, commanding presence. As her engineer and later her exec, Frank had been one of the original shapers of the *Harder*, and he brought much of that great tradition to the *Haddo*. He had revived and restored the required paperwork and made the boat conform more to regulations. But far more importantly, Frank had continued Chester's atmosphere of intellectual energy and curiosity. Everyone on board was trying to find a new and different way to do things. With its fearless aggressiveness and its strong wardroom, the *Haddo* was becoming a new edition of the *Harder*.

By contrast the *Jack* had been, as I have said, the USS *Dykers*. His personality, which had molded the ship far more than those of her other skippers, was of the old school. Paperwork and record keeping were done meticulously, according to Navy regulations. The officers called the men only by their last names. No one came into the wardroom except in a complete uniform. Meals in the wardroom were always served with linen, silver, and china. The boat had a general atmosphere of clean, quiet orderliness.

I think I have made it clear that none of this old-Navy style interfered in any way with the battle aggressiveness of the *Jack*. Her whole tradition, from day one, had been to get in there and slug— right up to the point of senseless bravery, but not beyond.

The *Haddo* was different in some ways, very much alike in others. Her battle tradition, under both Nimitz and Lynch, had been every bit as (if not more) aggressive and determined as that of the *Jack*. But her atmosphere was different. Wardroom conversation ignored the Civil War and ventured into some stimulating areas, mainly led by Lynch but also by some of her younger officers, all of whom, save one, were reserves. The relationship between the men and the officers was less formal, but the job still got done and done well.

Lynch, sensing he now had an exec brought up in the old school, had put me in charge of an effort to restore the record-keeping structure of the *Haddo*. It was not easy. As far as I could see, every Title A card and similar record had simply been thrown away. We had to start from scratch, but we got it done. (I think a number of the young *Haddo* officers caught up in the storm of paperwork wondered just what the hell this had to do with winning the war.)

We arrived in Sagami-nada in early August and had begun the same sort of routine we had followed in the *Jack* more than two years earlier. We conducted submerged periscope patrol by day, getting in as close to the coast as possible. Then at night we would surface and pull out at least partway to the center of Sagami-nada for battery charging.

The huge bulk of Mount Fuji continued to loom in the distance to the northwest as it had in early 1943. War does not change such things, but it somehow looked different to us now. Instead of being the symbol of a mighty and threatening nation, it was now only a strikingly beautiful mountain in a beaten nation that was soon going to witness some of the fiercest hand-to-hand combat the world had ever seen. Or so we thought; for we knew, generally, that plans for the invasion of both Kyushu and Honshu were taking final shape. These invasions were to take place, rumors told, before the end of 1945, and it was expected that Allied casualties could amount to over a quarter of a million men.

The *Haddo* had been busy with this kind of patrolling for only a couple of days when the fateful message about the new U.S. weapon arrived. As we had said in our wardroom conversation, this changed everything. Perhaps now that dreaded invasion would never take place.

We received no further instructions and so, in the best Navy tradition, kept on doing what we had been doing—patrolling as before. Needless to say, we watched the radio room like hawks. People were continually walking in through the normally closed door of the radio room to ask if there was any news. The radiomen got so tired of this that they made a sign for the door saying

NO NEWS ABOUT ANYTHING. WHEN WE HAVE SOME WE'LL TELL YOU.

Three days later, on August 9, we got word of the explosion of the second weapon over Nagasaki. Along with this information, we got more detail on the nature of this new device. We were told that it was a bomb that employed nuclear energy and that it had been developed in secret by the U.S. Government in cooperation with Great Britain.

We also learned, soon after, that on the same day the second bomb was dropped, Russia declared war on Japan.

"They're a little late catching the train," observed Al Viebranz wryly.

Like the *Jack* the *Haddo* had a ship's newspaper, and we did our best to put all of this information in a form that would make sense to everyone on board. I would hate to see that newspaper now because I am certain our attempts to explain the new weapon were not only rudimentary but also, in many respects, just plain wrong. Explaining the Russian move was a little simpler. We said only that everyone loves to be on board with a winner.

We still received no instructions to do anything different. If we saw a Japanese ship, we were to torpedo it. But we didn't see any. It appeared that traffic, at least through Sagami-nada, had come to a halt.

Then on August 15, we heard on the regular news broadcast that the emperor of Japan had decided to sue for peace. He was broadcasting an appeal to his nation to surrender.

Later that same night, we received a message originated by Admiral Nimitz and addressed to all Naval units in the Pacific:

CEASE OFFENSIVE OPERATIONS AGAINST JAPANESE FORCES. CONTINUE SEARCH AND PATROLS. MAINTAIN DEFENSIVE AND INTERNAL SECURITY MEASURES AT HIGHEST LEVEL AND BEWARE OF TREACHERY OR LAST MOMENT ATTACKS BY ENEMY FORCES OR INDIVIDUALS.

This sounded pretty final, but the next day we received a message from Admiral Halsey, commander of the Third Fleet, relayed to us by Admiral Lockwood:

HOSTILITIES HAVE CEASED BUT IF APPROACHED BY ANY JAPANESE AIRCRAFT, SHOOT THEM DOWN IN FRIENDLY FASHION.

What had caused this singular message with its vintage Halsey phrasing? It was several days before we learned that it had been caused, at least in part, by a Japanese bombing attack a few hours *after* receipt of the "Cease offensive operations" message on a fellow American submarine off the coast of Honshu, less than a hundred miles from us.

Since we did not have the ability to shoot down any attacking aircraft, in friendly fashion or otherwise, we defended ourselves the only way we could in daytime—we stayed submerged.

While we were spending these seemingly endless days waiting for instructions, I could not help but reflect on where I would have been had Captain Warder not stepped in and shortstopped my application for flight training. I would probably have been on my way to Pensacola with no certain knowledge of whether any more naval aviators would be trained for months or even years to come. I would have been trying to work into naval aviation just as it was being shrunk to peacetime size. I would, in short, have been in professional limbo. As it was, I was exec of a fleet submarine and, having completed nine war patrols, was in as good a professional situation as anyone could have wanted.

As usual, Captain Warder had known what he was doing when he tore up those papers.

Within a week it was clear that the hostilities were genuinely over and that we could stay surfaced twenty-four hours a day. Still, we remained in Sagami-nada, waiting for instructions on just what to do.

They soon came. The formal surrender ceremony was to be in Tokyo Bay on board the *Missouri*, probably in early September. We were also told that the *Missouri* and the *Duke of York*, flagship of the British Pacific Fleet, would be anchoring in Sagami-nada on August 27, and we were to remain clear. They would go into Tokyo Bay later.

A day later we were told that the *Haddo* would be among the twelve submarines chosen to be in Tokyo Bay for the surrender. What a thrill that was! We were finally to enter the Uraga Strait in safety and see the inside of fabled Tokyo Bay.

It is always exciting to enter a new harbor after long days at sea. But when that harbor is at the nerve center of a long-respected and often-feared enemy nation, the excitement rises to a fever pitch.

On August 30, if my memory is correct, the *Haddo* came to its assigned berth in the nest, alongside the submarine tender *Proteus*. She was anchored almost in the center of Tokyo Bay and not far from where the *Missouri* was moored.

The sight of that Allied armada of warships, anchored right in the sanctum sanctorum of the Japanese Empire, thrilled me even more than the sight of the B-29 formation. There were over 250 warships in a relatively compact area, representing every Allied nation that had fought against Japan. Although there were many aircraft carriers present, we were told that a number of carriers had stayed outside, in Sagami-nada, so that they could launch airplanes for an appropriate salute the day of the surrender, which was now scheduled for September 2.

All of the ships were anchored in orderly rows, with larger lanes left for the main passages of ships still to come. On the day after our arrival in the Tokyo Bay anchorage, I was sitting alone on the bridge of the *Haddo* taking a tour of all the magnificent warships with my binoculars. Many, many nations were represented—the British, the Free French, the Australians, the Dutch, the New Zealanders, the Canadians, and others. All of them were there, anchored in Tokyo Bay, and all as resplendent as they could manage to be with their war paint still on.

There were still some latecomers moving about looking for their places, and I idly noticed a new, spick-and-span American cruiser coming down one of the main thoroughfares that had been arranged in the anchorage. She looked as though she were just out of the building yard and showed none of the signs of the battle wear or sea-weariness that characterized so many of the other ships present.

Suddenly a small submarine chaser, looking very battle-worn, and perhaps ninety or so feet long, came zooming out of one of the small byways in the anchorage and cut right across the bow of the new cruiser. There was a sudden sounding of the cruiser's danger signal—five short, angry blasts on her horn—then black smoke from her stacks as she backed emergency. All this time the tiny submarine chaser putted calmly across the big ship's bow.

Without delay there came a rapid-fire blinker message from the signal bridge of the cruiser, aimed right at the bridge of the little fellow. It came at such blazing speed that I was unable to catch it. I sent for the quartermaster to help me, but before he could get there the little sub chaser had asked for a repeat. On the second time it came more slowly, and I got it:

REQUEST SIGNAL NUMBER OF COMMANDING OFFICER.

I asked the quartermaster to stay and help me with the blinker messages in the event there was more to this exchange.

The skipper of the new cruiser must have been buried in the bowels of some dark office in Washington until finally getting his sea command, because he certainly wasn't up-to-date on signal numbers.

These were numbers assigned, in the pre–World War II Navy, to each graduate of the Naval Academy, signifying his ranking in the list of officers of the regular Navy. In the 1920s and 1930s, these numbers were used to identify, quickly and accurately, the rank and lineal position of any naval officer. After Pearl Harbor the huge influx of reserve and mustang officers was interspersed all through the various Academy classes depending on their date of entry. The reserve and mustang officers were not assigned signal numbers, and thus these numbers became totally meaningless except as a relic of bygone days.

I doubted if the sub chaser skipper even knew what a signal

number was. He was almost surely a reserve officer, counting the days until his release from active duty.

Slowly, haltingly, but still easily readable came the response from the tiny ship:

COMMANDING OFFICER HAS NO SIGNAL NUMBER BUT HAS FIFTY-NINE POINTS.

A recently announced message from the Bureau of Naval Personnel had promulgated a point system for reserve officers, determining their date of release from active duty. It had to do with total length of service, number of days in the war zone, combat decorations, and so on. Various release dates were thus determined, but if you had fifty-nine points or more you were eligible for immediate release from active duty—and, incidentally, from the wrath of any regular Navy cruiser skippers.

I reflected that the sub chaser skipper was certainly off the hook, and I imagined that someone on the bridge of the new cruiser was now explaining the reserve release-point system as the steam continued to jet out of the cruiser skipper's ears.

14

Tokyo—Hail and Farewell

While we were deeply honored to be present at the surrender and found the experience of being anchored in such an impressive and historic fleet most interesting, there was actually not much to do.

The twelve submarines present were moored, six to each side of the submarine tender *Proteus*. With her huge bulk, she obscured our view of a large part of the historic anchorage. Interestingly, the *Proteus* was named after the Greek sea god who could change his shape at will. He didn't choose to do it on this occasion, however.

We were disappointed that our old tender, the *Griffin*, could not have been so honored, but the *Proteus* was a new, built-for-the-purpose tender, and we regretfully had to admit she was much better looking.

In a day or two, however, we were informed of something very exciting to us. Permission had been arranged for "any submarine officers who are interested" to go ashore to see the Japanese Submarine Base at Yokosuka, the naval base south of Yokohama at the southernmost curve of Tokyo Bay.

We were interested, to put it mildly.

After we signed up, we were instructed to wear side arms and under no conditions to leave the submarine base. When we had seen it, we were to return to our ships. We were not to go farther than the submarine base, and there was to be no looting and no souvenir hunting. Any violation of any of these orders would be a court-martial offense.

So, dressed in khakis with no ties and wearing short jackets of the style that General Eisenhower had made popular, we buckled on our forty-five-caliber automatics, complete with ammunition, put on our best gold-strapped caps, which we never wore at sea, and took off for the Yokosuka submarine base. Our khaki-colored jackets had USS *Haddo* stenciled in large letters across the back, along with a colored cartoon fish insignia that made it clear we were from an American submarine.

After disembarking at the submarine base, we were immediately struck by its run-down condition. It had been hit by bombs several times, but it clearly had not been a showplace to begin with. The buildings were small, low, and poorly built; their interiors had not been kept clean. Everything looked in need of repair and painting. It was a drab and dreary-looking place.

There were several old Japanese submarines moored alongside, looking as though they needed a lot of tender loving care and weren't getting it. I couldn't tell whether they were capable of going to sea or not—they didn't look like it to me. There was no sign of people on board any of them.

Up on the base were a number of midget submarines, supported on pedestals, as well as some of the suicide *kaitens*. These latter were torpedoes capable of carrying a man whose job was to guide the torpedo to its target, then to die with it when it exploded against its objective. We were told that kaitens were being produced in significant numbers to oppose the expected Allied invasion of the Japanese mainland.

The Japanese had used a kaiten successfully in the Ulithi anchorage (in the Carolines) during the Leyte operations, sinking a fleet tanker there. The kaitens were launched from I-class submarines, the largest of the regularly built Japanese submarines. We were also told that there never had been a shortage of volunteers to man the kaitens.

The willingness of Japanese submarine men to undertake such a task offered some insight into the Japanese war mentality. To even the most patriotic Western mind, such a mission would have been unthinkable. Our submariners were as brave men as any I have ever known, but I doubt if any of them would have volunteered to guide a human torpedo to certain death.

We wanted at least a fighting chance to survive.

There really wasn't much else to see, and we were beginning to get ready to go back to the *Haddo* when we passed a large hole in the base's exterior wall, caused by a bomb that had exploded outside the base with enough force to blow a hole perhaps ten feet in diameter in the wall.

It's hard to explain why we acted as we did then, but we stepped right through the hole and out onto the streets of Yokosuka—something we had been explicitly ordered not to do. I suppose the only way to explain it is to describe our state of mind. We really felt on top of the world. The war, which had occupied almost our every waking thought for nearly four years, was over. Also, to be frank, we had a very inflated idea of what part the submarines had played in that victory. Ignoring the 250 or more ships anchored out in the bay, we truly imagined the submarines had won the war pretty much by themselves.

While there was no denying the major role played by the American submarines, had we thought soberly for a moment, we would have admitted what a team effort the Allied victory had been. But we weren't thinking soberly. We were so exhilarated by the end of the war, so confident of our own part in that victory, so jubilant at seeing the conquered nation at firsthand, that we just stepped through the hole in the wall without much thought about what we were doing.

"Why don't we try to get the train to Tokyo?" asked Joe McCune, a handsome, blond officer who was usually quiet but had succumbed to the same virus that had struck all of us.

Why not, indeed? Who could stop us? We were the conquerors—let us see the conquered land.

Al Viebranz went up to an intelligent-looking pedestrian and asked the way to the train station in careful, slow English. The man showed no sign of understanding. Then Al made a motion with his arms like the driving rods of a locomotive.

"Ahhh!" said our new friend with a vigorous nod of his head as he pointed down the street we were already on.

As we walked down the avenue, passing many civilians, we noted the almost total absence of men except for very elderly ones. It was like Australia—the men had all gone to war. Most of the women we saw were poorly clad and seemed depressed and discouraged. The great majority of them carried either umbrellas or parasols. They looked at us keenly, but if it was with active hate, it was well disguised. It was more a look of stolid acceptance. In the street hundreds of bicycles went by.

The train station was dirty and looked in need of maintenance. How would we get the tickets to Tokyo? Al Viebranz, with his shining look of good humor, went to the ticket window and, pointing to all of us, said: "Tokyo." We were all waved on to the waiting platform with no mention of money. In about ten minutes, the train pulled in, and we got on board with no sign of anyone wanting tickets from us.

The train was crowded; there were almost no vacant seats. We believed the better course was to remain standing, so we grabbed the straps and, swaying like commuters, became preoccupied with looking out the windows. We were conscious of all the passengers staring at us closely, examining our jacket insignia, our gold-strapped uniform caps, our side arms. On the average we were nearly a foot taller than our Japanese traveling companions. For the first time, I thought seriously about the danger we were in. Probably almost everyone was resigned to the nation's fate, but we had seen how fanatical at least some of these people could be.

On the other hand, I could not but think that these women were glad to have this wretched war over. They had been losing their husbands and sons, and their homes were being wrecked. Maybe they looked on us as liberators. If so, they kept their oriental restraint and showed us nothing. Their faces were inscrutable.

The train cars themselves looked like something out of the 1920s or earlier. The black-leather-covered padding on the seats was desperately thin and hard as a rock. The wooden floor had knotholes through which could be seen the rail bed below as it whizzed by. The train was electric, with the power taken from a wire strung above the cars—no third rails here.

As we bumped along (the rail bed was not very well maintained) an elderly man came up to Joe McCune, who was standing beside me, and grasped his arm firmly while saying, almost in a whisper, "We are very grad to see you here—*very* grad."

Joe, wisely, only nodded in acknowledgment. There was no telling where that conversation could lead.

We were now going through the open country between Yokosuka and Yokohama. Every square inch of land was under cultivation. Somewhat surprisingly, it appeared that the rice paddies had plenty of water. Everything was green. It was a pastoral scene with no sign of war damage.

As we got closer to Yokohama, however, we began to see the destruction that the B-29s and the carrier planes had wrought. We were going through a wasteland. Factory after factory had been burned to the ground. Not even a portion of a wall had been left standing. The rusted remains of lathes, drill presses, and other machine tools stood on a gray medley of ashes and concrete foundations. The reddish brown of the rusted machinery contrasted starkly with the gray ashes. The brown and gray desolation stretched as far as one could see. Here and there weeds were starting to spring up among the ashes, providing a touch of green to the awful scene. But the heavily overcast sky maintained the air of dreariness and gloom.

In each factory the office safe stood as a mute, rusted memorial to what had gone on there before the bombing. In my mind's eye, I could see people at the lathes, at the forges, at the foundry furnaces, people with green eye shades in the offices, all working at top speed to produce war material for the Empire.

Then the unthinkable had happened: air-raid warnings—the accursed Americans were daring to invade the sacred homeland. Then bombs falling, then fire. So much fire that there was an actual firestorm over Yokohama. Strong winds generated by and fanning the center of the conflagration roared in like demons of destruction. Block after block of factories and homes and warehouses were consumed in little more than minutes.

Now the busy factories and homes had become the ruins—and in many cases the tombs—of a silent wasteland.

The train stopped at a ruined station in Yokohama, where a number of Japanese soldiers in uniform got on board. They looked at us, and we looked at them. No one nodded, and no one blinked or looked away for a long time. Nothing was said by anyone. There was none of the bowing that, I had noticed, was common on the train. The soldiers wore khaki-colored burlap-strip leggings, and their plain, visored caps were worn absolutely straight—no jaunty angles here. They looked strong, mean, and tough. They did not talk to each other or to anyone else. I felt somewhat uneasy, but there was nothing we could do at this point—and none of us wanted to turn back.

The train left Yokohama and began to cross the more open country on the way to Tokyo. On the rugged terrain, we could see scrawny juniper trees hanging on to the steep hills. Plainly visible in the hills were tunnels; some of the hills honeycombed with them. Having heard about how the Japanese had fought from tunnels on some Pacific islands, I thanked God that our troops would not have to be fighting the Japanese on these honeycombed hillsides. If they had fought desperately and fiercely in the Pacific islands, imagine how they would have fought for their homeland.

I thought to myself that the estimates we had heard of two hundred to three hundred thousand Allied casualties would have proved to be low.

As we approached Tokyo, we began to see more signs of bombing. Blackened, ruined trees were everywhere. Bombed-out apartment buildings lined the area through which the train traveled. Occasionally we would see a Shinto shrine, shaped in the style of a small pagoda. Some were upright, some were ruined, and some had been roughly and crudely repaired.

As we passed these ruined buildings, I thought again of Frank Lynch's words in the wardroom the morning we had learned of the bomb on Hiroshima: "The Japanese wanted war, and they got it . . . in spades."

Oh, Lord, how they got it . . . how they got it, I thought—and not only in Hiroshima, but everywhere.

Shortly before noon we arrived at the main Tokyo railroad station. The station had been damaged by bombing but was still essentially standing. It was crowded, with both civilians and military personnel milling in every direction.

"OK, we're here. Now what do we do?" asked Al Viebranz with a grin.

"I don't know. Let's wait and see what happens," I replied without much confidence.

Jack Keller, the only Academy graduate on board the *Haddo* besides the skipper and me, showed more initiative. He went and talked to a sort of police headquarters office that was in the station and asked for help.

Before long an elderly man in a long, faded-blue cotton coat came up to us and, in fairly good English, said, "I am a railway guide. Can I help you?"

We told him we were from one of the American ships in the bay and would like to see as much of Tokyo as possible.

"How much time do you have?"

"We'd like to leave about three," I replied.

"I would be happy to escort you," he said politely.

"Can you take that much time?" I asked.

"Certainly."

We were off.

Jack Keller offered Mr. Shirato—for that was our guide's name—a cigarette as we walked along.

"Oh, yes! Camels! I know them! Thank you very much."

This reminded him of other American things he knew.

"I like baseball. I saw Babe Ruth when he toured Japan."

He began to show us the sights. We went by the huge Mitsubishi Bank building and the main Tokyo Post Office. Both seemed to have survived the war reasonably well.

The next thing was to see the emperor's palace, but taking Mr. Shirato's advice we viewed it only from a comfortable distance. We could, however, see that, war or no war, the palace had not been damaged, and its grounds had been meticulously cared for and trimmed. Ducks swam leisurely in quiet ponds within the grounds.

Mr. Shirato interrupted this pastoral peace by saying, "Not a good idea to stay here long. Black Dragon Society people may be here."

Mr. Shirato was referring to a group of men sworn to defend Japan to the end, no matter what the emperor said. They were reputed to be dangerous, and I couldn't think of a more obvious target for them than a group of American submarine officers gawking around Tokyo. We left.

We told Mr. Shirato we were interested in food if that was a possibility. Without another word he headed in the direction of the Imperial Hotel, Frank Lloyd Wright's claim to immortality in Japan. We passed the building of the Imperial Japanese Diet, the closest counterpart to our Capitol building in Washington. It reminded some of us of the New York Stock Exchange building. We also walked by the Foreign Office, a rather ugly redbrick building. I reflected that these buildings must certainly have been the sites of some anguished and emotional scenes in the past few days.

Entering the Imperial Hotel, we were promptly and without question ushered into a sort of grillroom, clearly not the main dining room. We asked Mr. Shirato to eat with us, but he said he did not think that would be appropriate. He promised to wait outside for us.

We were no sooner seated than two or three Red Cross men came over to see us in astonishment.

"What in the *hell* are you guys doing here? Do you have authority to be here?" was their rather heated question.

"No, we just came," I replied.

"Kee-*rist* Almighty. You could be screwing up the whole peace process," said one of them with an English accent.

"Well, what are *you* guys doing here?" I retorted somewhat defensively.

"We've been interned in Tokyo for the whole damned war," was the response from the English gentleman, who, judging from his very thick glasses, must have been ineligible for any kind of military duty.

Bit by bit we learned that there had been Red Cross representatives from many nations in Tokyo during most of the war. As we talked we asked them about living conditions in Tokyo. "Grim" was the one-word reply. They told us they lived in various places but frequently got together in the Imperial Hotel's grillroom for lunch.

We asked them if Tokyo Rose ever came here. We had heard her so often and for so long—she was someone we wanted to learn more about.

"We've never seen her here, but we've seen her other places. She's disappeared since the Bomb," said the Englishman.

"You haven't missed a thing—she's as homely as a mud fence," chipped in another Red Cross type.

"How's the food here?" asked ever-practical Joe McCune.

"Not very good at the start of the war, and it's been getting steadily worse ever since."

We were soon to learn what they meant. The head waiter came over to see us, speaking fluent American English. He was a slight, graceful-looking man who, we learned, was half Japanese and half French.

He said that we should call him Eddie, and he told us that he had gone to but not graduated from the University of Southern California. He had all the American slang phrases to prove it.

Our tables were set with regular English silverware—no chopsticks—and the table linen, while worn, was clean. The china and glassware were modest but also clean.

"I'm not sure you guys are gonna like our menu. Due to the exigencies of the war, as they say, there is only one selection. But it's a complete lunch," said our maître d'.

"Sign us up, Eddie," I answered.

The lunch started with hard black bread and pea soup. Not great, but better than I had expected. But with this we had had the best of it. The main course was some kind of fish boiled with cabbage and then covered with oil. The dish also contained bits of octopus legs, complete with suction cups. That was too much for us.

None of us could eat much of it, so it was all carefully taken away, and Eddie told us it would be saved.

When everything was cleared away, we had tea. It was boiling hot and bitter but fairly good.

"Sorry it wasn't more to your liking, but this is the best meal you can get in Tokyo," Eddie shrugged. "Every damned bit of food raised in this country goes to the troops."

Eddie brought the check for our lunches and, in the best tourist style, I asked him how much that was in dollars.

"Just sign the bill 'U.S. Navy.' You're gonna own the whole damned place anyway," answered Eddie with a grin.

As we left the hotel, Mr. Shirato asked us all to keep close together and not to straggle. He said that as long as we were seen with him, we would be safer.

As we walked along, I talked with our Japanese friend and learned that he had been a schoolteacher for most of his life. After reaching retirement age, he had then taken up the railway guide job. It never was clear to me just what a Japanese railway guide does from day to day.

We wanted to see the Ginza, the major shopping and entertainment center of Tokyo, so Mr. Shirato took us there, somewhat reluctantly I thought. There were many more people on the streets and the first real signs of hostility. We passed a group of Japanese Army officers who did nothing to hide their hostile feelings. One of them stared directly at me, possibly because I was the tallest, and gave me a look of pure, unadulterated hatred. His hand reached briefly under his uniform jacket, and I'll admit that my heart skipped a beat. As I think back, he may have just been scratching himself, but at the time I was certain, for a moment, that he was reaching for a revolver.

Either he wasn't, or he changed his mind.

We passed through one large department store, which was almost barren of goods. We began to understand just what desperate shape this country was in.

As we made our way back to the station, we were hissed as we passed a small group of men in civilian clothes—a rare sight in itself—but I didn't see any of them reaching for a gun.

I was becoming increasingly uneasy, and I wasn't altogether sorry to see our gang back safely in the train station. Since we had to wait for the train, Mr. Shirato thoughtfully arranged some tea for us. It was better than the tea at the hotel and was served by two very attractive little girls, about ten years old I would guess.

They brought the tea on little trays that held rather pretty blue-and-white cups along with the piping hot teapot. The girls were very courteous with their bows, and I felt we looked like rubes with our inability to return their courtesy.

Mr. Shirato had disappeared, but he came back with a copy of the Tokyo English-language newspaper, the *Mainichi*. Its headlines were all about the bombs dropped on Hiroshima and Nagasaki. The stories explained very graphically the horror of the destruction and the unbelievable force of the explosions.

There were smaller stories about the surrender, the emperor's message, and a plea for all Japanese to stick together during the coming winter.

Without any request from us, Mr. Shirato went to the ticket office and got a pass for all of us to return to Yokosuka. When the train pulled in, he told us we would be in first class and that we would have seats. He gave the conductor instructions as to just where we were to be let off the train, and he wished us good luck.

I thanked him as sincerely as I could and offered him a ten-dollar bill, "not as a tip but simply as a way of saying thank you."

He politely refused. "No, I work for the railroad—they pay me for this."

He did, however, accept some cigars and an unbroken pack of Camels from two of our officers who smoked.

And so we said goodbye to the first citizen we had gotten to know in the conquered country. We thought he represented them well. But he did not change our basic feeling about the Japanese nation—it was going to take more than a courteous guide to accomplish that.

After a day of walking, the seats felt good, and we had a chance to observe all of the destruction again. It looked just as bad going south as it had going north. What a task it will be to rebuild this nation—it will take decades, I thought.

On arrival at Yokosuka, we stepped onto the station platform and, almost literally, into the arms of an irate U.S. Marine Colonel. He was taller and much heavier than any of us, looked larger than life, and had a face as red as a tomato.

"Who's the senior officer here?" he yelled in a voice loud enough to be heard a block away.

"I am, sir," I replied.

"Let me see your ID card."

As he looked it over, he said, "Goddamn it, we've been hearing about you guys all day. Don't you realize your presence in Tokyo could cause a real mess? You disobeyed direct orders in doing what you have done. You think you own the whole damned country?"

I thought it best, all things considered, not to answer that question.

"Don't you realize that part of the Japanese Army still considers itself undefeated and may start fighting for its homeland at any minute? What in the *hell* were you guys thinking about?" yelled the Colonel with ever-increasing volume.

Once again I couldn't see much to be gained by answering.

"Lieutenant," he said, glaring right at me, "Are all of you people from the same ship?"

"Yessir, the USS *Haddo*," I answered, not feeling nearly as confident at I sounded.

"Lieutenant Calvert, I am placing all of these officers under military arrest. You are to retain them in your custody and return them all to the *Haddo* without delay. The formal instructions for your courts-martial will come later. Every damned one of you is going to fry—is that clear?"

"Yessir."

I looked over the papers he had handed to me. It was clear that he meant what he said. Not much could have dampened my spirits that day, but those papers did.

As we walked back to the Submarine Base, I reflected that most of my companions had, indeed, accumulated fifty-nine points, and all would be heading for home and civilian life soon, court-martial or no court-martial. Only Jack Keller and I were regular Navy and planning to stay in the service after the war—and Jack, as a much more recent entry into submarines, had a lot less at stake. I didn't want the rest of them to know how I felt, so I said nothing. But inside I was crushed.

What a *stupid* way this was to end my Naval career—all for a silly trip to Tokyo, which I more than anyone else involved should have had enough sense to realize was not only wrong but crazy. When the authorities gave us written orders not to leave the Submarine Base, they meant exactly what they said. The notice had even made it clear that a violation would result in a court-martial. We had no, absolutely no, excuse.

As the senior officer with this group and the executive officer of their ship, I was responsible for the whole mess. And I knew I would pay for it in the court-martial.

My career in the Navy was finished.

As we took the long ride in the motor launch back to where the *Haddo* was anchored, I began to think what all this would mean. I would have to tell Nancy that the Navy, for us, was over. I would have to tell my parents, which would break my father's heart.

I began to reflect again on my long-interrupted plans for medical school. I would have to take at least one more full year of undergraduate work to get the courses I would need to apply for medical school. Then four more years of medical school, assuming I could get in. Then at least three years of a residency before I could begin to practice.

Eight years—where was the money going to come from? Neither my family nor Nancy's could begin to support us through this long program. For the first time in my life, I began to think seriously of borrowing money to go to school. We would be in our fifties before we could have it all paid back, I thought. Still, I was determined. I had really blown my future with this damned trip to Tokyo, but I resolved to attempt to salvage it from this point on.

First, I would have to write to Nancy and my parents and tell them what had happened. As soon as I returned to the States, I would begin looking around for a loan and a college where I could do the necessary undergraduate work. Nancy would have to go to work, but I was confident that she would pitch in and help.

Next, I resolved I would write to the Western Reserve and University of Pennsylvania medical schools—the two I had been most interested in—to see what financial aid I could get. Finally I would write to Washington and see what veteran's benefit there might be for medical school. Surely a beneficent government could not ignore my nine war patrols in the Pacific.

I even went so far as to consider the possibility that the court-martial could result in a dishonorable discharge, in which case I would not be eligible for any benefits. Even in my depressed state, however, this seemed a bit far-fetched.

But before I did any of these things, I would have to tell my skipper what had happened—and how I had been dumb enough to let it happen.

As soon as I got on board, I went to his room and told him the whole story, handing him the documents of arrest from the Marine Colonel. He read them carefully.

"Well, you've really ripped your knickers this time, Jim," came the none too reassuring assessment from Lynch.

"Yessir," I replied somberly.

"I'll talk to the people higher up to see what the next step is going to be," he said quietly, and I got up and excused myself.

All the other officers were waiting in the wardroom.

"What did he say?" they asked almost in one voice.

I told them and noticed that, despite their fifty-nine points, no one seemed to be very cheerful. After all of their fine service, they didn't want to leave the Navy with such a black mark on their records.

Despite the exciting events of the day, there wasn't much conversation at dinner that night.

The next morning at breakfast, the skipper told us that he would be attending the surrender on board the *Missouri*. While he was gone, we were to make all preparations for getting under way the next day. We would transit to Pearl Harbor and, after refueling there and staying one or two days, would leave for New London via the Panama Canal. On reaching New London, the *Haddo* would probably be mothballed and placed in wartime reserve.

All of this would normally have put me in high good humor, but the thought of the looming courts-martial hung over all of us like a black cloud.

All of the submarines alongside the *Proteus* were refueling for the long voyage home, and we had to wait our turn. Soon, however, the hoses were fitted and refueling commenced. Stores began to come on board, and when I saw that all the preparations were under way satisfactorily, I sat down to write to Nancy and to my parents. How could I explain such an idiotic act? Weren't we supposed to be grown men? Why had we acted like schoolboys? What a *stupid, foolish* thing we had done, I thought.

Despite all these self-incriminations, I finished the letters. I told everyone of my plans for medical school, and I wrote to Nancy in some detail as to how I thought we might finance that eight-year stretch.

Aware that, court-martial or no court-martial, a great deal of history was being made on board the *Missouri* not far away, I went up to the bridge about a quarter to nine in the morning to see what I could see. I couldn't see very much because the *Proteus* was blocking part of the view. So, taking a pair of binoculars with me, I went to a point high in the *Proteus* superstructure where I could see everything happening on the *Missouri*—though from a distance.

I wasn't alone. Everyone who was not actively engaged in fueling or loading stores had sought out some vantage point from which to see what was happening on board the *Missouri*.

We were pretty far away, but with the binoculars, I could see a large group of Admirals and Generals, obviously of several nations, gathered near a table on which documents were spread. Behind them—and, like those of us in the *Proteus*, perched in every vantage point—were officers of more modest rank. Among them, I was sure, was our skipper.

I knew that President Truman had appointed General MacArthur Supreme Commander of the Allied Powers for the purposes of the surrender, but I could not see any sign of him through my binoculars. I could, however, see the five-starred flags of both Admiral Nimitz and General MacArthur fluttering at the main, so I knew that both of them were on board the *Missouri*.

"There they come!" shouted someone on deck, pointing to several small, somewhat stooped men, some in uniform, some in civilian formal clothing, coming up the gangway of the *Missouri*. The civilians wore black top hats, as though they were nineteenth-century New Yorkers going to the opera. One of them had a noticeable limp.

"Is it the emperor himself?" someone asked.

Clearly it wasn't, but I could not make out who or exactly what the civilians were. Except that they were Japanese—there was no mistaking that. I could see the sideboys giving them honors and could hear faintly the shrill sound of the boatswain's pipe as the Japanese representatives came on board the *Missouri* to sign the surrender documents. All in all, the Japanese did not make a very impressive delegation, but perhaps this was fitting from everyone's point of view.

Shortly after the Japanese took their appointed places, both General MacArthur and Admiral Nimitz appeared. The tall, distinguished-looking figure of the general was recognizable, even from our distance, as he stepped up to a microphone and spoke. We, of course, could not hear what he said.

When he had finished, one of the Japanese civilians sat at the document-filled table and signed. I could not see what he was actually doing, but it appeared to be satisfactory because, without delay, General MacArthur sat down and signed the documents. After him a long string of Allied flag and general officers followed, one at a time, seating themselves at the table and apparently signing.

I learned later from Frank Lynch that the long trail of document signers had been the senior military representatives of all the Allied Powers—the United States, Great Britain, Australia, New Zealand, Canada, the Netherlands, France, China, and Russia. Admiral Chester W. Nimitz had been chosen to sign for the United States—certainly a fitting choice.

About the time I thought everything was over, the flight of carrier aircraft, of which we had heard earlier, zoomed over the *Missouri* in a final salute to those participating. There were hundreds of them, and it was a thrilling sight.

The ceremony and the war with Japan were both over.

The skipper did not return for lunch, and we were all a bit disappointed, for we were anxious to get a direct eyewitness account of the surrender ceremony.

About two in the afternoon, Frank Lynch returned and said he wanted to see me in his room. With a heavy heart, I went in and shut the door.

"I've talked with Captain Warder and told him the whole story of your Tokyo frolic and read him the papers you brought back with you from the Marine Colonel," Lynch said with a smile that I thought was a bit out of place, considering the situation.

"After a short delay, he said not to worry about it. The Marine General in charge of this kind of thing is a good friend of his. He said he would talk to the Marines."

"But that Marine Colonel did everything except attack me physically. Maybe he won't give up so easily," I said.

"Captain Warder said if we didn't hear anything more about it before tomorrow morning to forget about it—the whole thing would be dropped."

I could hardly believe my ears. This was too good to be true.

Once again Captain Frederick B. Warder had come to Jim Calvert's rescue. How many more times was he going to have to bail me out?

I vowed to myself right then and there that I would demonstrate to him, somehow, that he had not made a mistake in helping me out.

I went directly to my room, tore up the letters I had written, and, sitting there with tears in my eyes, made another vow to myself that

I would give the Navy the best that I had. It had, through men like Tommy Dykers and Captain Warder, given me both instruction in the profession and forgiveness when I had erred. I wanted to follow in their footsteps. All thought of the medical profession would be set aside once and for all.

The next morning dawned with no further word of the courts-martial, and with further exultation in our hearts for our miraculous delivery, we took off our mooring lines, carefully keeping them this time, and prepared to leave Tokyo Bay.

So, we were homeward bound, with hearts so light that I find it impossible to convey just how happy we really were. Not only was the war over, but we were going home, and the threat of doom that had so recently destroyed all our happiness had vanished.

We threaded our way southward, out through the Uraga Strait, on a bright sunny morning and soon were saying our last goodbyes to Sagami-nada. No tears were shed as we saw the last of that place of such bittersweet memories. There had been sheer terror, great victories, humiliating defeats, and long days of boredom in those dark waters. I thought to myself, If I never see them again, I will not be disappointed.

Day after day we plied our lonely way across the broad Pacific. We made a trim dive every day to be sure we were in balance, but there was no diving for patrol planes. The skies were empty. We ran with running lights at night and had to accustom ourselves to the glare they made after the pitch blackness we had lived with for so long.

Now that the threat of the courts-martial was gone, all the memories of that trip to Tokyo came flooding back. At mealtime the talk was of nothing else. We hashed over every detail, and some of the events were growing more interesting with every telling.

Quite clearly Frank Lynch regretted missing this great experience—although I knew that had he been with us, he would have had too much sense and maturity to have walked out through that hole in the submarine base wall and taken the train to Tokyo. Nevertheless, he listened to the same Tokyo stories over and over again, with far more patience than most skippers would have shown in similar circumstances. We should have had the sense to see that enough was enough and talked about something else.

But we didn't, and one day at lunch Lynch banged the wardroom table so hard with his fist that all the china jumped.

"Dammit! If you guys don't stop talking about that trip to Tokyo, I'm going to do something drastic. If I hear just one more word about that trip, I'm going to send Captain Warder a message recommending that he do his best to get those court-martial orders reinstated! I have *had* it!"

We weren't absolutely sure whether we should take this threat seriously or not, but from then on the tales of Tokyo were shared only on the bridge or some other place where we knew we were well out of earshot of the skipper.

As we made our way across the Pacific, I took sun lines every morning and afternoon, and stars in the evening as well as the next dawn. Slowly but surely, at about 350 miles a day, we were transiting eastward.

As I took my ease on the bridge, enjoying the sun and chatting with the OOD, I thought back on all this war had brought in the way of experiences. The flail of getting into Submarine School directly. The school itself. Building the *Jack*. Getting to know Tommy Dykers.

There is an old saying in the Navy that your first skipper is the most important one you will ever have. I believed it, and I realized how incredibly lucky I had been to have Tommy Dykers for that first skipper. He had combined all the traits and abilities that a good commanding officer should, and I knew how much I owed him.

I thought of the successes we had had with the ship that Dykers had done so much to shape. The sinking of the troop transports on the first patrol. The brilliant success of the third patrol, where we sank almost all of a five-ship tanker convoy and won the title of *Jack* the Pack. I also thought of the fine patrols made by Art Krapf and of our successes under Al Fuhrman. I had been blessed with competent skippers.

But I also thought about our defeats. The heartbreaking troubles with the HOR engines. The torpedoes that didn't work. The backbreaking work of training a new crew for every patrol. Newton's hideously broken leg during one of those training periods. And the missed chances on the two big cruisers.

I thought about Australia and the bittersweet memories it brought. I reflected that any trouble I had gotten into there had been my own doing alone. No one else was to blame, least of all Kathie. And, perhaps as a result of the upheaval in my emotions that Australia had caused, my relationship with Nancy was stronger than it had ever been.

I would never forget the friends I had made. Tommy Dykers, Beetle Roach, Miles Refo, and Kent Lukingbeal would be part of my memories for the rest of my life, I was sure. In the past two and a half years, we had survived many dangers together and developed those bonds that men do in such circumstances. Leyton Goodman had been lost in his new submarine, the *Barbel*. And many of my Submarine School classmates were gone.

I was also aware that the bottom of the Pacific Ocean we were crossing was the final resting place of more than fifty American submarines lost in the war against Japan. The submarines had won a great victory, but at a heavy price.

I was only twenty-four in years but much older in experience, and best of all, I had lived through the war. Despite having made nine war patrols, despite having been bombed by airplanes, depth charged by escorts, shot at by several different kinds of Japanese ships, and scared nearly to death dozens of times, I had lived through the war. I had beaten the odds, and there would be more to come after all.

Kathie and I had been wrong about that.

Each Sunday on the long trek back to New London, we held church services, as most submarines had done all through the war. Joe McCune usually conducted them, but one Sunday he asked me to do it, and I included two longtime favorites of mine. All of us attending that day recited in unison:

> God is our refuge and strength, a very present help in trouble.
> Therefore will we not fear, though the earth be removed, and
>   though the mountains be carried into the midst of the sea;
> Though the waters thereof roar and be troubled, though the
>   mountains shake with the swelling thereof . . .
> The Lord of hosts is with us.

We had, indeed, seen the waters roar and be troubled, and we had seen, from a distance, the mountains shake. He had been with us and had been our refuge in our time of trouble.

Fittingly, we completed the service with the Nunc Dimittis:

Lord, now lettest thou thy servant depart in peace,
according to thy word.
For mine eyes have seen thy salvation.

We had without doubt been delivered out of death and destruction—and against fairly heavy odds.
We were grateful, grateful indeed.

Afterword

After the end of the war, Tommy Dykers retired from the Navy and originated a television series called *The Silent Service*. Some fifty episodes, each one devoted to a factual representation of a U.S. submarine war patrol in the Pacific, were filmed. They ran on NBC-TV for many years. Tommy retired as a Rear Admiral and passed on in 1975. Beetle Roach had preceded him in 1967.

Art Krapf is comfortably retired and living in California. Miles Refo is also retired and lives in Virginia. He and I are the only two of the original *Jack* officers still alive. Leyton Goodman was lost later in the war, in the *Barbel*. Kent Lukingbeal became a senior partner in a large New York law firm and died prematurely of cancer. Billy Coleman was a Charleston, South Carolina, banker for many years; he organized several big-game hunting safaris to Africa before his death. Earl Archer, Jack O'Brien, and Al Fuhrman are also gone.

Kathie Aberdeen married a prominent Australian physician in 1946, and they live in a suburb of Perth. Kathie still plays golf but says her handicap has gone up a bit. They have two sons and two daughters, now grown, of course. This book was the catalyst that caused me to relocate her, and we have had several wonderful phone conversations, talking over events now a half-century past.

Frederick Warder, now a retired Admiral, lives quietly in Florida and has reviewed this text for possible errors. At the time of this writing, he is ninety-one and is, without doubt, the grand old man of surviving World War II submariners. I never forget that anything I have accomplished in the Navy has been due to the generosity and kindness of this great officer.

Chester Nimitz, Jr., is a retired Admiral and, after the war, became Chief Executive Officer of Perkin Elmer, the large scientific-equipment company. He and his wife, Joan, divide their time between Florida and Cape Cod. Over the years since the war, he has been a good friend and a helper on several occasions.

Frank Lynch, while commanding a destroyer, was seriously injured in a tragic automobile accident in Sri Lanka and had to be retired physically from the Navy. He died in 1987.

After the war a Joint Army-Navy Assessment Committee (JANAC) was sent to Japan to compile, as accurately as possible, an accounting of just what ships American submarines actually sank according to Japanese records. JANAC also used Japanese sources to confirm the sizes (tonnage) of ships sunk. When the JANAC results were finally promulgated, the *Jack* ranked ninth in tonnage sunk, out of over two hundred American submarines, and it was in the top twenty-five for numbers of ships sunk.

After decommissioning, the *Jack* was given to the Greek Navy, who operated with it for several years and renamed it the *Amfitriti*. After retirement from the Greek Navy, the *Jack* was sent to her final resting place in the Mediterranean after being intentionally destroyed in a torpedo test firing by the U.S. Sixth Fleet.

After the end of the war, I had command of a new, postwar diesel submarine, the *Trigger*, named after the famous submarine of that name, lost in World War II.

Later I was interviewed and selected by Admiral Rickover as the third skipper for his fleet of nuclear-powered submarines. I took the *Skate* on two voyages under the Arctic ice to the North Pole, in 1958 and 1959. On the second voyage, we broke through the ice with the *Skate* to surface directly at the North Pole—the first ship of any kind to reach that part of the earth on the surface. My first book, *Surface at the Pole*, tells the story of these two voyages.

Nancy and I lived together very happily as I pursued my Navy career in various locations. She was a major help to me every step of the way. We had three children before her premature death in 1965. Jim, the oldest, is a physician. Charley, the youngest, is an engineer in the computer software industry in California. Margaret, our only daughter, died in 1994. She was a wonderful person, and her memory will be with us as long as we live.

I was promoted to Rear Admiral in 1965 and, in December of 1967, in what was the most fortunate event of my life, met Peggy Harrison Battle of Princeton, New Jersey. We were married in Athens, Greece, in the spring of 1968 while I was commanding part of the Sixth Fleet in the Mediterranean. I have had many wonderful breaks in my life but none more so than meeting Peggy and persuading her to become my wife. Her beauty and grace, as well as her wonderful sense of fun, have made my years with her the happiest in my life.

Shortly after our marriage I became Superintendent of the Naval Academy at Annapolis. I served as Superintendent from 1968 to 1972 and was promoted to Vice Admiral halfway through this tour of duty.

After commanding the First Fleet in the Pacific, I left the Navy at age fifty-two and joined Texaco, Inc., as Assistant to the Chairman of the Board. Two years later I became Vice President in Charge of Operations and a member of the board of directors at Combustion Engineering, a diversified company prominent in public utility power plants, oil field equipment, and large engineering and construction projects.

After retiring from Combustion Engineering in 1984, I became Chairman of the Board of Aqua-Chem, Inc., a Milwaukee-based manufacturer of boilers and water treatment equipment.

I am now Chairman Emeritus of Aqua-Chem, and Peggy and I divide our time between our home on the Eastern Shore of Maryland, our summer place on Martha's Vineyard, and a small apartment in New York City.

Between us we have six children. Now, after Margaret's death, they are all young men, ranging from thirty-eight to forty-nine years old. Among Peggy's sons are two investment bankers, one commercial banker, and one sculptor. We have twelve grandchildren.

Index